SAS Users Say It Best

"I was particularly impressed with two areas of this book: The examples pose problems that every programmer has faced, and the solutions address those problems using both traditional approaches and novel strategies.

"Programmers in their early stages often don't recognize the benefits of using functions. Ron has presented the examples in a way that allows programmers to consider functions from the angle, 'Ok, I've got this same problem. How can functions help me treat it?' The text explanation with accompanying code makes it a snap to apply the techniques to your own programs. The examples don't make you assume what the outcome will be, and Ron alerts you to any side-effects or unexpected results.

"Programmers in later stages of development often rely on the same traditional bag of functions, supplemented with lots of work-around code. These professionals will find relief using 'alternative therapies' like Perl expressions and the new V9 functions presented in the book. In the old days, data was usually entered by trained personnel using set protocols. Today, programs need to be able to accept data entered by untrained users from Web-forms. This has resulted in a plague of bad data. Ron's book provides a function Rx for almost every conceivable data entry malady. I've been programming in SAS for about 15 years, and found myself saying over and over again, 'I didn't know about that function. I can use **that!**' "

Jeanne Spicer
Manager, Data Management & Programming Services
Social Science Research Institute
Penn State University

"Ron Cody has done a great job of putting together a SAS functions "cookbook" that will be a big time saver when trying to easily use and transform your data. There are examples for every function and each is well explained and easy to follow. The author is well experienced in many types of data and programming languages. For example, in Chapter 2 he concentrates on Perl expressions, and Chapter 12 is devoted to trigonometric functions. This book would appeal to beginning and seasoned SAS programmers, as it is very difficult to remember how to use every function you'd need to complete assignments. Just like it would be very hard to remember the details of all your favorite recipes, this book is a similar reference."

Diane Marie Goldschmidt
Anthem Blue Cross Blue Shield of CT

SAS Publishing

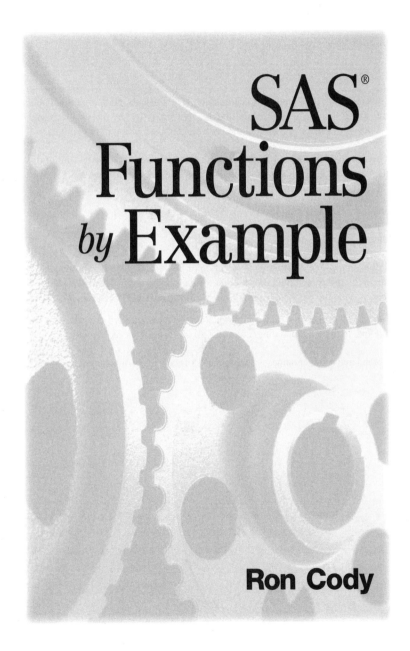

SAS®
Functions
by Example

Ron Cody

Table of Contents

Chapter 1 Character Functions

Chapter 2 Perl Regular Expressions

Chapter 8   Mathematical Functions

Chapter 9   Random Number Functions

Chapter 10   Special Functions

Chapter 11   State and Zip Code Functions

Chapter 12   Trigonometric Functions

Chapter 13   Macro Functions

Chapter 14   SAS File I/O Functions

Chapter 15   Variable Information Functions

Chapter 16   Bitwise Logical Functions

List of Programs

Programs in Chapter 1

Programs in Chapter 2

Programs in Chapter 3

Programs in Chapter 4

Programs in Chapter 5

Programs in Chapter 6

Programs in Chapter 7

Programs in Chapter 8

Programs in Chapter 9

Programs in Chapter 10

Programs in Chapter 11

Programs in Chapter 12

Programs in Chapter 13

Programs in Chapter 14

Programs in Chapter 15

Programs in Chapter 16

Preface

SAS functions provide some of the real power of SAS. This book covers almost two hundred of the most common and useful functions and call routines—I did not attempt to describe every one. Unlike SAS language manuals or other reference materials where SAS functions are merely described, this book shows you the functions and one or more examples of how they can be used. These examples are complete working programs. Sometimes the examples demonstrate a common usage of the function; at other times, the use is non-traditional, but still very practical. Some of the examples show how several functions can be used in combination to produce a desired result.

This book contains useful information for veteran SAS users as well. Versions 8 and 9 added some new functions and even whole new categories of functions. For example, a handful of functions now exist that address Version 9 regular expressions. Functions that are new for SAS 9 are marked with this icon in the text: **SAS9.1**

One of the strengths of SAS is its ability to manipulate character data. You will find extensive examples of character manipulation in this book. For example, there are complete programs to perform "fuzzy matching" using a combination of functions, including the SPEDIS (spelling distance) function.

For those who are statistically inclined, there are examples of random number functions performing Monte Carlo simulations, including the use of the SAS Output Delivery System (ODS) to capture values from a procedure to a SAS data set.

I have decided to stay with the same function categories described in the latest version of the SAS OnlineDoc. Because some of these functions have other important uses besides the obvious one described by its category, I have provided two lists to allow you to look up a function by name, and by program. There is also a traditional index that includes functions and tasks. Note: The wording of arguments in this book might differ from the wording of arguments in the *SAS OnlineDoc 9.1*.

Besides providing a nearly complete description of the Base SAS functions, I have provided programs that I hope you will find useful in your daily programming tasks. For example, did you realize that you can sort the values in an array using the ORDINAL function or use the SPEDIS function to perform a "fuzzy merge"?

Several of the more useful examples here are also presented as SAS macros. All the programs in this book can be downloaded from the companion Web site for this book, located at **support.sas.com/companionsites**. The programs can be used as is, or modified to fit your particular application.

By the way, this is the first book I have ever written while on sabbatical. In fact, this is the first sabbatical I have ever had. I have truly enjoyed writing this book, even though I was "forced" to embark on research trips to Virgin Gorda and Italy (a villa in the Chianti region). After several bottles of excellent wine, I was able to conjure up some interesting examples to add to this book.

Acknowledgments

The last part of writing a book is the acknowledgments page. This is the fun part. Most of the work is done and you can sit back, relax, and think about the people who helped make all this possible.

First, my sincere thanks to Judy Whatley, my acquisitions editor and friend. This is the second or third book (who's counting) that I have written with Judy's help. It's so nice to work with someone who knows you so well and has such a depth of experience.

This time, some of my reviewers had to do "double duty." Several of the reviewers felt that the organization of my first draft, alphabetically by function name within function categories, was fine for a reference book. However, they felt that structuring the book by logical grouping of functions would allow the book to serve both as a textbook that could be read cover-to-cover and as a reference. Uncharacteristically, I chose to take their advice and restructure the entire book. The changes were so major that several of the reviewers were given the "opportunity" to look at the material a second time. Thus, the "double duty."

Now for the names: My reviewers were Paul Grant, Jason Secosky, Kevin Hobbs, Lynn Mackay, Richard Bell, Kent Reeve, and Sharon Hamrick, all from SAS Institute and Mike Zdeb, my friend and a professor at the School of Public Health at Albany. These folks did a spectacular job. Thank you.

Version 9 has increased the number of functions and even added entirely new function categories to the SAS arsenal. I sincerely thank the SAS developers who were so generous with their time in helping me to understand these new and wonderful functions.

On the production side, I wish to thank Candy Farrell (technical publishing specialist), Patrice Cherry (cover and format designer), Caroline Brickley (copyeditor), and Patricia Spain and Liz Villani (marketing analysts).

Ron Cody
Winter 2004

Introduction: A Brief Discussion of SAS Functions and Call Routines

SAS functions take the form of a function name, followed by a set of parentheses. In these parentheses are usually one or more arguments. (Certain functions such as TODAY take no arguments, but you need to follow the function name with an opening parenthesis and a closing parenthesis anyway to tell SAS that you are referring to the TODAY function, not to a variable called TODAY.) These arguments provide information that the function needs to return a result. For example, the statement DAY_OF_WEEK = WEEKDAY(DATE); computes the day of the week from a SAS date and assigns it to the variable DAY_OF_WEEK. This function, as with all other SAS functions, returns a single value that is either assigned to a variable or used in a SAS expression. When the function executes, the values of its arguments do not change.

Call routines have some similarity to SAS functions because they often perform similar operations. However, there are some important differences. Call routines are not used in assignment statements. Instead, they stand alone as SAS statements. Multiple arguments in a call routine can be assigned new values by the routine. For example, the statement CALL SCAN(string, n, position, length); returns the position and the length of the nth "word" in the string. The SCAN function, on the other hand, returns only a single value—the nth word in the string.

Functions and call routines in this book are arranged by category and topic. For example, in Chapter 1, "Character Functions," there are topics such as, "Functions That Search for Characters" or "Functions That Remove Leading and Trailing Blanks from Strings."

C h a p t e r   1

Character Functions

Introduction

A major strength of SAS is its ability to work with character data. The SAS character functions are essential to this. The collection of functions and call routines in this chapter allow you to do extensive manipulation on all sorts of character data.

SAS users who are new to Version 9 will notice the tremendous increase in the number of SAS character functions. You will also want to review the next chapter on Perl regular expressions, another way to process character data.

Before delving into the realm of character functions, it is important to understand how SAS stores character data and how the length of character variables gets assigned.

Storage Length for Character Variables

It is in the compile stage of the DATA step that SAS variables are determined to be character or numeric, that the storage lengths of SAS character variables are determined, and that the descriptor portion of the SAS data set is written. The program below will help you to understand how character storage lengths are determined:

Program 1.1: How SAS determines storage lengths of character variables

```
DATA EXAMPLE1;
   INPUT GROUP $
      @10 STRING $3.;
   LEFT  = 'X    '; *X AND 4 BLANKS;
   RIGHT = '    X'; *4 BLANKS AND X;
   SUB = SUBSTR(GROUP,1,2);
   REP = REPEAT(GROUP,1);
DATALINES;
ABCDEFGH 123
XXX         4
Y           5
;
```

Explanation

The purpose of this program is not to demonstrate SAS character functions. That is why the functions in this program are not highlighted as they are in all the other programs in this book. Let's look at each of the character variables created in this DATA step. To see the storage length for each of the variables in data set EXAMPLE1, let's run PROC CONTENTS. Here is the program:

Program 1.2: Running PROC CONTENTS to determine storage lengths

```
PROC CONTENTS DATA=EXAMPLE1 VARNUM;
   TITLE "PROC CONTENTS for Data Set EXAMPLE1";
RUN;
```

The VARNUM option requests the variables to be in the order that they appear in the SAS data set, rather than the default, alphabetical order. The output is shown next:

```
-----Variables Ordered by Position-----

     #    Variable    Type    Len

     1    GROUP       Char      8
     2    STRING      Char      3
     3    LEFT        Char      5
     4    RIGHT       Char      5
     5    SUB         Char      8
     6    REP         Char    200
```

First, GROUP is read using list input. No informat is used, so SAS will give the variable the default length of 8. Since STRING is read with an informat, the length is set to the informat width of 3. LEFT and RIGHT are both created with an assignment statement. Therefore the length of these two variables is equal to the number of bytes in the literals following the equal sign. Note that if a variable appears several times in a DATA step, its length is determined by the **first** reference to that variable.

For example, beginning SAS programmers often get in trouble with statements such as:

```
IF SEX = 1 THEN GENDER = 'MALE';
ELSE IF SEX = 2 THEN GENDER = 'FEMALE';
```

The length of GENDER in the two lines above is 4, since the statement in which the variable first appears defines its length.

There are several ways to make sure a character variable is assigned the proper length. Probably the best way is to use a LENGTH statement. So, if you precede the two lines above with the statement:

```
LENGTH GENDER $ 6;
```

the length of GENDER will be 6, not 4. Some lazy programmers will "cheat" by adding two blanks after MALE in the assignment statement (me, never!). Another trick is to place the line for FEMALE first.

So, continuing on to the last two variables. You see a length of 8 for the variable SUB. As you will see later in this chapter, the SUBSTR (substring) function can extract some or all of one string and assign the result to a new variable. Since SAS has to determine variable lengths in the compile stage and since the SUBSTR arguments that define the starting point and the length of the substring could possibly be determined in the execution stage (from data values, for example), SAS does the logical thing: it gives the variable defined by the SUBSTR function the longest length it possibly could—the length of the string from which you are taking the substring.

Finally, the variable REP is created by using the REPEAT function. As you will find out later in this chapter, the REPEAT function takes a string and repeats it as many times as directed by the second argument to the function. Using the same logic as the SUBSTR function, since the length of REP is determined in the compile stage and since the number of repetitions could vary, SAS gives it a default length of 200. A note of historical interest: Prior to Version 7, the maximum length of character variables was 200. With the coming of Version 7, the maximum length of character variables was increased to 32,767. SAS made a very wise decision to leave the default length for situations such as the REPEAT function described here, at 200. The take-home message is that you should always be sure that you know the storage lengths of your character variables.

Functions That Change the Case of Characters

Two old functions, UPCASE and LOWCASE, change the case of characters. A new function (as of Version 9), PROPCASE (proper case) capitalizes the first letter of each word.

Function: **UPCASE**

Purpose: To change all letters to uppercase.
Note: The corresponding function LOWCASE changes uppercase to
lowercase.

Syntax: UPCASE(*character-value*)

character-value is any SAS character expression.

If a length has not been previously assigned, the length of the resulting
variable will be the length of the argument.

Examples

For these examples CHAR = "ABCxyz"

Function	Returns
UPCASE(CHAR)	"ABCXYZ"
UPCASE("a1%m?")	"A1%M?"

Program 1.3: Changing lowercase to uppercase for all character variables in a data set

```
***Primary function: UPCASE
***Other function: DIM;

DATA MIXED;
   LENGTH A B C D E $ 1;
   INPUT A B C D E X Y;
DATALINES;
M f P p D 1 2
m f m F M 3 4
;
DATA UPPER;
   SET MIXED;
   ARRAY ALL_C[*] _CHARACTER_;
   DO I = 1 TO DIM(ALL_C);
      ALL_C[I] = UPCASE(ALL_C[I]);
   END;
```

```
    DROP I;
RUN;

PROC PRINT DATA=UPPER NOOBS;
    TITLE 'Listing of Data Set UPPER';
RUN;
```

Explanation

Remember that upper- and lowercase values are represented by different internal codes, so if you are testing for a value such as Y for a variable and the actual value is y, you will not get a match. Therefore it is often useful to convert all character values to either upper- or lowercase before doing your logical comparisons. In this program, _CHARACTER_ is used in the array statement to represent all the character variables in the data set MIXED. Inspection of the listing below verifies that all lowercase values were changed to uppercase.

```
              Listing of Data Set UPPER

          A    B    C    D    E    X    Y

          M    F    P    P    D    1    2
          M    F    M    F    M    3    4
```

Function: **LOWCASE**

Purpose: To change all letters to lowercase.

Syntax: LOWCASE(*character-value*)

character-value is any SAS character expression.

Note: The corresponding function UPCASE changes lowercase to uppercase.

If a length has not been previously assigned, the length of the resulting variable will be the length of the argument.

Examples

For these examples CHAR = "ABCxyz"

Function	Returns
LOWCASE(CHAR)	"abcxyz"
LOWCASE("A1%M?")	"a1%m?"

Program 1.4: Program to capitalize the first letter of the first and last name (using SUBSTR)

```
***Primary functions: LOWCASE, UPCASE
***Other function: SUBSTR (used on the left and right side of the equal
sign);

DATA CAPITALIZE;
   INFORMAT FIRST LAST $30.;
   INPUT FIRST LAST;
   FIRST = LOWCASE(FIRST);
   LAST = LOWCASE(LAST);
   SUBSTR(FIRST,1,1) = UPCASE(SUBSTR(FIRST,1,1));
   SUBSTR(LAST,1,1) = UPCASE(SUBSTR(LAST,1,1));
DATALINES;
ronald cODy
THomaS eDISON
albert einstein
;
PROC PRINT DATA=CAPITALIZE NOOBS;
   TITLE "Listing of Data Set CAPITALIZE";
RUN;
```

Explanation

Before we get started on the explanation, I should point out that as of Version 9, the PROPCASE function capitalizes the first letter of each word in a string. However, it provides a good demonstation of the LOWCASE and UPCASE functions and this method will still be useful for SAS users using earlier versions of SAS software.

This program capitalizes the first letter of the two character variables FIRST and LAST. The same technique could have other applications. The first step is to set all the letters to lowercase using the LOWCASE function. The first letter of each name is then turned back to uppercase using the SUBSTR function (on the right side of the equal sign) to select the first letter in the first and last names, and the UPCASE function to capitalize it. The

SUBSTR function on the left side of the equal sign is used to place this letter in the first position of each of the variables. The listing below shows that this program worked as desired:

```
                      Listing of Data Set CAPITALIZE

              FIRST     LAST

              Ronald    Cody
              Thomas    Edison
              Albert    Einstein
```

SAS9.1 **Function: PROPCASE**

Purpose: To capitalize the first letter of each word in a string.

Syntax: PROPCASE(*character-value*)

character-value is any SAS character expression.

If a length has not been previously assigned, the length of the resulting variable will be the length of the argument.

Examples
For these examples CHAR = "ABCxyz"

Function	Returns
PROPCASE(CHAR)	"Abcxyz"
PROPCASE("al%m?")	"Al%m?"
PROPCASE("mr. george w. bush")	"Mr. George W. Bush"

Program 1.5: Capitalizing the first letter of each word in a string

```
***Primary function: PROPCASE;

DATA PROPER;
   INPUT NAME $60.;
   NAME = PROPCASE(NAME);
```

```
DATALINES;
ronald cODy
THomaS eDISON
albert einstein
;
PROC PRINT DATA=PROPER NOOBS;
    TITLE "Listing of Data Set PROPER";
RUN;
```

Explanation

In this program, you use the PROPCASE function to capitalize the first letter of the first and last names. The listing is shown below:

```
               Listing of Data Set PROPER

          NAME

          Ronald Cody
          Thomas Edison
          Albert Einstein
```

Program 1.6: Alternative program to capitalize the first letter of each word in a string

```
***First and last name are two separate variables.

DATA PROPER;
    INFORMAT FIRST LAST $30.;
    INPUT FIRST LAST;
    LENGTH NAME $ 60;
    CALL CATX(' ', NAME, FIRST, LAST);
    NAME = PROPCASE(NAME);
DATALINES;
ronald cODy
THomaS eDISON
albert einstein
;
PROC PRINT DATA=PROPER NOOBS;
    TITLE "Listing of Data Set PROPER";
RUN;
```

Explanation

In this alternative program, the CATX call routine is used to concatenate the first and last name with a blank as the separator character. The PROPCASE function is then used the same way as above. The listing is identical to the listing above.

Functions That Remove Characters from Strings

COMPBL (compress blanks) can replace multiple blanks with a single blank. The COMPRESS function can remove not only blanks, but also any characters you specify from a string.

Function: COMPBL

Purpose: To replace all occurrences of two or more blanks with a single blank character. This is particularly useful for standardizing addresses and names where multiple blanks may have been entered.

Syntax: COMPBL(*character-value*)

character-value is any SAS character expression.

If a length has not been previously assigned, the length of the resulting variable will be the length of the argument.

Example

For these examples CHAR = "A C   XYZ"

Function	Returns
COMPBL(CHAR)	"A C XYZ"
COMPBL("X Y Z LAST")	"X Y Z LAST"

Program 1.7: Using the COMPBL function to convert multiple blanks to a single blank

```
***Primary function: COMPBL;

DATA SQUEEZE;
   INPUT #1 @1  NAME     $20.
         #2 @1  ADDRESS $30.
         #3 @1  CITY     $15.
            @20 STATE    $2.
            @25 ZIP      $5.;
   NAME = COMPBL(NAME);
   ADDRESS = COMPBL(ADDRESS);
   CITY = COMPBL(CITY);
DATALINES;
RON CODY
89 LAZY BROOK ROAD
FLEMINGTON       NJ    08822
BILL      BROWN
28   CATHY   STREET
NORTH   CITY      NY   11518
;
PROC PRINT DATA=SQUEEZE;
   TITLE 'Listing of Data Set SQUEEZE';
   ID NAME;
   VAR ADDRESS CITY STATE ZIP;
RUN;
```

Explanation

Each line of the addresses was passed through the COMPBL function to replace any sequence of two or more blanks to a single blank. A listing of data set SQUEEZE is shown below:

```
                   Listing of Data Set SQUEEZE

     NAME             ADDRESS           CITY       STATE     ZIP

   RON CODY       89 LAZY BROOK ROAD   FLEMINGTON    NJ     08822
   BILL BROWN     28 CATHY STREET      NORTH CITY    NY     11518
```

Function: COMPRESS

Purpose: To remove specified characters from a character value.

Syntax: COMPRESS(*character-value* <,'*compress-list*'>)

character-value is any SAS character expression.

compress-list is an optional list of the characters you want to remove. If this argument is omitted, the default character to be removed is a blank. If you include a list of values to remove, only those characters will be removed. If a blank is not included in the list, blanks will not be removed.

If a length has not been previously assigned, the length of the resulting variable will be the length of the argument.

Examples

In the examples below, CHAR = "A C123XYZ"

Function	Returns
COMPRESS("A C XYZ")	"ACXYZ"
COMPRESS("(908) 777-1234"," (-)")	"9087771234"
COMPRESS(CHAR,"0123456789")	"A CXYZ"

Program 1.8: Removing dashes and parentheses from phone numbers

```
***Primary function: COMPRESS;

DATA PHONE_NUMBER;
   INPUT PHONE $ 1-15;
   PHONE1 = COMPRESS(PHONE);
   PHONE2 = COMPRESS(PHONE,'(-) ');
DATALINES;
(908)235-4490
(201) 555-77 99
;
PROC PRINT DATA=PHONE_NUMBER;
   TITLE 'Listing of Data Set PHONE_NUMBER';
RUN;
```

Explanation

For the variable PHONE1, the second argument is omitted from the COMPRESS function; therefore, only blanks are removed. For PHONE2, left and right parentheses, dashes, and blanks are listed in the second argument so all of these characters are removed from the character value. You can verify this by inspecting the listing below:

```
                     Listing of Data Set PHONE_NUMBER

        Obs          PHONE             PHONE1            PHONE2

         1       (908)235-4490     (908)235-4490      9082354490
         2       (201) 555-77 99   (201)555-7799      2015557799
```

Converting Social Security Numbers to Numeric Form

Here is another example where the COMPRESS function makes it easy to convert a standard social security number, including the dashes, to a numeric value.

Program 1.9: Converting social security numbers from character to numeric

```
***Primary function: COMPRESS
***Other function:  INPUT;

DATA SOCIAL;
   INPUT @1 SS_CHAR $11.
         @1 MIKE_ZDEB COMMA11.;
   SS_NUMERIC = INPUT(COMPRESS(SS_CHAR,'-'),9.);
   SS_FORMATTED = SS_NUMERIC;
   FORMAT SS_FORMATTED SSN.;
DATALINES;
123-45-6789
001-11-1111
;
PROC PRINT DATA=SOCIAL NOOBS;
   TITLE "Listing of Data Set SOCIAL";
RUN;
```

Explanation

The COMPRESS function is used to remove the dashes from the social security number and the INPUT function does the character to numeric conversion.

It should be noted here that the social security number, including dashes, can be read directly into a numeric variable using the comma11. informat. This trick was brought to light by Mike Zdeb in a NESUG workshop in Buffalo in the Fall of 2002. Here, the variable SS_FORMATTED is set equal to the variable SS_NUMERIC so that you can see the effect of adding the SSN. format. (Note: SSN. is equivalent to SSN11.) This format prints numeric values with leading zeros and dashes in the proper places, as you can see in the listing below:

```
                   Listing of Data Set SOCIAL

    SS_CHAR       MIKE_ZDEB     SS_NUMERIC    SS_FORMATTED

   123-45-6789    123456789      123456789    123-45-6789
   001-11-1111     1111111        1111111     001-11-1111
```

Counting the Number of Digits in a Character String

This program computes the number of numerals (i.e., digits) in a string by a novel method. It uses the COMPRESS function to remove all digits from the string and then subtracts the resulting length from the original length for the computation.

Program 1.10: Counting the number of numerals in a string

```
***Primary functions: COMPRESS, LENGTHN;

DATA COUNT;
   INPUT STRING $20.;
   ONLY_LETTERS = COMPRESS(STRING,'0123456789');
   NUM_NUMERALS = LENGTHN(STRING) - LENGTHN(ONLY_LETTERS);
DATALINES;
ABC123XYZ
XXXXX
12345
1234X
;
```

```
PROC PRINT DATA=COUNT NOOBS;
   TITLE "Listing of Data Set COUNT";
RUN;
```

Explanation

This is an interesting application of the COMPRESS function. By computing the length of the string before and after removing the numerals, this program sets the difference in the lengths to the number of numerals in the original string. Notice the use of the LENGTHN function instead of the LENGTH function. When the COMPRESS function operates on the third observation (all digits), the result is a null string. The LENGTH function returns a value of 1 in this situation; the LENGTHN function returns a value of 0. See LENGTH and LENGTHN function descriptions for a detailed explanation.

```
              Listing of Data Set COUNT


                          ONLY_       NUM_
            STRING       LETTERS    NUMERALS

            ABC123XYZ    ABCXYZ         3
            XXXXX        XXXXX          0
            12345                       5
            1234X        X              4
```

Functions That Search for Characters

Functions in this category allow you to search a string for specific characters or for a character category (such as a digit). Some of these functions can also locate the first position in a string where a character does not meet a particular specification. Quite a few of the functions in this section are new to Version 9 and they provide some new and useful capabilities.

The "ANY" functions (ANYALNUM, ANYALPHA, ANYDIGIT, ANYPUNCT, and ANYSPACE)

This group of functions is described together because of the similarity of their use. New as of Version 9, these functions return the location of the first alphanumeric, letter, digit, punctuation, or space in a character string. Note that there are other "ANY" functions besides those presented here—these are the most common ones (see the *SAS OnlineDoc 9.1* for a complete list). The functionality of this group of functions is similar to many of the Perl regular expressions that are also available in Version 9.

It is important to note that it may be necessary to use the TRIM function (or STRIP function) with the ANY and NOT functions since leading or, especially, trailing blanks will affect the results. For example, if X = "ABC   " (ABC followed by three blanks), Y = NOTALNUM(X) will be 4, the location of the first blank. Therefore, you may want to routinely use TRIM (or STRIP) like this:

```
Y = NOT or ANY function(TRIM(X));
```

Note that there are a group of similar functions NOTALPHA, NOTDIGIT, etc. that work in a similar manner and are described together later in the next section. One program example follows the description of these five functions.

SAS9.1 Function: ANYALNUM

Purpose: To locate the first occurrence of an alphanumeric character (any upper- or lowercase letter or number) and return its position. If none is found, the function returns a 0. With the use of an optional parameter, this function can begin searching at any position in the string and can also search from right to left, if desired.

Syntax: ANYALNUM(*character-value* <,*start*>)

character-value is any SAS character expression.

start is an optional parameter that specifies the position in the string to begin the search. If it is omitted, the search starts at the beginning of the string. If it is non-zero, the search begins at the position in the string of the absolute value of the number (starting from the left-most position in the string). If the start value is positive, the search goes from left to right; if the value is negative, the search goes from right to left. A negative value larger than the length of the string results in a scan from right to left, starting at the end of the string. If the value of *start* is a positive number longer than the length of the string, or if it is 0, the function returns a 0.

Examples

For these examples, STRING = "ABC 123 ?xyz_n_"

Function	Returns
ANYALNUM(STRING)	1 (the position of "A")
ANYALNUM("??$$%%")	0 (no alpha-numeric characters)
ANYALNUM(STRING,5)	5 (the position of "1")
ANYALNUM(STRING,-4)	3 (the position of "C")
ANYALNUM(STRING,6)	6 (the position of "2")

SAS9.1 **Function:**   **ANYALPHA**

Purpose: To locate the first occurrence of an alpha character (any upper- or lowercase letter) and return its position. If none is found, the function returns a 0. With the use of an optional parameter, this function can begin searching at any position in the string and can also search from right to left, if desired.

Syntax: ANYALPHA(*character-value* <,*start*>)

character-value is any SAS character expression.

start is an optional parameter that specifies the position in the string to begin the search. If it is omitted, the search starts at the beginning of the string. If it is non-zero, the search begins at the position in the string of the absolute value of the number (starting from the left-most position in the string). If the start value is positive, the search goes from left to right; if the value is negative, the search goes from right to left. A negative value larger than the length of the string results in a scan from right to left, starting at the end of the string. If the value of *start* is a positive number longer than the length of the string, or if it is 0, the function returns a 0.

Examples

For these examples, STRING = "ABC 123 ?xyz_n_"

Function	Returns	
ANYALPHA(STRING)	1	(position of "A")
ANYALPHA("??$$%%")	0	(no alpha characters)
ANYALPHA(STRING,5)	10	(position of "x")
ANYALPHA(STRING,-4)	3	(position of "C")
ANYALPHA(STRING,6)	10	(position of "x")

SAS9.1 Function: **ANYDIGIT**

Purpose: To locate the first occurrence of a digit (numeral) and return its position. If none is found, the function returns a 0. With the use of an optional parameter, this function can begin searching at any position in the string and can also search from right to left, if desired.

Syntax: ANYDIGIT(*character-value* <,*start*>)

character-value is any SAS character expression.

start is an optional parameter that specifies the position in the string to begin the search. If it is omitted, the search starts at the beginning of the string. If it is non-zero, the search begins at the position in the string of the absolute value of the number (starting from the left-most position in the string). If the start value is positive, the search goes from left to right; if the value is negative, the search goes from right to left. A negative value larger than the length of the string results in a scan from right to left, starting at the end of the string. If the value of *start* is a positive number longer than the length of the string, or if it is 0, the function returns a 0.

Examples

For these examples, STRING = "ABC 123 ?xyz_n_"

Function	Returns
ANYDIGIT(STRING)	5 (position of "1")
ANYDIGIT("??$$%%")	0 (no digits)
ANYDIGIT(STRING,5)	5 (position of "1")
ANYDIGIT(STRING,-4)	0 (no digits from position 4 to 1)
ANYDIGIT(STRING,6)	6 (position of "2")

SAS9.1 Function: ANYPUNCT

Purpose: To locate the first occurrence of a punctuation character and return its position. If none is found, the function returns a 0. With the use of an optional parameter, this function can begin searching at any position in the string and can also search from right to left, if desired.

In the ASCII character set, the following characters are considered punctuation:

```
!    "    #   $   %   &   '   (   )   *   +   ,   -   .   /   :   ;
<   =   >   ?   @   [   \   ]   ^   _   `   {   |   }   ~
```

Syntax: ANYPUNCT(*character-value* <,*start*>)

character-value is any SAS character expression.

start is an optional parameter that specifies the position in the string to begin the search. If it is omitted, the search starts at the beginning of the string. If it is non-zero, the search begins at the position in the string of the absolute value of the number (starting from the left-most position in the string). If the start value is positive, the search goes from left to right; if the value is negative, the search goes from right to left. A negative value larger than the length of the string results in a scan from right to left, starting at the end of the string. If the value of *start* is a positive number longer than the length of the string, or if it is 0, the function returns a 0.

Examples

For these examples, STRING = "A!C 123 ?xyz_n_"

Function	Returns
ANYPUNCT(STRING)	2 (position of "!")
ANYPUNCT("??$$%%")	1 (position of "?")
ANYPUNCT(STRING,5)	9 (position of "?")
ANYPUNCT(STRING,-4)	2 (starts at position 4 and goes left, position of "!")
ANYPUNCT(STRING,-3)	2 (starts at "C" and goes left, position of "!")

SAS9.1 Function: ANYSPACE

Purpose: To locate the first occurrence of a white space character (a blank, horizontal or vertical tab, carriage return, linefeed, and form-feed) and return its position. If none is found, the function returns a 0. With the use of an optional parameter, this function can begin searching at any position in the string and can also search from right to left, if desired.

Syntax: ANYSPACE(*character-value* <,*start*>)

character-value is any SAS character expression.

start is an optional parameter that specifies the position in the string to begin the search. If it is omitted, the search starts at the beginning of the string. If it is non-zero, the search begins at the position in the string of the absolute value of the number (starting from the left-most position in the string). If the start value is positive, the search goes from left to right; if the value is negative, the search goes from right to left. A negative value larger than the length of the string results in a scan from right to left, starting at the end of the string. If the value of *start* is a positive number longer than the length of the string, or if it is 0, the function returns a 0.

Examples

For these examples, STRING = "ABC 123 ?xyz_n_"

Function	Returns
ANYSPACE(STRING)	4 (position of the first blank)
ANYSPACE("??$$%%")	0 (no spaces)
ANYSPACE(STRING,5)	8 (position of the second blank)
ANYSPACE(STRING,-4)	4 (position of the first blank)
ANYSPACE(STRING,6)	8 (position of the second blank)

Program 1.11: Demonstrating the "ANY" character functions

```
***Primary functions: ANYALNUM, ANYALPHA, ANYDIGIT, ANYPUNCT, and
ANYSPACE;

DATA ANYWHERE;
   INPUT STRING $CHAR20.;
   ALPHA_NUM    = ANYALNUM(STRING);
   ALPHA_NUM_9  = ANYALNUM(STRING,-999);
   ALPHA        = ANYALPHA(STRING);
   ALPHA_5      = ANYALPHA(STRING,-5);
   DIGIT        = ANYDIGIT(STRING);
   DIGIT_9      = ANYDIGIT(STRING,-999);
   PUNCT        = ANYPUNCT(STRING);
   SPACE        = ANYSPACE(STRING);
DATALINES;
Once upon a time 123
HELP!
987654321
;
PROC PRINT DATA=ANYWHERE NOOBS HEADING=H;
   TITLE "Listing of Data Set ANYWHERE";
RUN;
```

Explanation

Each of these "ANY" functions works in a similar manner, the only difference being in the types of character values it is searching for. The two statements using a starting value of –999 demonstrate an easy way to search from right to left, without having to know the length of the string (assuming that you don't have any strings longer than 999, in which case you could choose a larger number). Functions such as ANYALPHA and ANYDIGIT can be very useful for extracting values from strings where the positions of digits or letters are not fixed. An alternative to using this group of functions would be the Perl regular expressions. See the following chapter for a complete discussion of regular expressions. Notice in the listing below that the position of the first space in lines two and three are 6 and 10, respectively. These are the positions of the first trailing blank in each of the two strings (remember that the length of STRING is 20).

```
                       Listing of Data Set ANYWHERE


                    ALPHA_  ALPHA_
    STRING            NUM    NUM_9  ALPHA  ALPHA_5  DIGIT  DIGIT_9  PUNCT  SPACE

    Once upon a time 123    1      20     1        4      18     20     0      5
    HELP!                   1       4     1        4       0      0     5      6
    987654321               1       9     0        0       1      9     0     10
```

Program 1.12: Using the functions ANYDIGIT and ANYSPACE to find the first number in a string

```
***Primary functions: ANYDIGIT and ANYSPACE
***Other functions: INPUT and SUBSTR;

DATA SEARCH_NUM;
   INPUT STRING $60.;
   START = ANYDIGIT(STRING);
   END = ANYSPACE(STRING,START);
   IF START NE 0 THEN
      NUM = INPUT(SUBSTR(STRING,START,END-START),9.);
DATALINES;
This line has a 56 in it
two numbers 123 and 456 in this line
No digits here
;
PROC PRINT DATA=SEARCH_NUM NOOBS;
   TITLE "Listing of Data Set SEARCH_NUM";
RUN;
```

Explanation

This program identifies the first number in any line of data that contains a numeric value (followed by one or more blanks). The ANYDIGIT function determines the position of the first digit of the number; the ANYSPACE function searches for the first blank following the number (the starting position of this search is the position of the first digit). The SUBSTR function extracts the digits (starting at the value of START with a length determined by the difference between END and START). Finally, the INPUT function performs the character to numeric conversion. Inspect the listing below to see that this program works as expected.

```
                    Listing of Data Set SEARCH_NUM

     STRING                                    START    END    NUM

     This line has a 56 in it                    17      19     56
     two numbers 123 and 456 in this line        13      16    123
     No digits here                               0       0      .
```

The "NOT" functions (NOTALNUM, NOTALPHA, NOTDIGIT, and NOTUPPER)

This group of functions is similar to the "ANY" functions (such as ANYALNUM, ANYALPHA, etc.) except that the function returns the position of the first character value that is **not** a particular value (alphanumeric, character, digit, or uppercase character). Note that this is not a complete list of the "NOT" functions. See the *SAS OnlineDoc 9.1* for a complete list.

As with the "ANY" functions, there is an optional parameter that specifies where to start the search and in which direction to search.

SAS9.1 **Function: NOTALNUM**

Purpose: To determine the position of the first character in a string that is **not** an alphanumeric (any upper- or lowercase letter or a number). If none is found, the function returns a 0. With the use of an optional parameter, this function can begin searching at any position in the string and can also search from right to left, if desired.

Syntax: NOTALNUM(*character-value* <,*start*>)

character-value is any SAS character expression.

start is an optional parameter that specifies the position in the string to begin the search. If it is omitted, the search starts at the beginning of the string. If it is non-zero, the search begins at the position in the string of the absolute value of the number (starting from the left-most position in the string). If the start value is positive, the search goes from left to right; if the value is negative, the search goes from right to left. A negative value larger than the length of the string results in a scan from right to left, starting at the end of the string. If the value of *start* is a positive number longer than the length of the string, or if it is 0, the function returns a 0.

Examples

For these examples, STRING = "ABC 123 ?xyz_n_"

Function	Returns
NOTALNUM(STRING)	4 (position of the 1st blank)
NOTALNUM("Testing123")	0 (all alpha-numeric values)
NOTALNUM("??$$%%")	1 (position of the "?")
NOTALNUM(STRING,5)	8 (position of the 2nd blank)
NOTALNUM(STRING,-6)	4 (position of the 1st blank)
NOTALNUM(STRING,8)	9 (position of the "?")

SAS9.1 Function: NOTALPHA

Purpose: To determine the position of the first character in a string that is **not** an upper- or lowercase letter (alpha character). If none is found, the function returns a 0. With the use of an optional parameter, this function can begin searching at any position in the string and can also search from right to left, if desired.

Syntax: NOTALPHA(*character-value* <,*start*>)

character-value is any SAS character expression.

start is an optional parameter that specifies the position in the string to begin the search. If it is omitted, the search starts at the beginning of the string. If it is non-zero, the search begins at the position in the string of the absolute value of the number (starting from the left-most position in the string). If the start value is positive, the search goes from left to right; if the value is negative, the search goes from right to left. A negative value larger than the length of the string results in a scan from right to left, starting at the end of the string. If the value of *start* is a positive number longer than the length of the string, or if it is 0, the function returns a 0.

Examples

For these examples, STRING = "ABC 123 ?xyz_n_"

Function	Returns
NOTALPHA(STRING)	4 (position of 1st blank)
NOTALPHA("ABCabc")	0 (all alpha characters)
NOTALPHA("??$$%%")	1 (position of first "?")
NOTALPHA(STRING,5)	5 (position of "1")
NOTALPHA(STRING,-10)	9 (start at position 10 and search left, position of "?")
NOTALPHA(STRING,2)	4 (position of 1st blank)

SAS9.1 Function: **NOTDIGIT**

Purpose: To determine the position of the first character in a string that is **not** a digit. If none is found, the function returns a 0. With the use of an optional parameter, this function can begin searching at any position in the string and can also search from right to left, if desired.

Syntax: NOTDIGIT(*character-value* <,*start*>)

character-value is any SAS character expression.

start is an optional parameter that specifies the position in the string to begin the search. If it is omitted, the search starts at the beginning of the string. If it is non-zero, the search begins at the position in the string of the absolute value of the number (starting from the left-most position in the string). If the start value is positive, the search goes from left to right; if the value is negative, the search goes from right to left. A negative value larger than the length of the string results in a scan from right to left, starting at the end of the string. If the value of start is a positive number longer than the length of the string, or if it is 0, the function returns a 0.

Examples

For these examples, STRING = "ABC 123 ?xyz_n_"

Function	Returns
NOTDIGIT(STRING)	1 (position of "A")
NOTDIGIT("123456")	0 (all digits)
NOTDIGIT("??$$%%")	1 (position of "?")
NOTDIGIT(STRING,5)	8 (position of 2nd blank)
NOTDIGIT(STRING,-6)	4 (position of 1st blank)
NOTDIGIT(STRING,6)	8 (position of 2nd blank)

SAS9.1 Function: NOTUPPER

Purpose: To determine the position of the first character in a string that is **not** an uppercase letter. If none is found, the function returns a 0. With the use of an optional parameter, this function can begin searching at any position in the string and can also search from right to left, if desired.

Syntax: NOTUPPER(*character-value* <,*start*>)

character-value is any SAS character expression.

start is an optional parameter that specifies the position in the string to begin the search. If it is omitted, the search starts at the beginning of the string. If it is non-zero, the search begins at the position in the string of the absolute value of the number (starting from the left-most position in the string). If the start value is positive, the search goes from left to right; if the value is negative, the search goes from right to left. A negative value larger than the length of the string results in a scan from right to left, starting at the end of the string. If the value of *start* is a positive number longer than the length of the string, or if it is 0, the function returns a 0.

Examples

For these examples, STRING = "ABC 123 ?xyz_n_"

Function	Returns
NOTUPPER("ABCDabcd")	5 (position of "a")
NOTUPPER("ABCDEFG")	0 (all uppercase characters)
NOTUPPER(STRING)	4 (position of 1st blank)
NOTUPPER("??$$%%")	1 (position of "?")
NOTUPPER(STRING,5)	5 (position of "1")
NOTUPPER(STRING,-6)	6 (position of "2")
NOTUPPER(STRING,6)	6 (position of "2")

Program 1.13: Demonstrating the "NOT" character functions

```
***Primary functions: NOTALNUM, NOTALPHA, NOTDIGIT, AND NOTUPPER;

DATA NEGATIVE;
   INPUT STRING $5.;
   NOT_ALPHA_NUMERIC = NOTALNUM(STRING);
   NOT_ALPHA        = NOTALPHA(STRING);
   NOT_DIGIT        = NOTDIGIT(STRING);
   NOT_UPPER     .  = NOTUPPER(STRING);
DATALINES;
ABCDE
abcde
abcDE
12345
:#$%&
ABC
;
PROC PRINT DATA=NEGATIVE NOOBS;
   TITLE "Listing of Data Set NEGATIVE";
RUN;
```

Explanation

This straightforward program demonstrates each of the "NOT" character functions. As with most character functions, be careful with trailing blanks. Notice that the last observation ("ABC") contains only three characters but since STRING is read with a $5. informat, there are two trailing blanks following the letters 'ABC'. That is the reason you obtain a value of 4 for all the functions except NOTDIGIT, which returns a 1 (the first character is not a digit). A listing of the data set NEGATIVE is shown next:

```
                        Listing of Data Set NEGATIVE


                      NOT_ALPHA_     NOT_      NOT_      NOT_
            STRING      NUMERIC      ALPHA     DIGIT     UPPER

            ABCDE          0           0         1         0
            abcde          0           0         1         1
            abcDE          0           0         1         1
            12345          0           1         0         1
            :#$%&          1           1         1         1
            ABC            4           4         1         4
```

FIND and FINDC

This pair of functions shares some similarities to the INDEX and INDEXC functions. FIND and INDEX both search a string for a given substring. FINDC and INDEXC both search for individual characters. However, both FIND and FINDC have some additional capability over their counterparts. For example, this pair of functions has the ability to declare a starting position for the search, the direction of the search, and to ignore case or trailing blanks.

SAS9.1 **Function:** **FIND**

Purpose: To locate a substring within a string. With optional arguments, you can define the starting point for the search, the direction of the search, and ignore case or trailing blanks.

Syntax: FIND(*character-value, find-string* <,*'modifiers'*> <,*start*>)

character-value is any SAS character expression.

find-string is a character variable or string literal that contains one or more characters that you want to search for. The function returns the first position in the *character-value* that contains the *find-string*. If the *find-string* is not found, the function returns a 0.

The following modifiers (in upper- or lowercase), placed in single or double quotation marks, may be used with FIND:

i ignore case.

t ignore trailing blanks in both the character variable and the *find-string*.

start is an optional parameter that specifies the position in the string to begin the search. If it is omitted, the search starts at the beginning of the string. If it is non-zero, the search begins at the position in the string of the absolute value of the number. If the value is positive, the search goes from left to right; if the value is negative, the search goes from right to left. A negative value larger than the length of the string results in a scan from right to left, starting at the end of the string. If the value of *start* is a positive number longer than the length of the string, or if it is 0, the function returns a 0.

Examples

For these examples STRING1 = "Hello hello goodbye" and STRING2 = "hello"

Function	Returns
FIND(STRING1, STRING2)	7
FIND(STRING1, STRING2, 'I')	1
FIND(STRING1,"bye")	17
FIND("abcxyzabc","abc",4)	7
FIND(STRING1, STRING2, "i", -99)	7

SAS9.1 **Function:**   **FINDC**

Purpose: To locate a character that appears or does not appear within a string. With optional arguments, you can define the starting point for the search, the direction of the search, to ignore case or trailing blanks, or to look for characters except the ones listed.

Syntax: FINDC(*character-value, find-characters*
<,*'modifiers'*> <,*start*>)

character-value is any SAS character expression.

find-characters is a list of one or more characters that you want to search for.

The function returns the first position in the *character-value* that contains one of the *find-characters*. If none of the characters are found, the function returns a 0. With an optional argument, you can have the function return the position in a character string of a character that is not in the *find-characters* list.

modifiers (in upper- or lowercase), placed in single or double quotation marks, may be used with FINDC as follows:

   i ignore case.

   t ignore trailing blanks in both the character variable and the *find-characters*.

   v count only characters that are not in the list of find characters.

   o process the modifiers and find characters only once to a specific call to the function. In subsequent calls, changes to these arguments will have no effect.

start is an optional parameter that specifies the position in the string to begin the search. If it is omitted, the search starts at the beginning of the string. If it is non-zero, the search begins at the position in the string of the absolute value of the number. If the value is positive, the search goes from left to right; if the value is negative, the search goes from right to left. A negative value larger than the length of the string results in a scan from right to left, starting at the end of the string. If the value of $start$ is a positive number longer than the length of the string, or if it is 0, the function returns a 0.

Note: You can switch the positions of $start$ and $modifiers$ and the function will work the same.

Examples

For these examples STRING1 = "Apples and Books" and STRING2 = "abcde"

Function	Returns
FINDC(STRING1, STRING2)	5
FINDC(STRING1, STRING2, 'i')	1
FINDC(STRING1,"aple",'vi')	6
FINDC("abcxyzabc","abc",4)	7

Program 1.14: Using the FIND and FINDC functions to search for strings and characters

```
***Primary functions: FIND and FINDC;

DATA FIND_VOWEL;
   INPUT @1 STRING $20.;
   PEAR = FIND(STRING,"Pear");
   POS_VOWEL = FINDC(STRING,"aeiou",'I');
   UPPER_VOWEL = FINDC(STRING,"aeiou");
   NOT_VOWEL = FINDC(STRING,"AEIOU",'IV');
DATALINES;
XYZABCabc
XYZ
Apple and Pear
;
PROC PRINT DATA=FIND_VOWEL NOOBS;
   TITLE "Listing of Data Set FIND_VOWEL";
RUN;
```

Explanation

The FIND function returns the position of the characters "Pear" in the variable STRING. Since the i modifier is not used, the search is case-sensitive. The first use of the FINDC function looks for any upper- or lowercase vowel in the string (because of the i modifier). The next statement, without the i modifier, locates only lowercase vowels. Finally, the v modifier in the last FINDC function reverses the search to look for the first character that is not a vowel (upper- or lowercase because of the i modifier).

Program 1.15: Demonstrating the o modifier with FINDC

```
***Primary function: FINDC;

DATA O_MODIFIER;
   INPUT STRING       $15.
         @16 LOOK_FOR $1.;
   POSITION = FINDC(STRING,LOOK_FOR,'IO');
DATALINES;
Capital A here A
Lower a here   X
Apple          B
;
PROC PRINT DATA=O_MODIFIER NOOBS HEADING=H;
   TITLE "Listing of Data Set O_MODIFIER";
RUN;
```

Explanation

In the first call to FINDC, the value of LOOK_FOR is an uppercase A. Since the o modifier was used, changing the value of LOOK_FOR in the next two observations has no effect— the function continues to look for the letter A. Note that another use of FINDC in this DATA step would not be affected by the previous use of the o modifier, even if the name of the variable (in this case POSITION) were the same. The o modifier is most likely useful in reducing processing time when looping through multiple strings, looking for the same string with the same modifiers. The listing of data set O_MODIFIER below shows that, even though the LOOK_FOR value was changed to X in the second observation and B in the third observation, the function continues to search for the letter A.

```
                  Listing of Data Set O_MODIFIER

          STRING           LOOK_FOR    POSITION

          Capital A here      A           2
          Lower a here        X           7
          Apple               B           1
```

INDEX, INDEXC, and INDEXW

This group of functions all search a string for a substring of one or more characters. INDEX and INDEXW are similar, the difference being that INDEXW looks for a word (defined as a string bounded by spaces or the beginning or end of the string) while INDEX simply searches for the designated substring. INDEXC searches for one or more individual characters and always searches from right to left. Note that these three functions are all case-sensitive.

Function: INDEX

Purpose: To locate the starting position of a substring in a string.

Syntax: INDEX(*character-value, find-string*)

character-value is any SAS character expression.

find-string is a character variable or string literal that contains the substring for which you want to search.

The function returns the first position in the *character-value* that contains the *find-string*. If the *find-string* is not found, the function returns a 0.

Examples

For these examples STRING = "ABCDEFG"

Function	Returns
INDEX(STRING,'C')	3 (the position of the 'C')
INDEX(STRING,'DEF')	4 (the position of the 'D')
INDEX(STRING,'X')	0 (no "X" in the string)
INDEX(STRING,'ACE')	0 (no "ACE" in the string)

Program 1.16: Converting numeric values of mixed units (e.g., kg and lbs) to a single numeric quantity

```
***Primary functions: COMPRESS, INDEX, INPUT
***Other function: ROUND;

DATA HEAVY;
   INPUT CHAR_WT $ @@;
   WEIGHT = INPUT(COMPRESS(CHAR_WT,'KG'),8.);
   IF INDEX(CHAR_WT,'K') NE 0 THEN WEIGHT = 2.22 * WEIGHT;
   WEIGHT = ROUND(WEIGHT);
   DROP CHAR_WT;
DATALINES;
60KG 155 82KG 54KG 98
;
PROC PRINT DATA=HEAVY NOOBS;
   TITLE "Listing of Data Set HEAVY";
   VAR WEIGHT;
RUN;
```

Explanation

The data lines contain numbers in kilograms, followed by the abbreviation KG or in pounds (no units used). As with most problems of this type, when you are reading a combination of numbers and characters, you usually need to first read the value as a character. Here the COMPRESS function is used to remove the letters KG from the character value. The INPUT function does its usual job of character to numeric conversion. If the INDEX function returns any value other than a 0, the letter K was found in the string and the WEIGHT value is converted from KG to pounds. Finally, the value is rounded to the nearest pound, using the ROUND function. The listing of data set HEAVY follows:

```
                   Listing of Data Set HEAVY

                   WEIGHT

                     133
                     155
                     182
                     120
                      98
```

Function: **INDEXC**

Purpose: To search a character string for one or more characters. The INDEXC function works in a similar manner to the INDEX function, with the difference being it can be used to search for any one in a list of character values.

Syntax: INDEXC(*character-value*, '*char1*','*char2*','*char3*', ...)

INDEXC(*character-value*, '*char1char2char3*...')

character-value is any SAS character expression.

char1, *char2*, ... are individual character values that you wish to search for in the *character-value*.

The INDEXC function returns the first occurrence of any of the *char1*, *char2*, etc., values in the string. If none of the characters is found, the function returns a 0.

Examples

For these examples STRING = "ABCDEFG"

Function	Returns
INDEXC(STRING,'F','C','G')	3 (position of the "C")
INDEXC(STRING, 'FCG')	3 (position of the "C")
INDEXC(STRING,'FCG')	3 (position of the "C")
INDEXC(STRING,'X','Y','Z')	0 (no "X", "Y", or "Z" in STRING)

Note: It makes no difference if you list the search characters as 'ABC' or 'A','B','C'.

Program 1.17: Searching for one of several characters in a character variable

```
***Primary function: INDEXC;

DATA CHECK;
   INPUT TAG_NUMBER $ @@;
   ***If the tag number contains an X, Y, or Z, it indicates
      an international destination, otherwise, the destination
      is domestic;
   IF INDEXC(TAG_NUMBER,'X','Y','Z') GT 0 THEN
      DESTINATION = 'INTERNATIONAL';
   ELSE DESTINATION = 'DOMESTIC';
DATALINES;
T123 TY333 1357Z UZYX 888 ABC
;
PROC PRINT DATA=CHECK NOOBS;
   TITLE "Listing of Data Set CHECK";
   ID TAG_NUMBER;
   VAR DESTINATION;
RUN;
```

Explanation

Rather than use three statements using the INDEX function, you can use the INDEXC function, which allows you to check for any one of a number of character values. Here, if an X, Y, or Z is found in the variable TAG_NUMBER, the function returns a number greater than 0 and DESTINATION will be set to INTERNATIONAL. As you can see in the listing below, this use of the INDEXC function works as advertised.

```
                    Listing of Data Set CHECK

               TAG_
               NUMBER    DESTINATION

               T123      DOMESTIC
               TY333     INTERNATIONAL
               1357Z     INTERNATIONAL
               UZYX      INTERNATIONAL
               888       DOMESTIC
               ABC       DOMESTIC
```

Program 1.18: Reading dates in a mixture of formats

```
***Primary function: INDEXC
***Other function: INPUT;

***Note: Version 9 has some enhanced date reading ability;

***Program to read mixed dates;
DATA MIXED_DATES;
    INPUT @1 DUMMY $15.;
    IF INDEXC(DUMMY,'/-:') NE 0 THEN DATE = INPUT(DUMMY,MMDDYY10.);
    ELSE DATE = INPUT(DUMMY,DATE9.);
    FORMAT DATE WORDDATE.;
    DROP DUMMY;
DATALINES;
10/21/1946
06JUN2002
5-10-1950
7:9:57
;
PROC PRINT DATA=MIXED_DATES NOOBS;
    TITLE "Listing of Data Set MIXED_DATES";
    VAR DATE;
RUN;
```

Explanation

In this somewhat trumped-up example, dates are entered either in *mm/dd/yyyy* or *ddMONyyyy* form. Also, besides a slash, dashes and colons are used. Any string that includes either a slash, dash, or colon is a date that needs the mmddyy10. informat.

Otherwise, the date9. informat is used. A list of the data set MIXED_DATES is shown below:

```
Listing of Data Set MIXED_DATES

            DATE

October 21, 1946
   June 6, 2002
   May 10, 1950
   July 9, 1957
```

Function: **INDEXW**

Purpose: To search a string for a word, defined as a group of letters separated on both ends by a word boundary (a space, the beginning of a string, end of the string). Note that punctuation is not considered a word boundary.

Syntax: INDEXW(*character-value, find-string*)

character-value is any SAS character expression.

find-string is the word for which you want to search.

The function returns the first position in the *character-value* that contains the *find-string*. If the *find-string* is not found, the function returns a 0.

Examples

For these examples STRING1 = "there is a the here" and
STRING2 = "end in the."

Function	Result
INDEXW(STRING1,"the")	12 (the word "the")
INDEXW("ABABAB","AB")	0 (no word boundaries around "AB")
INDEXW(STRING1,"er")	0 (not a word)
INDEXC(STRING2,"the")	0 (punctuation is not a word boundary)

Program 1.19: Searching for a word using the INDEXW function

```
***Primary functions: INDEX and INDEXW;

DATA FIND_WORD;
   INPUT STRING $40.;
   POSITION_W = INDEXW(STRING,"the");
   POSITION   = INDEX(STRING,"the");
DATALINES;
there is a the in this line
ends in the
ends in the.
none here
;
PROC PRINT DATA=FIND_WORD;
   TITLE "Listing of Data Set FIND_WORD";
RUN;
```

Explanation

This program demonstrates the difference between INDEX and INDEXW. Notice in the first observation in the listing below, the INDEX function returns a 1 because the letters "the" as part of the word "there" begin the string. Since the INDEXW function needs either white space at the beginning or end of a string to delimit a word, it returns a 12, the position of the word "the" in the string. Observation 3 emphasizes the fact that a punctuation mark does not serve as a word separator. Finally, since the string "the" does not appear anywhere in the fourth observation, both functions return a 0. Here is the listing:

```
              Listing of Data Set FIND_WORD

   Obs    STRING                      POSITION_W    POSITION

    1     there is a the in this line     12           1
    2     ends in the                      9           9
    3     ends in the.                     0           9
    4     none here                        0           0
```

Function: VERIFY

Purpose: To check if a string contains any unwanted values.

Syntax: VERIFY(*character-value*, *verify-string*)

character-value is any SAS character expression.

verify-string is a SAS character variable or a list of character values in quotation marks.

This function returns the first position in the *character-value* that is **not** present in the *verify-string*. If the *character-value* does not contain any characters other than those in the *verify-string*, the function returns a 0. Be especially careful to think about trailing blanks when using this function. If you have an 8-byte character variable equal to 'ABC' (followed by five blanks), and if the verify string is equal to 'ABC', the VERIFY function returns a 4, the position of the first blank (which is not present in the verify string). Therefore, you may need to use the TRIM function on either the *character-value*, the *verify-string*, or both.

Examples

For these examples STRING = "ABCXABD" and V = "ABCDE"

Function	Returns
VERIFY(STRING,V)	4 ("X" is not in the verify string)
VERIFY(STRING,"ABCDEXYZ")	0 (no "bad" characters in STRING)
VERIFY(STRING,"ACD")	2 (position of the "B")
VERIFY("ABC ","ABC")	4 (position of the 1st blank)
VERIFY(TRIM("ABC "),"ABC")	0 (no invalid characters)

Program 1.20: Using the VERIFY function to check for invalid character data values

```
***Primary function: VERIFY;

DATA VERY_FI;
   INPUT ID      $ 1-3
         ANSWER $ 5-9;
   P = VERIFY(ANSWER,'ABCDE');
   OK = P EQ 0;
DATALINES;
001 ACBED
002 ABXDE
003 12CCE
004 ABC E
;
PROC PRINT DATA=VERY_FI NOOBS;
   TITLE "listing of Data Set VERY_FI";
RUN;
```

Explanation

In this example, the only valid values for ANSWER are the uppercase letters A–E. Any time there are one or more invalid values, the result of the VERIFY function (variable P) will be a number from 1 to 5. The SAS statement that computes the value of the variable OK needs a word of explanation. First, the logical comparison P EQ 0 returns a value of true or false, which is equivalent to a 1 or 0. This value is then assigned to the variable OK. Thus, the variable OK is set to 1 for all valid values of ANSWER and to 0 for any invalid values. This use of the VERIFY function is very handy in some data cleaning applications. A listing of data set VERI_FI is shown below:

```
              listing of Data Set VERY_FI

        ID      ANSWER    P    OK

        001     ACBED     0    1
        002     ABXDE     3    0
        003     12CCE     1    0
        004     ABC E     4    0
```

Functions That Extract Parts of Strings

The functions described in this section can extract parts of strings. When used on the left hand side of the equal sign, the SUBSTR function can also be used to insert characters into specific positions of an existing string.

Function: **SUBSTR**

Purpose: To extract part of a string. When the SUBSTR function is used on the left side of the equal sign, it can place specified characters into an existing string.

Syntax: SUBSTR(*character-value, start <,length>*)

character-value is any SAS character expression.

start is the starting position within the string.

length if specified, is the number of characters to include in the substring. If this argument is omitted, the SUBSTR function will return all the characters from the start position to the end of the string.

If a length has not been previously assigned, the length of the resulting variable will be the length of the *character-value*.

Examples

For these examples, let STRING = "ABC123XYZ"

Function	Returns
SUBSTR(STRING,4,2)	"12"
SUBSTR(STRING,4)	"123XYZ"
SUBSTR(STRING,LENGTH(STRING))	"Z" (last character in the string)

Program 1.21: Extracting portions of a character value and creating a character variable and a numeric value

---

```
***Primary function: SUBSTR
***Other function: INPUT;

DATA SUBSTRING;
   INPUT ID $ 1-9;
   LENGTH STATE $ 2;
   STATE = SUBSTR(ID,1,2);
   NUM = INPUT(SUBSTR(ID,7,3),3.);
DATALINES;
NYXXXX123
NJ1234567
;
PROC PRINT DATA=SUBSTRING NOOBS;
   TITLE 'Listing of Data Set SUBSTRING';
RUN;
```

Explanation

In this example, the ID contains both state and number information. The first two characters of the ID variable contain the state abbreviations and the last three characters represent numerals that you want to use to create a numeric variable. Extracting the state codes is straightforward. To obtain a numeric value from the last 3 bytes of the ID variable, it is necessary to first use the SUBSTR function to extract the three characters of interest and to then use the INPUT function to do the character to numeric conversion. A listing of data set SUBSTRING is shown next:

```
             Listing of Data Set SUBSTRING

             ID          STATE    NUM

             NYXXXX123    NY       123
             NJ1234567    NJ       567
```

Program 1.22:　Extracting the last two characters from a string, regardless of the length

```
***Primary functions: LENGTH, SUBSTR;

DATA EXTRACT;
   INPUT @1 STRING $20.;
     LAST_TWO = SUBSTR(STRING,LENGTH(STRING)-1,2);
DATALINES;
ABCDE
AX12345NY
126789
;
PROC PRINT DATA=EXTRACT NOOBS;
   TITLE "Listing of Data Set EXTRACT";
     VAR STRING LAST_TWO;
RUN;
```

Explanation

This program demonstrates how you can use the LENGTH and SUBSTR functions together to extract portions of a string when the strings are of different or unknown lengths. To see how this program works, take a look at the first line of data. The LENGTH function will return a 5 and (5–1) = 4, the position of the next to the last (penultimate) character in STRING. See the listing below:

```
                    Listing of Data Set EXTRACT

              STRING        LAST_TWO

              ABCDE           DE
              AX12345NY       NY
              126789          89
```

Program 1.23: Using the SUBSTR function to "unpack" a string

```
***Primary function: SUBSTR
***Other functions: INPUT;

DATA PACK;
    INPUT STRING $ 1-5;
DATALINES;
12345
8 642
;
DATA UNPACK;
    SET PACK;
    ARRAY X[5];
    DO J = 1 TO 5;
        X[J] = INPUT(SUBSTR(STRING,J,1),1.);
    END;
    DROP J;
RUN;
PROC PRINT DATA=UNPACK NOOBS;
    TITLE "Listing of Data Set UNPACK";
RUN;
```

Explanation

There are times when you want to store a group of one-digit numbers in a compact, space-saving way. In this example, you want to store five one-digit numbers. If you stored each one as an 8-byte numeric, you would need 40 bytes of storage for each observation. By storing the five numbers as a 5-byte character string, you need only 5 bytes of storage. However, you need to use CPU time to turn the character string back into the five numbers.

The key here is to use the SUBSTR function with the starting value as the index of a DO loop. As you pick off each of the numerals, you can use the INPUT function to do the character-to-numeric conversion. Notice that the ARRAY statement in this program does not include a list of variables. When this list is omitted and the number of elements is placed in parentheses, SAS automatically uses the array name followed by the numbers from 1 to n, where n is the number in parentheses. A listing of data set UNPACK is shown below:

```
              Listing of Data Set UNPACK

        STRING    X1    X2    X3    X4    X5

        12345     1     2     3     4     5
        8 642     8     .     6     4     2
```

Function: SUBSTR (on the left-hand side of the equal sign)

As we mentioned in the description of the SUBSTR function, there is an interesting and useful way it can be used—on the left-hand side of the equal sign.

Purpose: To place one or more characters into an existing string.

Syntax: SUBSTR(*character-value, start <, length>*) = *character-value*

character-value is any SAS character expression.

start is the starting position in a string where you want to place the new characters.

length is the number of characters to be placed in that string. If *length* is omitted, all the characters on the right-hand side of the equal sign replace the characters in *character-value*.

Examples

In these examples EXISTING = "ABCDEFGH", NEW = "XY"

Function	Returns
SUBSTR(EXISTING,3,2) = NEW	EXISTING is now = "ABXYEFGH"
SUBSTR(EXISTING,3,1) = "*"	EXISTING is now = "AB*DEFGH"

Program 1.24: Demonstrating the SUBSTR function on the left-hand side of the equal sign

```
***Primary function: SUBSTR
***Other function: PUT;

DATA STARS;
   INPUT SBP DBP @@;
   LENGTH SBP_CHK DBP_CHK $ 4;
   SBP_CHK = PUT(SBP,3.);
   DBP_CHK = PUT(DBP,3.);
   IF SBP GT 160 THEN SUBSTR(SBP_CHK,4,1) = '*';
   IF DBP GT 90 THEN SUBSTR(DBP_CHK,4,1) = '*';
DATALINES;
120 80 180 92 200 110
;
PROC PRINT DATA=STARS NOOBS;
   TITLE "Listing of Data Set STARS";
RUN;
```

Explanation

In this program, you want to "flag" high values of systolic and diastolic blood pressure by placing an asterisk after the value. Notice that the variables SBP_CHK and DBP_CHK are both assigned a length of 4 by the length statement. The fourth position needs to be there in case you want to place an asterisk in that position, to flag the value as abnormal. The PUT function places the numerals of the blood pressures into the first 3 bytes of the corresponding character variables. Then, if the value is above the specified level, an asterisk is placed in the fourth position of these variables.

```
             Listing of Data Set STARS

        SBP    DBP    SBP_CHK    DBP_CHK

        120    80      120        80
        180    92      180*       92*
        200    110     200*       110*
```

SAS9.1 Function: SUBSTRN

Purpose: This function serves the same purpose as the SUBSTR function with a few added features. Unlike the SUBSTR function, the starting position and the length arguments of the SUBSTRN function can be 0 or negative without causing an error. In particular, if the length is 0, the function returns a string of 0 length. This is particularly useful when you are using regular expression functions where the length parameter may be 0 when a pattern is not found (with the PRXSUBSTR function, for example). You can use the SUBSTRN function in any application where you would use the SUBSTR function. The effect of 0 or negative parameters is discussed in the description of the arguments below.

Syntax: SUBSTRN(*character-value, start <, length>*)

character-value is any SAS character variable.

start is the starting position in the string. If this value is non-positive, the function returns a substring starting from the first character in *character-value* (the length of the substring will be computed by counting, starting from the value of *start*). See the program below.

length is the number of characters in the substring. If this value is non-positive (in particular, 0), the function returns a string of length 0. If this argument is omitted, the SUBSTRN function will return all the characters from the start position to the end of the string.

If a length has not been previously assigned, the length of the resulting variable will be the length of the *character-value*.

Examples

For these examples, STRING = "ABCDE"

Function	Returns
SUBSTRN(STRING,2,3)	"BCD"
SUBSTRN(STRING,-1,4)	"AB"
SUBSTRN(STRING,4,5)	"DE"
SUBSTRN(STRING,3,0)	string of zero length

Program 1.25: Demonstrating the unique features of the SUBSTRN function

```
***Primary function: SUBSTRN;

DATA HOAGIE;
   STRING = 'ABCDEFGHIJ';
   LENGTH RESULT $5.;
   RESULT = SUBSTRN(STRING,2,5);
   SUB1 = SUBSTRN(STRING,-1,4);
   SUB2 = SUBSTRN(STRING,3,0);
   SUB3 = SUBSTRN(STRING,7,5);
   SUB4 = SUBSTRN(STRING,0,2);
   FILE PRINT;
   TITLE "Demonstrating the SUBSTRN Function";
   PUT "Original String ="       @25 STRING   /
       "SUBSTRN(STRING,2,5) ="   @25 RESULT   /
       "SUBSTRN(STRING,-1,4) ="  @25 SUB1     /
       "SUBSTRN(STRING,3,0) ="   @25 SUB2     /
       "SUBSTRN(STRING,7,5) ="   @25 SUB3     /
       "SUBSTRN(STRING,0,2) ="   @25 SUB4;
RUN;
```

Explanation

In data set HOAGIE (sub-strings, get it?) the storage lengths of the variables SUB1–SUB4 are all equal to the length of STRING (which is 10). Since a LENGTH statement was used to define the length of RESULT, it has a length of 5.

Examine the results below and the brief explanation that follows the results.

```
              Demonstrating the SUBSTRN Function

          Original String =        ABCDEFGHIJ
          SUBSTRN(STRING,2,5) =    BCDEF
          SUBSTRN(STRING,-1,4) =   AB
          SUBSTRN(STRING,3,0) =
          SUBSTRN(STRING,7,5) =    GHIJ
          SUBSTRN(STRING,0,2) =    A
```

The first function call (RESULT) gives the same result as the SUBSTR function. The resulting substring starts at the second position in STRING (B) and has a length of 5. All the remaining SUBSTRN functions would have resulted in an error if the SUBSTR function had been used instead.

The starting position of –1 and a length of 4 results in the characters "AB." To figure this out, realize that you start counting from –1 (–1, 0, 1, 2) and the result is the first two characters in STRING.

When the LENGTH is 0, the result is a string of length 0.

When you start at position 7 and have a length of 5, you go past the end of the string, so that the result is truncated and the result is "GHIJ."

Finally, when the starting position is 0 and the length is 2, you get the first character in string, "A."

Functions That Join Two or More Strings Together

There are three call routines and four functions that concatenate character strings. Although you can use the ‖ concatenation operator in combination with the STRIP, TRIM, or LEFT functions, these routines and functions make it much easier to put strings together and, if you wish, to place one or more separator characters between the strings. The three call routines are discussed first, followed by the four concatenation functions.

Call Routines

These three call routines, new with Version 9, concatenate two or more strings. Note that there are four concatenation functions as well (CAT, CATS, CATT, and CATX). The differences among these routines involve the handling of leading and/or trailing blanks as well as spacing between the concatenated strings. The traditional concatenation operator (‖) is still useful, but it sometimes takes extra work to strip leading and trailing blanks (LEFT and TRIM functions, or the new STRIP function) before performing the concatenation operation. These call routines are a convenience, and you will probably want to use them in place of the older form of concatenation. There are corresponding concatenation functions described in the next section.

One advantage of using the call routines over their corresponding functions is improved performance. For example, CALL CATS(R, X, Y, Z) is faster than R = CATS(R, X, Y, Z).

We will describe all three call routines and follow with one program demonstrating all three.

SAS9.1 Function: CALL CATS

Purpose: To concatenate two or more strings, removing both leading and trailing blanks before the concatenation takes place.   To help you remember that this call routine is the one that strips the leading and trailing blanks before concatenation, think of the S at the end of CATS as "strip blanks."
Note: To call our three cats, I usually just whistle loudly.

Syntax: CALL CATS(*result, string-1 <,string-n>*)

result is the concatenated string. It can be a new variable or, if it is an existing variable, the other strings will be added to it. **Be sure that the length of result is long enough to hold the concatenated results.** If not, the resulting string will be truncated, and you will see an error message in the log.

string-1 and *string-n* are the character strings to be concatenated. Leading and trailing blanks will be stripped prior to the concatenation.

Example

For these examples
A = "Bilbo" (no blanks)
B = "   Frodo" (leading blanks)
C = "Hobbit   " (trailing blanks)
D = "   Gandalf   " (leading and trailing blanks)

Function	Returns
CALL CATS(RESULT, A, B)	"BilboFrodo"
CALL CATS(RESULT, B, C, D)	"FrodoHobbitGandalf"
CALL CATS(RESULT, "Hello", D)	"HelloGandalf"

SAS9.1 Function: **CALL CATT**

Purpose: To concatenate two or more strings, removing only trailing blanks before the concatenation takes place.   To help you remember this, think of the T at the end of CATT as "trailing blanks" or "trim blanks."

Syntax: CALL CATT(*result, string-1 <,string-n>*)

result is the concatenated string.   It can be a new variable or, if it is an existing variable, the other strings will be added to it. **Be sure that the length of result is long enough to hold the concatenated results.** If not, the program will terminate and you will see an error message in the log.

string-1 and *string-n* are the character strings to be concatenated. Trailing blanks will be stripped prior to the concatenation.

Example

For these examples
A = "Bilbo" (no blanks)
B = "   Frodo" (leading blanks)
C = "Hobbit   " (trailing blanks)
D = "   Gandalf   " (leading and trailing blanks)

Function	Returns
CALL CATT(RESULT, A, B)	"Bilbo Frodo"
CALL CATT(RESULT, B, C, D)	" FrodoHobbit Gandalf"
CALL CATT(RESULT, "Hello", D)	"Hello Gandalf"

SAS9.1 Function: **CALL CATX**

Purpose: To concatenate two or more strings, removing both leading and trailing blanks before the concatenation takes place, and place a single space, or one or more characters of your choice, between each of the strings.   To help you remember this, think of the X at the end of CATX as "add eXtra blank."

Syntax: CALL CATX(*separator, result, string-1 <,string-n>*)

separator is one or more characters, placed in single or double quotation marks, that you want to use to separate the strings

result is the concatenated string. It can be a new variable or, if it is an existing variable, the other strings will be added to it. **Be sure that the length of result is long enough to hold the concatenated results.** If not, the program will terminate and you will see an error message in the log.

String-1 and *string-n* are the character strings to be concatenated. Leading and trailing blanks will be stripped prior to the concatenation and a single blank will be placed between the strings.

Example

For these examples
```
A = "Bilbo"  (no blanks)
B = "   Frodo"  (leading blanks)
C = "Hobbit    "  (trailing blanks)
D = "   Gandalf    "  (leading and trailing blanks)
```

Function	Returns
CALL CATX(" ", RESULT, A, B)	"Bilbo Frodo"
CALL CATX(",", RESULT, B, C, D)	"Frodo,Hobbit,Gandalf"
CALL CATX(":", RESULT, "Hello", D)	"Hello:Gandalf"
CALL CATX(", ", RESULT, "Hello", D)	"Hello, Gandalf"
CALL CATX("***", RESULT, A, B)	"Bilbo***Frodo"

Program 1.26: Demonstrating the three concatenation call routines

```
***Primary functions: CALL CATS, CALL CATT, CALL CATX;

DATA CALL_CAT;
   STRING1 = "ABC";       * No spaces;
   STRING2 = "DEF   ";    * Three trailing spaces;
   STRING3 = "   GHI";    * Three leading spaces;
   STRING4 = "   JKL   "; * Three leading and trailing spaces;
   LENGTH RESULT1 - RESULT4 $ 20;
   CALL CATS(RESULT1, STRING2, STRING4);
```

```
      CALL CATT(RESULT2, STRING2, STRING1);
      CALL CATX(" ", RESULT3 ,STRING1,STRING3);
      CALL CATX(",", RESULT4,STRING3,STRING4);
RUN;
PROC PRINT DATA=CALL_CAT NOOBS;
   TITLE "Listing of Data Set CALL_CAT";
RUN;
```

Explanation

The three concatenation call routines each perform concatenation operations. The CATS call routine strips leading and trailing blanks; the CATT call routine removes trailing blanks before performing the concatenation; the CATX call routine is similar to the CATS call routine except that it inserts a separator character (specified as the first argument) between each of the concatenated strings.

According to SAS documentation, the call routines are more efficient to use than the concatenation operator combined with the TRIM and LEFT functions. For example:

```
RESULT5 = TRIM(STRING2) || " " || TRIM(LEFT(STRING3));
```

```
RESULT5 would be: "DEF GHI"
```

A listing of data set CALL_CAT is shown below:

Listing of Data Set CALL_CAT							
STRING1	STRING2	STRING3	STRING4	RESULT1	RESULT2	RESULT3	RESULT4
ABC	DEF	GHI	JKL	DEFJKL	DEFABC	ABC GHI	GHI,JKL

The "CAT" Functions (CAT, CATS, CATT, and CATX)

These four concatenation functions are very similar to the concatenation call routines described above. However, since they are functions and not call routines, you need to name the new character variable to be created on the left-hand side of the equal sign and the function, along with its arguments, on the right-hand side of the equal sign. As with the concatenation call routines, we will describe the four functions together and then use a single program to demonstrate them.

SAS9.1 Function: CAT

Purpose: To concatenate (join) two or more character strings, leaving leading and/or trailing blanks unchanged. This function accomplishes the same task as the concatenation operator (‖).

Syntax: CAT(*string-1, string-2 <,string-n>*)

string-1, string-2 <,string-n> are the character strings to be concatenated. These arguments can also be written as: CAT(OF C1-C5) where C1 to C5 are character variables.

Note: It is **very important to set the length of the resulting character string**, using a LENGTH statement (or other method), before using any of the concatenation functions. Otherwise, the length of the resulting string will default to 200.

Example

For these examples
A = "Bilbo" (no blanks)
B = "   Frodo" (leading blanks)
C = "Hobbit   " (trailing blanks)
D = "   Gandalf   " (leading and trailing blanks)
C1-C5 are five character variables, with the values of 'A', 'B', 'C', 'D', and 'E' respectively.

Function	Returns
CAT(A, B)	"Bilbo Frodo"
CAT(B, C, D)	" FrodoHobbit Gandalf "
CAT("Hello", D)	"Hello Gandalf "
CAT(OF C1-C5)	"ABCDE"

SAS9.1 Function: **CATS**

Purpose: To concatenate (join) two or more character strings, stripping both leading and trailing blanks.

Syntax: CATS(*string-1, string-2 <,string-n>*)

string-1, string-2, and *string-n* are the character strings to be concatenated. These arguments can also be written as: CATS(OF C1-C5) where C1 to C5 are character variables.

Note: It is **very important to set the length of the resulting character string**, using a LENGTH statement or other method, before calling any of the concatenation functions. Otherwise, the length of the resulting string will default to 200.

Example

For these examples
A = "Bilbo" (no blanks)
B = " Frodo" (leading blanks)
C = "Hobbit " (trailing blanks)
D = " Gandalf " (leading and trailing blanks)
C1-C5 are five character variables, with the values of 'A', 'B', 'C', 'D', and 'E' respectively.

Function	Returns
CATS(A, B)	"BilboFrodo"
CATS(B, C, D)	"FrodoHobbitGandalf"
CATS("Hello", D)	"HelloGandalf"
CATS(OF C1-C5)	"ABCDE"

SAS9.1 **Function: CATT**

Purpose: To concatenate (join) two or more character strings, stripping only trailing blanks.

Syntax: CATT(*string-1, string-2 <,string-n>*)

string1, string-2, and *string-n* are the character strings to be concatenated. These arguments can also be written as: CATT(OF C1-C5) where C1 to C5 are character variables.

Note: It is **very important to set the length of the resulting character string**, using a LENGTH statement or other method, before calling any of the concatenation functions. Otherwise, the length of the resulting string will default to 200.

Example:

For these examples
A = "Bilbo" (no blanks)
B = "   Frodo" (leading blanks)
C = "Hobbit   " (trailing blanks)
D = "   Gandalf   " (leading and trailing blanks)
C1-C5 are five character variables, with the values of 'A', 'B', 'C', 'D', and 'E' respectively.

Function	Returns
CATT(A, B)	"Bilbo Frodo"
CATT(B, C, D)	" FrodoHobbit Gandalf"
CATT("Hello", D)	"Hello Gandalf"
CATT(OF C1-C5)	"ABCDE"

SAS9.1 **Function:**   **CATX**

Purpose: To concatenate (join) two or more character strings, stripping both leading and trailing blanks and inserting one or more separator characters between the strings.

Syntax: CATX(*separator, string-1, string-2 <,string-n>*)

separator is one or more characters, placed in single or double quotation marks, to be used as separators between the concatenated strings.

string-1, string-2, string-n are the character strings to be concatenated. These arguments can also be written as: CATX(" ",OF C1-C5), where C1 to C5 are character variables.

Note: It is **very important to set the length of the resulting character string** using a LENGTH statement (or other method), before calling any of the concatenation functions. Otherwise, the length of the resulting string will default to 200.

Example

For these examples
A = "Bilbo" (no blanks)
B = "   Frodo" (leading blanks)
C = "Hobbit   " (trailing blanks)
D = "   Gandalf   " (leading and trailing blanks)
C1-C5 are five character variables, with the values of 'A', 'B', 'C', 'D', and 'E' respectively.

Function	Returns
CATX(" ", A, B)	"Bilbo Frodo"
CATX(":"B, C, D)	"Frodo:Hobbit:Gandalf"
CATX("***", "Hello", D)	"Hello***Gandalf"
CATX("," ,OF C1-C5)	"A,B,C,D,E"

Program 1.27: Demonstrating the four concatenation functions

```
***Primary functions: CAT, CATS, CATT, CATX;

DATA CAT_FUNCTIONS;
   STRING1 = "ABC";       * No spaces;
   STRING2 = "DEF   ";    * Three trailing spaces;
   STRING3 = "   GHI";    * Three leading spaces;
   STRING4 = "   JKL   "; * Three leading and trailing spaces;
   LENGTH JOIN1 - JOIN5 $ 20;
   JOIN1 = CAT(STRING2, STRING3);
   JOIN2 = CATS(STRING2, STRING4);
   JOIN3 = CATT(STRING2, STRING1);
   JOIN4 = CATX(" ",STRING1,STRING3);
   JOIN5 = CATX(",",STRING3,STRING4);
RUN;
PROC PRINT DATA=CAT_FUNCTIONS NOOBS;
   TITLE "Listing of Data Set CAT_FUNCTIONS";
RUN;
```

Explanation

Notice that each of the STRING variables differs with respect to leading and trailing blanks. The CAT function is identical to the || operator. The CATS function removes both leading and trailing blanks and is equivalent to TRIM(LEFT(STRING2)) || TRIM(LEFT(STRING4)). The CATT function, trims only trailing blanks. The last two statements use the CATX function, which removes leading and trailing blanks. It is just like the CATS function but adds one or more separator characters (specified as the first argument), between each of the strings to be joined. Inspection of the listing below will help make all this clear:

```
            Listing of Data Set CAT_FUNCTIONS

     STRING1    STRING2    STRING3    STRING4      JOIN1

       ABC        DEF        GHI        JKL      DEF   GHI

     JOIN2      JOIN3      JOIN4      JOIN5

     DEFJKL     DEFABC     ABC GHI    GHI,JKL
```

Functions That Remove Blanks from Strings

There are times when you want to remove blanks from the beginning or end of a character string. The two functions LEFT and RIGHT merely shift the characters to the beginning or the end of the string, respectively. The TRIM, TRIMN, and STRIP functions are useful when you want concatenate strings (although the new concatenation functions will do this for you).

LEFT and RIGHT

These two functions left- or right-align text. Remember that the length of a character variable will not change when you use these two functions. If there are leading blanks, the LEFT function will shift the first non-blank character to the first position and move the extra blanks to the end; if there are trailing blanks, the RIGHT function will shift the non-blank text to the right and move the extra blanks to the left.

Function:	**LEFT**
Purpose:	To left-align text values. A subtle but important point: LEFT doesn't "remove" the leading blanks; it moves them to the end of the string. Thus, it doesn't change the storage length of the variable, even when you assign the result of LEFT to a new variable. The LEFT function is particularly useful if values were read with the $CHAR informat, which preserves leading blanks. Note that the STRIP function removes both leading and trailing blanks from a string.
Syntax:	LEFT(*character-value*)
	character-value is any SAS character expression.

Example
In these examples STRING = "   ABC"

Function	Returns
LEFT(STRING)	"ABC "
LEFT(" 123 ")	"123 "

Program 1.28: Left-aligning text values from variables read with the $CHAR informat

```
***Primary function: LEFT;

DATA LEAD_ON;
   INPUT STRING $CHAR15.;
   LEFT_STRING = LEFT(STRING);
DATALINES;
ABC
   XYZ
 Ron Cody
;
PROC PRINT DATA=LEAD_ON NOOBS;
   TITLE "Listing of Data Set LEAD_ON";
   FORMAT STRING LEFT_STRING $QUOTE17.;
RUN;
```

Explanation

If you want to work with character values, you will usually want to remove any leading
blanks first. The $CHARw. informat differs from the $w. informat. $CHARw. maintains
leading blanks; $w. left-aligns the text. Programs involving character variables sometimes
fail to work properly because careful attention was not paid to either leading or trailing
blanks.

Notice the use of the $QUOTE format in the PRINT procedure. This format adds double
quotation marks around the character value. This is especially useful in debugging programs
involving character variables since it allows you to easily identify leading blanks in a
character value.

The listing of data set LEAD_ON is shown below.   Notice that the original variable
STRING contains leading blanks. The length of LEFT_STRING is also 15.

```
                    Listing of Data Set LEAD_ON

            STRING                 LEFT_STRING

            "ABC"                  "ABC"
            "   XYZ"               "XYZ"
            " Ron Cody"            "Ron Cody"
```

Function: **RIGHT**

Purpose: To right-align a text string. Note that if the length of a character variable has previously been defined and it contains trailing blanks, the RIGHT function will move the characters to the end of the string and add the blanks to the beginning so that the final length of the variable remains the same.

Syntax: `right(`*`character-value`*`)`

character-value is any SAS character expression.

Example

In these examples STRING = "ABC   "

Function	Returns
RIGHT(STRING)	" ABC"
RIGHT(" 123 ")	" 123"

Program 1.29: Right-aligning text values

```
***Primary function: RIGHT;

DATA RIGHT_ON;
   INPUT STRING $CHAR10.;
   RIGHT_STRING = RIGHT(STRING);
DATALINES;
   ABC
   123 456
Ron Cody
;
PROC PRINT DATA=RIGHT_ON NOOBS;
   TITLE "Listing of Data Set RIGHT_ON";
   FORMAT STRING RIGNT_STRING $QUOTE12.;
RUN;
```

Explanation

Data lines one and two both contain three leading blanks; lines one and three contain trailing blanks.

Notice the use of the $QUOTE format in the PRINT procedure. This format adds double quotation marks around the character value. This is especially useful in debugging programs involving character variables since it allows you to easily identify leading blanks in a character value.

Notice in the listing below, that the values are right-aligned and that blanks are moved to the beginning of the string:

```
             Listing of Data Set RIGHT_ON

             STRING            RIGHT_STRING

             "   ABC"          "        ABC"
             "   123 456"      "   123 456"
             "Ron Cody"        "   Ron Cody"
```

TRIM, TRIMN, and STRIP

This group of functions trims trailing blanks (TRIM and TRIMN) and both leading and trailing blanks (STRIP).

The two functions TRIM and TRIMN are similar: they both remove trailing blanks from a string. The functions work identically except when the argument contains only blanks. In that case, TRIM returns a single blank (length of 1) and TRIMN returns a null string with a length of 0. The STRIP function removes both leading and trailing blanks.

Function: TRIM

Purpose: To remove trailing blanks from a character value. This is especially useful when you want to concatenate several strings together and each string may contain trailing blanks.

Syntax: TRIM(*character-value*)

character-value is any SAS character expression.

Important note: The length of the variable returned by the TRIM function will be the same length as the argument, unless the length of this variable has been previously defined. If the result of the TRIM function is assigned to a variable with a length longer than the trimmed argument, the resulting variable will be padded with blanks.

Examples

For these examples, STRING1 = "ABC   " and STRING2 = "   XYZ"

Function	Returns
TRIM(STRING1)	"ABC"
TRIM(STRING2)	" XYZ"
TRIM("A B C ")	"A B C"
TRIM("A ") || TRIM("B ")	"AB"
TRIM(" ")	" " (length = 1)

Program 1.30: Creating a program to concatenate first, middle, and last names into a single variable

```
***Primary function: TRIM;

DATA PUT_TOGETHER;
   LENGTH NAME $ 45;
   INFORMAT NAME1-NAME3 $15.;
   INFILE DATALINES MISSOVER;
   INPUT NAME1 NAME2 NAME3;
   NAME = TRIM(NAME1) || ' ' || TRIM(NAME2) || ' ' || TRIM(NAME3);
   WITHOUT = NAME1 || NAME2 || NAME3;
   KEEP NAME WITHOUT;
DATALINES;
Ronald Cody
Julia     Child
Henry     Ford
Lee Harvey Oswald
;
PROC PRINT DATA=PUT_TOGETHER NOOBS;
   TITLE "Listing Of Data Set PUT_TOGETHER";
RUN;
```

Explanation

Note that this program would be much simpler using the concatenation functions or call routines. However, this method was used to demonstrate the TRIM function.

This program reads in three names, each up to 15 characters in length. Note the use of the INFILE option MISSOVER. This options sets the value of NAME3 to missing when there are only two names.

To put the names together, you use the concatenate operator (||). The TRIM function is used to trim trailing blanks from each of the words (which are all 15 bytes in length), before putting them together. Without the TRIM function, there are extra spaces between each of the names (see the variable WITHOUT). The listing below demonstrates that the program works as desired.

```
                    Listing Of Data Set PUT_TOGETHER

        NAME                    WITHOUT


        Ronald Cody             Ronald          Cody
        Julia Child             Julia           Child
        Henry Ford              Henry           Ford
        Lee Harvey Oswald       Lee             Harvey          Oswald
```

Function: **TRIMN**

Purpose: To remove trailing blanks from a character value. This is especially useful when you want to concatenate several strings together and each string may contain trailing blanks. The difference between TRIM and TRIMN is that the TRIM function returns a single blank for a blank string while TRIMN returns a null string (zero blanks).

Syntax: `TRIMN(character-value)`

character-value is any SAS character expression.

Important note: The length of the variable returned by the TRIMN function will be the same length as the argument, unless the length of this variable has been previously defined. If the result of the TRIMN function is assigned to a variable with a length longer than the trimmed argument, the resulting variable will be padded with blanks.

Examples

For these examples, `STRING1 = "ABC    "` and `STRING2 = "    XYZ"`

Function	Returns
`TRIMN(STRING1)`	`"ABC"`
`TRIMN(STRING2)`	`"    XYZ"`
`TRIMN("A  B  C  ")`	`"A  B  C"`
`TRIMN("A  ") || TRIM("B  ")`	`"AB"`
`TRIMN("    ")`	`""` (length = 0)

Program 1.31: Demonstrating the difference between the TRIM and TRIMN functions

```
***Primary functions: TRIM, TRIMN, and LENGTHC
***Other function: COMPRESS;

DATA ALL_THE_TRIMMINGS;
   A = "AAA";
   B = "BBB";
   LENGTH_AB = LENGTHC(A || B);
   LENGTH_AB_TRIM = LENGTHC(TRIM(A) || TRIM(B));
   LENGTH_AB_TRIMN = LENGTHC(TRIMN(A) || TRIMN(B));
   LENGTH_NULL = LENGTHC(COMPRESS(A,"A") || COMPRESS(B, "B"));
   LENGTH_NULL_TRIM = LENGTHC(TRIM(COMPRESS(A,"A")) ||
                   TRIM(COMPRESS(B,"B")));
   LENGTH_NULL_TRIMN = LENGTHC(TRIMN(COMPRESS(A,"A")) ||
                   TRIMN(COMPRESS(B,"B")));
   PUT A= B= /
       LENGTH_AB= LENGTH_AB_TRIM= LENGTH_AB_TRIMN= /
       LENGTH_NULL= LENGTH_NULL_TRIM= LENGTH_NULL_TRIMN=;
RUN;
```

Explanation

First, remember that the LENGTHC function returns the length of its argument, including trailing blanks. As the listing from the SAS log (below) shows, the two functions TRIM and TRIMN yield identical results when there are no null strings involved. When you compress an 'A' from the variable A, or 'B' from variable B, the result is null. Notice that when you trim these compressed values and concatenate the results, the length is 2 (1 + 1); when you use the TRIMN function, the length is 0. Here are the lines written to the SAS log:

```
A=AAA B=BBB
LENGTH_AB=6 LENGTH_AB_TRIM=6 LENGTH_AB_TRIMN=6
LENGTH_NULL=0 LENGTH_NULL_TRIM=2 LENGTH_NULL_TRIMN=0
```

SAS9.1 Function: STRIP

Purpose: To strip leading and trailing blanks from character variables or strings. STRIP(CHAR) is equivalent to TRIMN(LEFT(CHAR)), but more convenient.

Syntax: STRIP(*character-value*)

character-value is any SAS character expression.

If the STRIP function is used to create a new variable, the length of that new variable will be equal to the length of the argument of the STRIP function. If leading or trailing blanks were trimmed, trailing blanks will be added to the result to pad out the length as necessary. The STRIP function is useful when using the concatenation operator. However, note that there are several new concatenation functions and call routines that also perform trimming before concatenation.

Examples

For these examples, let STRING = " abc "

Function	Returns
`STRIP(STRING)`	`"abc"` (if result was previously assigned a length of three, otherwise trailing blanks would be added)
`STRIP("   LEADING AND TRAILING   ")`	`"LEADING AND TRAILING"`

Program 1.32: Using the STRIP function to strip both leading and trailing blanks from a string

```
***Primary function: STRIP;

DATA _NULL_;
   ONE = "   ONE   "; ***Note: three leading and trailing blanks;
   TWO = "   TWO   "; ***Note: three leading and trailing blanks;
   CAT_NO_STRIP = ":" || ONE || "-" || TWO || ":";
   CAT_STRIP    = ":" || STRIP(ONE) || "-" || STRIP(TWO) || ":";
   PUT ONE= TWO= / CAT_NO_STRIP= / CAT_STRIP=;
RUN;
```

Explanation

Without the STRIP function, the leading and trailing blanks are maintained in the concatenated string. The STRIP function, as advertised, removed the leading and trailing blanks. The following lines were written to the SAS log:

```
ONE=ONE TWO=TWO
CAT_NO_STRIP=:   ONE   -   TWO   :
CAT_STRIP=:ONE-TWO:
```

Functions That Compare Strings (Exact and "Fuzzy" Comparisons)

Functions in this section allow you to compare strings that are exactly alike (similar except for case) or close (not exact matches). Programmers find this latter group of functions useful in matching names that may be spelled differently in separate files.

SAS9.1 **Function:** **COMPARE**

Purpose: To compare two character strings. When used with one or more modifiers, this function can ignore case, remove leading blanks, truncate the longer string to the length of the shorter string, and strip quotation marks from SAS n-literals. While all of these tasks can be accomplished with a variety of SAS functions, use of the COMPARE function can simplify character comparisons.

Syntax: COMPARE(*string-1*, *string-2* <,'*modifiers*'>)

string-1 is any SAS character expression.

string-2 is any SAS character expression.

modifiers are one or more modifiers, placed in single or double quotation marks as follows:

i or I	ignore case.
l or L	remove leading blanks.
n or N	remove quotation marks from any argument that is an n-literal and ignore case.
	An n-literal is a string in quotation marks, followed by an 'n', useful for non-valid SAS names.
: (colon)	truncate the longer string to the length of the shorter string.

Note that the default is to pad the shorter string with blanks before a comparison; this is similar to the =: comparison operator.

Note that the order of the modifiers is important. See the examples below.

The function returns a 0 when the two strings match (after any modifiers are applied). If the two strings differ, a non-zero result is returned. The returned value is negative if *string-1* comes before *string-2* in a sort sequence, positive otherwise. The magnitude of this value is the position of the first difference in the two strings.

Examples

For these examples, string1 = "AbC", string2 = "   ABC", string3 = "   'ABC'n", string4 = "ABCXYZ"

Function	Returns
COMPARE(string1,string4)	2 ("B" comes before "b")
COMPARE(string4,string1)	-2
COMPARE(string1,string2,'i')	1
COMPARE(string1,string4,':I')	0
COMPARE(string1,string3,'nl')	4
COMPARE(string1,string3,'ln')	1

Program 1.33: Comparing two strings using the COMPARE function

```
***Primary function: COMPARE
***Other function: UPCASE;

DATA COMPARE;
   INPUT @1 STRING1 $CHAR3.
         @5 STRING2 $CHAR10.;
   IF UPCASE(STRING1) = UPCASE(STRING2) THEN EQUAL = 'YES';
   ELSE EQUAL = 'NO';
   IF UPCASE(STRING1) =: UPCASE(STRING2) THEN COLON = 'YES';
   ELSE COLON = 'NO';
   COMPARE = COMPARE(STRING1,STRING2);
   COMPARE_IL = COMPARE(STRING1,STRING2,'IL');
   COMPARE_IL_COLON = COMPARE(STRING1,STRING2,'IL:');
DATALINES;
```

```
Abc    ABC
abc ABCDEFGH
123 311
;

PROC PRINT DATA=COMPARE NOOBS;
   TITLE "Listing of Data Set COMPARE";
RUN;
```

Explanation

The first two variables, EQUAL and COLON, use the UPCASE function to convert all the characters to uppercase before the comparison is made. The colon modifier following the equal sign (the variable COLON) is an instruction to truncate the longer variable to the length of the shorter variable before a comparison is made. Be careful here. If the variable STRING1 had been read with a $CHAR10. informat, the =: comparison operator would not have produced a match. The length truncation is done on the storage length of the variable, which may include trailing blanks.

The three COMPARE functions demonstrate the coding efficiency of using this function with its many modifiers. Use of this function without modifiers gives you no advantage over a simple test of equality using an equal sign. Using the IL and colon modifiers allows you to compare the two strings, ignoring case, removing leading blanks, and truncating the two strings to a length of 3 (the length of STRING1). Note the value of COMPARE_IL_COLON in the third observation is –1 since "1" comes before "3" in the ASCII collating sequence. The output from PROC PRINT is shown below:

```
                        Listing of Data Set COMPARE


                                                    COMPARE_      COMPARE_
    STRING1    STRING2    EQUAL    COLON   COMPARE      IL         IL_COLON

      Abc        ABC       NO       NO        1         0            0
      abc     ABCDEFGH     NO       YES       1        -4            0
      123       311        NO       NO       -1        -1           -1
```

CALL COMPCOST, COMPGED, and COMPLEV

The two functions, COMPGED and COMPLEV, are both used to determine the similarity between two strings. The COMPCOST call routine allows you to customize the scoring system when you are using the COMPGED function.

COMPGED computes a quantity called **generalized edit distance**, which is useful in matching names that are not spelled exactly the same. The larger the value, the more dissimilar the two strings. COMPLEV performs a similar function but uses a method called the **Levenshtein edit distance**. It is more efficient than the generalized edit distance, but may not be as useful in name matching. See the SPEDIS function for a discussion of fuzzy merging and for detailed programming examples.

SAS9.1 **Function:**   **CALL COMPCOST**

Purpose: To determine the similarity between two strings, using a method called the generalized edit distance. The cost is computed based on the difference between the two strings. For example, replacing one letter with another is assigned one cost and reversing two letters can be assigned another cost. Since there is a default cost associated with every operation used by COMPGED, you can use that function without using COMPCOST at all. You need to call this function only once in a DATA step. Since this is a very advanced and complicated routine, only a few examples of its use will be explained. See the *SAS OnlineDoc 9.1* for a complete list of operations and costs.

Syntax: `CALL COMPCOST('operation-1', cost-1 <,'operation-2', cost-2 ...>)`

    `operation` is a keyword, placed in quotation marks. A few keywords are listed here for explanation purposes, but see the *SAS OnlineDoc 9.1* documentation for a complete list of operations:

        Partial List of Operations
        `DELETE=`
        `REPLACE=`
        `SWAP=`
        `TRUNCATE=`

cost is a value associated with the operation. Valid values for cost range from –32,767 to +32,767.

Note: The wording of arguments in this book might differ from the wording of arguments in the *SAS OnlineDoc 9.1*.

Examples

```
CALL COMPCOST('REPLACE=', 100, 'SWAP=', 200);
CALL COMPCOST('SWAP=', 150);
```
Note: Operation can be upper- or lowercase

To see how CALL COMPCOST and COMPGED are used together, see Program 1.36.

SAS9.1 **Function:** **COMPGED**

Purpose: To compute the similarity between two strings, using a method called the generalized edit distance. See SPEDIS for a discussion of the possible uses of this function.

This function can be used in conjunction with CALL COMPCOST if you want to alter the default costs for each type of spelling error.

Syntax: COMPGED(*string-1*, *string-2* <,*maxcost*> <,'*modifiers*'>)

string-1 is any SAS character expression.
string-2 is any SAS character expression.

maxcost, if specified, is the maximum cost that will be returned by the COMPLEV function. If the cost computation results in a value larger than *maxcost*, the value of *maxcost* will be returned.

modifiers placed in single or double quotation marks as follows:

i or I	ignore case.
l or L	remove leading blanks.
n or N	remove quotation marks from any argument that is an n-literal and ignore case. An n-literal is a string in quotation marks, followed by an 'n', useful for non-valid SAS names.
: (colon)	truncate the longer string to the length of the shorter string.

Note: If multiple modifiers are used, the order of the modifiers is important. They are applied in the same order as they appear.

Examples

String1	String2	Function	Returns
SAME	SAME	COMPGED(STRING1, STRING2)	0
case	CASE	COMPGED(STRING1, STRING2)	500
case	CASE	COMPGED(STRING1,STRING2,'I')	0
case	CASE	COMPGED(STRING1, STRING2, 999, 'I')	0
Ron	Run	COMPGED(STRING1, STRING2)	100

Program 1.34: Using the COMPGED function with a SAS n-literal

```
***Primary function: COMPGED;

OPTIONS VALIDVARNAME=ANY;

DATA N_LITERAL;
   STRING1 = "'INVALID#'N";
   STRING2 = 'INVALID';
   COMP1 = COMPGED(STRING1,STRING2);
   COMP2 = COMPGED(STRING1,STRING2,'N:');
RUN;
```

```
PROC PRINT DATA=N_LITERAL NOOBS;
   TITLE "Listing of Data Set N_LITERAL";
RUN;
```

Explanation

This program demonstrates the use of the COMPGED function with a SAS n-literal. Starting with Version 7, SAS variable names could contain characters not normally allowed in SAS names. The system option VALIDVARNAME is set to "ANY" and the name is placed in quotation marks, followed by the letter N. Using the N modifier (which strips quotation marks and the 'n' from the string) and the colon modifier (which truncates the longer string to the length of the shorter string) results in a value of 0 for the variable COMP2. See the listing below:

```
                 Listing of Data Set N_LITERAL

            STRING1        STRING2    COMP1    COMP2

           'INVALID#'N     INVALID     310       0
```

SAS9.1 Function: **COMPLEV**

Purpose: To compute the similarity between two strings, using a method called the *Levenshtein edit distance*. It is similar to the COMPGED function except that it uses less computer resources but may not do as good a job of matching misspelled names.

Syntax: COMPLEV(*string-1*, *string-2* <,*maxcost*> <,*'modifiers'*>)

string-1 is any SAS character expression.

string-2 is any SAS character expression.

maxcost, if specified, is the maximum cost that will be returned by the COMPGED function. If the cost computation results in a value larger than *maxcost*, the value of *maxcost* will be returned.

modifiers (placed in single or double quotation marks)

i or I	ignore case.
l or L	remove leading blanks.
n or N	remove quotation marks from any argument that is an n-literal and ignore case.
	An n-literal is a string in quotation marks, followed by an 'n', that is useful for non-valid SAS names.
:(colon)	truncate the longer string to the length of the shorter string.

Note: If multiple modifiers are used, the order of the modifiers is important. They are applied in the same order as they appear.

Examples

String1	String2	Function	Returns
SAME	SAME	COMPLEV(STRING1, STRING2)	0
case	CASE	COMPLEV(STRING1, STRING2)	4
case	CASE	COMPLEV(STRING1,STRING2,'I')	0
case	CASE	COMPLEV(STRING1, STRING2, 999, 'I')	0
Ron	Run	COMPLEV(STRING1, STRING2)	1

Program 1.35: Demonstration of the generalized edit distance (COMPGED) and Levenshtein edit distance (COMPLEV) functions

```
***Primary functions: COMPGED and COMPLEV;

DATA _NULL_;
   INPUT @1  STRING1 $CHAR10.
         @11 STRING2 $CHAR10.;
   PUT "Function COMPGED";
   DISTANCE = COMPGED(STRING1, STRING2);
   IGNORE_CASE = COMPGED(STRING1, STRING2, 'I');
   LEAD_BLANKS = COMPGED(STRING1, STRING2, 'L');
   CASE_TRUNC = COMPGED(STRING1, STRING2, ':I');
   MAX = COMPGED(STRING1, STRING2, 250);
   PUT STRING1= STRING2= /
       DISTANCE= IGNORE_CASE= LEAD_BLANKS= CASE_TRUNC= MAX= /;

   PUT "Function COMPLEV";
   DISTANCE = COMPLEV(STRING1, STRING2);
   IGNORE_CASE = COMPLEV(STRING1, STRING2, 'I');
   LEAD_BLANKS = COMPLEV(STRING1, STRING2, 'L');
   CASE_TRUNC = COMPLEV(STRING1, STRING2, ':I');
   MAX = COMPLEV(STRING1, STRING2, 3);
   PUT STRING1= STRING2= /
       DISTANCE= IGNORE_CASE= LEAD_BLANKS= CASE_TRUNC= MAX= /;
DATALINES;
SAME      SAME
cAsE      case
Longer    Long
abcdef    xyz
   lead    lead
;
```

Explanation

In this program, all the default costs were used, so it was not necessary to call COMPCOST. Notice that the strings were read in with the $CHAR. informat so that leading blanks would be preserved. If you wish to use modifiers, you must enter them in quotation marks, in the order you want the modifying operations to proceed.   Careful inspection of the SAS log below demonstrates the COMPGED and COMPLEV functions and the effects of the modifiers and the *maxcost* parameter.

SAS Log from Program 1.35

```
Function COMPGED
STRING1=SAME STRING2=SAME
DISTANCE=0 IGNORE_CASE=0 LEAD_BLANKS=0 CASE_TRUNC=0 MAX=0

Function COMPLEV
STRING1=SAME STRING2=SAME
DISTANCE=0 IGNORE_CASE=0 LEAD_BLANKS=0 CASE_TRUNC=0 MAX=0

Function COMPGED
STRING1=cAsE STRING2=case
DISTANCE=200 IGNORE_CASE=0 LEAD_BLANKS=200 CASE_TRUNC=0 MAX=200

Function COMPLEV
STRING1=cAsE STRING2=case
DISTANCE=2 IGNORE_CASE=0 LEAD_BLANKS=2 CASE_TRUNC=0 MAX=2

Function COMPGED
STRING1=Longer STRING2=Long
DISTANCE=100 IGNORE_CASE=100 LEAD_BLANKS=100 CASE_TRUNC=100 MAX=100

Function COMPLEV
STRING1=Longer STRING2=Long
DISTANCE=2 IGNORE_CASE=2 LEAD_BLANKS=2 CASE_TRUNC=2 MAX=2

Function COMPGED
STRING1=abcdef STRING2=xyz
DISTANCE=550 IGNORE_CASE=550 LEAD_BLANKS=550 CASE_TRUNC=550 MAX=250

Function COMPLEV
STRING1=abcdef STRING2=xyz
DISTANCE=6 IGNORE_CASE=6 LEAD_BLANKS=6 CASE_TRUNC=6 MAX=3

Function COMPGED
STRING1=lead STRING2=lead
DISTANCE=320 IGNORE_CASE=320 LEAD_BLANKS=0 CASE_TRUNC=320 MAX=250

Function COMPLEV
STRING1=lead STRING2=lead
DISTANCE=3 IGNORE_CASE=3 LEAD_BLANKS=0 CASE_TRUNC=3 MAX=3
```

The program below demonstrates how to use CALL COMPCOST in combination with COMPGED and the resulting differences.

Program 1.36: Changing the effect of the call to COMPCOST on the result from COMPGED

```
***Primary functions: CALL COMPCOST and COMPGED;

DATA _NULL_;
   TITLE "Program without Call to COMPCOST";
   INPUT @1  STRING1 $CHAR10.
         @11 STRING2 $CHAR10.;
   DISTANCE = COMPGED(STRING1, STRING2);
   PUT STRING1= STRING2= /
       DISTANCE=;
DATALINES;
Ron       Run
ABC       AB
;
DATA _NULL_;
   TITLE "Program with Call to COMPCOST";
   INPUT @1  STRING1 $CHAR10.
         @11 STRING2 $CHAR10.;
   IF _N_ = 1 THEN CALL COMPCOST('APPEND=',33);
   DISTANCE = COMPGED(STRING1, STRING2);
   PUT STRING1= STRING2= /
       DISTANCE=;
DATALINES;
Ron       Run
ABC       AB
;
```

Explanation

The first DATA _NULL_ program is a simple comparison of STRING1 to STRING2, using the COMPGED function. The second DATA _NULL_ program makes a call to COMPCOST (note the use of _N_= 1) before the COMPGED function is used. In the SAS logs below, you can see that the distance in the second observation in the first program is 50, while in the second program it is 33. That is the result of overriding the default value of 50 points for an appending error and setting it equal to 33.

SAS Log from Program without CALL COMPCOST

```
STRING1=Ron STRING2=Run
DISTANCE=100
STRING1=ABC STRING2=AB
DISTANCE=50
```

SAS Log from Program with CALL COMPCOST

```
STRING1=Ron STRING2=Run
DISTANCE=100
STRING1=ABC STRING2=AB
DISTANCE=33
```

Function: SOUNDEX

The SOUNDEX function creates a phonetic equivalent of a text string to facilitate "fuzzy" matching. You can research the details of the SOUNDEX algorithm in the *SAS OnlineDoc 9.1*. Briefly, this algorithm makes all vowels equal, along with letters that sound the same (such as 'C' and 'K'). One feature of this algorithm is that the first letters in both words must be the same to obtain a phonetic match. For those readers interested in the topic of fuzzy matching, there is an algorithm called NYSIIS, similar to the SOUNDEX algorithm, that maintains vowel position information and allows mismatches on the initial letter. A copy of a macro to implement the NYSIIS algorithm is available on the companion Web site for this book, located at **support.sas.com/companionsites**. In addition, see the COMPGED and COMPLEV functions as well as the COMPCOST call routine for alternative matching algorithms.

Purpose: To create a phonetic equivalent of a text string. Often used to attempt to match names where there might be some minor spelling differences.

Syntax: SOUNDEX(*character-value*)

character-value is any SAS character expression.

Program 1.37: Fuzzy matching on names using the SOUNDEX function

```
***Primary function: SOUNDEX
***Prepare data sets FILE_1 and FILE_2 to be used in the match;

DATA FILE_1;
   INPUT @1  NAME  $10.
         @11 X       1.;
DATALINES;
Friedman  4
Shields   1
MacArthur 7
ADAMS     9
Jose      5
Lundquist 9
;
DATA FILE_2;
   INPUT @1  NAME  $10.
         @11 Y       1.;
DATALINES;
Freedman  5
Freidman  9
Schields  2
McArthur  7
Adams     3
Jones     6
Londquest 9
;
***PROC SQL is used to create a Cartesian Product, combinations of all
   the names in one data set against all the names in the other;

PROC SQL;
   CREATE TABLE BOTH AS
   SELECT FILE_1.NAME AS NAME1, X,
          FILE_2.NAME AS NAME2, Y
   FROM FILE_1 ,FILE_2
QUIT;

DATA POSSIBLE;
   SET BOTH;
   SOUND_1 = SOUNDEX(NAME1);
   SOUND_2 = SOUNDEX(NAME2);
   IF SOUND_1 EQ SOUND_2;
RUN;
PROC PRINT DATA=POSSIBLE NOOBS;
   TITLE "Possible Matches between two files";
   VAR NAME1 SOUND_1 NAME2 SOUND_2 X Y;
RUN;
```

Explanation

Each of the two SAS data sets (FILE_1 and FILE_2) contain names and data. One of the best ways to see which names may be possible matches is to use PROC SQL to create what is called a **Cartesian product** of the two data sets. This is a data set (table in SQLese) that matches each observation from FILE_1 to each observation from FILE_2. Since there are six observations in FILE_1 and seven observations in FILE_2, data set BOTH contains 6 x 7 = 42 observations. To be sure this is clear, see the listing of the first 15 observations from data set BOTH:

```
                    Listing of data set BOTH
                    First 15 Observations


        Obs     NAME1     X     NAME2        Y

         1     Friedman    4    Freedman     5
         2     Friedman    4    Freidman     9
         3     Friedman    4    Schields     2
         4     Friedman    4    McArthur     7
         5     Friedman    4    Adams        3
         6     Friedman    4    Jones        6
         7     Friedman    4    Londquest    9
         8     Shields     1    Freedman     5
         9     Shields     1    Freidman     9
        10     Shields     1    Schields     2
        11     Shields     1    McArthur     7
        12     Shields     1    Adams        3
        13     Shields     1    Jones        6
        14     Shields     1    Londquest    9
        15     MacArthur   7    Freedman     5
```

The next DATA step (the data set POSSIBLE) uses the SOUNDEX function to create a SOUNDEX equivalent for each of the two names. The subsetting IF statement selects all observations where the SOUNDEX values of NAME_1 and NAME_2 are the same. A more flexible approach is shown in Program 1.39, where you can choose various values of spelling distance in determining possible matches between two names.

```
                 Possible Matches between two files

     NAME1          SOUND_1     NAME2          SOUND_2     X     Y

     Friedman       F6355       Freedman       F6355       4     5
     Friedman       F6355       Freidman       F6355       4     9
     Shields        S432        Schields       S432        1     2
     MacArthur      M2636       McArthur       M2636       7     7
     ADAMS          A352        Adams          A352        9     3
     Lundquist      L53223      Londquest      L53223      9     9
```

Function: SPEDIS

The SPEDIS function is a relatively new addition to the SAS arsenal of character functions. It computes a "spelling distance" between two words. If the two words are identical, the spelling distance is 0; for each type of spelling error, SPEDIS assigns penalty points. For example, if the first letters of the two words do not match, there is a relatively large penalty. If two letters are reversed (such as ie or ei for example), there is a smaller penalty. The final spelling distance is also based on the length of the words being matched. A wrong letter in a long word results in a smaller score than a wrong letter in a shorter word.

Take a look at two new functions (COMPGED and COMPLEV) that are similar to the SPEDIS function. The COMPGED function even has an associated call routine (COMPCOST) that allows you to adjust the costs for various classes of spelling errors.

There are some very interesting applications of the SPEDIS, COMPGED, and COMPLEV functions. One, described next, allows you to match names that are not spelled exactly the same. You may want to try this same program with each of the alternative functions to compare matching ability and computer efficiency.

Purpose: To compute the spelling distance between two words. The more alike the two words are, the lower the score. A score of 0 indicates an exact match.

Syntax: SPEDIS(*word-1*, *word-2*);

word-1 is any SAS character expression.

word-2 is any SAS character expression.

The function returns the spelling distance between the two words. A zero indicates the words are identical. Higher scores indicate the words are more dissimilar. Note that SPEDIS is asymmetric—the order of the values being compared makes a difference. The value returned by the function is computed as a percentage of the length of the string to be compared. Thus, an error in two short words returns a larger value than the same error in two longer words.

A list of the operations and their "cost" is shown in the table below. This will give you an idea of the severity of different types of spelling errors. Swapping (interchanging) two letters has a smaller penalty than inserting a letter, and errors involving the first character in a string have a larger penalty than errors involving letters in the middle of the string.

Operation	Cost	Explanation
MATCH	0	no change
SINGLET	25	delete one of a double letter
DOUBLET	50	double a letter
SWAP	50	reverse the order of two consecutive letters
TRUNCATE	50	delete a letter from the end
APPEND	35	add a letter to the end
DELETE	50	delete a letter from the middle
INSERT	100	insert a letter in the middle
REPLACE	100	replace a letter in the middle
FIRSTDEL	100	delete the first letter
FIRSTINS	200	insert a letter at the beginning
FIRSTREP	200	replace the first letter

Examples

For these examples WORD1="Steven" WORD2 = "Stephen" and WORD3 = "STEVEN"

Function	Returns
SPEDIS(WORD1,WORD2)	25
SPEDIS(WORD2,WORD1)	28
SPEDIS(WORD1,WORD3)	83
SPEDIS(WORD1,"Steven")	0

Program 1.38: Using the SPEDIS function to match social security numbers that are the same or differ by a small amount

```
***Primary function: SPEDIS;

DATA FIRST;
   INPUT ID_1 : $2. SS : $11.;
DATALINES;
1A 123-45-6789
2A 111-45-7654
3A 999-99-9999
4A 222-33-4567
;
DATA SECOND;
   INPUT ID_2 : $2. SS : $11.;
DATALINES;
1B 123-45-6789
2B 111-44-7654
3B 899-99-9999
4B 989-99-9999
5B 222-22-5467
;
%LET CUTOFF = 10;
PROC SQL;
   TITLE "Output from SQL when CUTOFF is set to &CUTOFF";
   SELECT ID_1,
          FIRST.SS AS FIRST_SS,
          ID_2,
          SECOND.SS AS SECOND_SS
   FROM FIRST, SECOND
   WHERE SPEDIS(FIRST.SS, SECOND.SS) LE &CUTOFF;
QUIT;
```

Explanation

In this example, you want to match social security numbers between two files, where the two numbers may be slightly different (one digit changed or two digits transposed for example). Even though social security numbers are made up of digits, you can treat the values just like any other alphabetic characters. The program is first run with the cutoff value set to 10, with the result shown next:

```
         Output from SQL when CUTOFF is set to 10


         ID_1  FIRST_SS      ID_2  SECOND_SS

         ─────────────────────────────────────
         1A    123-45-6789   1B    123-45-6789
         2A    111-45-7654   2B    111-44-7654
         3A    999-99-9999   4B    989-99-9999
```

When you run the same program with the cutoff value set to 20, you obtain an additional match—numbers 3A and 3B. These two numbers differ in the first digit, which resulted in a larger penalty. Here is the listing with CUTOFF set to 20:

```
         Output from SQL when CUTOFF is set to 20


         ID_1  FIRST_SS      ID_2  SECOND_SS

         ─────────────────────────────────────
         1A    123-45-6789   1B    123-45-6789
         2A    111-45-7654   2B    111-44-7654
         3A    999-99-9999   3B    899-99-9999
         3A    999-99-9999   4B    989-99-9999
```

Program 1.39: Fuzzy matching on names using the spelling distance (SPEDIS) function

```
***Primary function: SPEDIS
***Other function: UPCASE;

***See Program 1-37 for the creation of data set BOTH and the
   explanation of the PROC SQL code.;

DATA POSSIBLE;
   SET BOTH;
   DISTANCE = SPEDIS(UPCASE(NAME1),UPCASE(NAME2));
RUN;

PROC PRINT DATA=POSSIBLE NOOBS;
   WHERE DISTANCE LE 15;
   TITLE "Possible Matches between two files";
   VAR NAME1 NAME2 DISTANCE X Y;
RUN;
```

Explanation

This program starts at the point following PROC SQL in Program 1.37.

The next DATA step (data set POSSIBLE) uses the SPEDIS function to compute the spelling distance between every pair of names in the data set BOTH. Notice that all the names are converted to uppercase, using the UPCASE function, to avoid missing possible matches because of case differences. (Note: the COMPGED and COMPLEV functions allow a modifier to ignore case in the comparison.) You might want to add a subsetting IF statement to this DATA step to limit pairs of names with a given spelling distance. For the purpose of demonstration, this was not done here, and the WHERE statement in the following PROC PRINT is used to select possible matches. The smaller the value of DISTANCE, the closer the match. If DISTANCE equals 0, the two names are an exact match. To see the results of all names within a spelling distance of 15, take a look at the output from the PROC PRINT. As you can see from the listing below, this method of fuzzy matching produces a different list of matches from the one produced using the SOUNDEX function.

```
                    Possible Matches between two files


            NAME1       NAME2       DISTANCE    X    Y

            Friedman    Freedman        12      4    5
            Friedman    Freidman         6      4    9
            Shields     Schields         7      1    2
            MacArthur   McArthur        11      7    7
            ADAMS       Adams            0      9    3
```

Functions That Divide Strings into "Words"

These extremely useful functions and call routines can divide a string into words. Words can be characters separated by blanks or other delimiters that you specify.

SCAN and SCANQ

The two functions, SCAN and SCANQ are similar. They both extract "words" from a string, **words** being defined as characters separated by a set of specified delimiters. Pay particular attention to the fact that the SCAN and SCANQ functions use different sets of default delimiters. The SCANQ function also has some additional useful features. Programs demonstrating both of these functions follow the definitions.

Function: SCAN

Purpose: Extracts a specified word from a character expression, where **word** is defined as the characters separated by a set of specified delimiters. The length of the returned variable is 200, unless previously defined.

Syntax: SCAN(*character-value, n-word <,'delimiter-list'>*)

character-value is any SAS character expression.

n-word is the *n*th "word" in the string. If *n* is greater than the number of words, the SCAN function returns a value that contains no characters. If *n* is negative, the character value is scanned from right to left. A value of zero is invalid.

delimiter-list is an optional argument. If it is omitted, the default set of delimiters are (for ASCII environments):

blank . < (+ & ! $ *) ; ^ - / , % |

For EBCDIC environments, the default delimiters are:

blank . < (+ | & ! $ *) ; ¬ - / , % | ¢

If you specify any delimiters, only those delimiters will be active. Delimiters before the first word have no effect. Two or more contiguous delimiters are treated as one.

Examples

For these examples STRING1 = "ABC DEF" and
STRING2 = "ONE?TWO THREE+FOUR|FIVE" This is an ASCII example.

Function	Returns
SCAN(STRING1,2)	"DEF"
SCAN(STRING1,-1)	"DEF"
SCAN(STRING1,3)	no characters
SCAN(STRING2,4)	"FIVE"
SCAN(STRING2,2," ")	"THREE+FOUR|FIVE"
SCAN(STRING1,0)	An error in the SAS log

SAS9.1 Function: SCANQ

Purpose: To extract a specified word from a character expression, **word** being defined as characters separated by a set of specified delimiters. The basic differences between this function and the SCAN function are the default set of delimiters (see syntax below) and the fact that a value of 0 for the word count does not result in an error message. SCANQ also ignores delimiters enclosed in quotation marks (SCAN recognizes them).

Syntax: SCANQ(*character-value, n-word* <,'*delimiter-list*'>)

character-value is any SAS character expression.

n-word is the *n*th "word" in the string (**word** being defined as one or more characters, separated by a set of specified delimiters. If *n* is negative, the scan proceeds from right to left. If *n* is greater than the number of words or 0, the SCANQ function will return a blank value. Delimiters located before the first word or after the last word are ignored. If two or more delimiters are located between two words, they are treated as one. If the character value contains sets of quotation marks, any delimiters within these marks are ignored.

delimiter-list is an optional argument. If it is omitted, the default set of delimiters are white space characters (blank, horizontal and vertical tab, carriage return, line feed, and form feed). **Note: this is a different set of default delimiters from the SCAN function.** If you specify any delimiters, only those delimiters will be active. You cannot specify single or double quotation marks as delimiters.

Examples

For these examples STRING1 = "ABC DEF", STRING2 = "ONE TWO THREE FOUR FIVE", STRING3 = "'AB CD' 'X Y'", and STRING4 = "ONE# ::TWO"

Function	Returns
SCANQ(STRING1,2)	"DEF"
SCANQ(STRING1,-1)	"DEF"
SCANQ(STRING1,3)	no characters
SCANQ(STRING2,4," ")	"FOUR"
SCANQ(STRING3,2)	"'X Y'"
SCANQ(STRING1,0)	no characters
SCANQ(STRING4,2," #:")	"TWO"

Program 1.40: A novel use of the SCAN function to convert mixed numbers to decimal values

```
***Primary function: SCAN
***Other function: INPUT;

DATA PRICES;
   INPUT @1 STOCK $3.
         @5 MIXED $6.;
   INTEGER = SCAN(MIXED,1,'/ ');
   NUMERATOR = SCAN(MIXED,2,'/ ');
   DENOMINATOR = SCAN(MIXED,3,'/ ');
   IF NUMERATOR = ' ' THEN VALUE = INPUT(INTEGER,8.);
   ELSE VALUE = INPUT(INTEGER,8.) +
                (INPUT(NUMERATOR,8.) / INPUT(DENOMINATOR,8.));
   KEEP STOCK VALUE;
DATALINES;
ABC 14 3/8
XYZ 8
TWW 5 1/8
;
PROC PRINT DATA=PRICES NOOBS;
   TITLE "Listing of Data Set PRICES";
RUN;
```

Explanation

The SCAN function has many uses besides merely extracting selected words from text expressions. In this program, you want to convert numbers such as 23 5/8 into a decimal value (23.675). An elegant way to accomplish this is to use the SCAN function to separate the mixed number into three parts: the integer, the numerator of the fraction, and the denominator. Once this is done, all you need to do is to convert each piece to a numerical value (using the INPUT function) and add the integer portion to the fractional portion. If the number being processed does not have a fractional part, the SCAN function returns a blank value for the two variables NUMERATOR and DENOMINATOR. The listing is shown below:

```
                 Listing of Data Set PRICES

                    STOCK     VALUE

                     ABC     14.375
                     XYZ      8.000
                     TWW      5.125
```

Program 1.41: Program to read a tab-delimited file

```
***Primary function: SCANQ;

DATA READ_TABS;
    INFILE 'C:\BOOKS\FUNCTIONS\TAB_FILE.TXT' PAD;
    INPUT @1 STRING $30.;
    LENGTH FIRST MIDDLE LAST $ 12;
    FIRST = SCANQ(STRING,1);
    MIDDLE = SCANQ(STRING,2);
    LAST = SCANQ(STRING,3);
    DROP STRING;
RUN;
PROC PRINT DATA=READ_TABS NOOBS;
    TITLE "Listing of Data Set READS_TABS";
RUN;
```

Explanation

This program reads values separated by tab characters. Although you can use the INFILE option DLM='09'X (the ASCII Hex value for a tab character, or '05'X for EBCDIC) to read this file, the SCANQ function provides an easy, alternate method. Here you take advantage of the fact that one of the default delimiters for the SCANQ function is a tab character. This method could be especially useful if you imported a file from another system, and individual character values contained tabs or other non-printing white space characters.

A listing of the resulting data set is shown next:

```
                    Listing of Data Set READS_TABS


                FIRST      MIDDLE     LAST


                Ron        P.         Cody
                Ralph      Waldo      Emerson
                Alfred     E.         Newman
```

Program 1.42: Alphabetical listing by last name when the name field
contains first name, possibly middle initial, and last name

```
***Primary function: SCAN;

***Making the problem a little harder.  Extracting the last name
   when there may or may not be a middle initial;

DATA FIRST_LAST;
   INPUT @1  NAME   $20.
         @21 PHONE $13.;
   ***Extract the last name from NAME;
   LAST_NAME = SCAN(NAME,-1,' '); /* Scans from the right */
DATALINES;
Jeff W. Snoker      (908)782-4382
Raymond Albert      (732)235-4444
Steven J. Foster    (201)567-9876
Jose Romerez        (516)593-2377
;
PROC REPORT DATA=FIRST_LAST NOWD;
   TITLE "Names and Phone Numbers in Alphabetical Order (by Last Name)";
   COLUMNS NAME PHONE LAST_NAME;
   DEFINE LAST_NAME / ORDER NOPRINT WIDTH=20;
   DEFINE NAME      / DISPLAY 'Name' LEFT WIDTH=20;
   DEFINE PHONE     / DISPLAY 'Phone Number' WIDTH=13 FORMAT=$13.;
RUN;
```

Explanation

It is easy to extract the last name by using a −1 as the second argument of the SCAN function. A negative value for this argument results in a scan from right to left. Output from the REPORT procedure is shown below:

```
         Names and Phone Numbers in Alphabetical Order (by Last Name)

                Name                    Phone Number
                Raymond Albert          (732)235-4444
                Steven J. Foster        (201)567-9876
                Jose Romerez            (516)593-2377
                Jeff W. Snoker          (908)782-4382
```

CALL SCAN and CALL SCANQ

The SCAN and SCANQ call routines are similar to the SCAN and SCANQ functions. But both call routines return a position and length of the *n*th word (to be used, perhaps, in a subsequent SUBSTR function) rather than the actual word itself.

Differences between CALL SCAN and CALL SCANQ are the same differences between the two functions, SCAN and SCANQ.

SAS9.1 **Function: CALL SCAN**

Purpose: To break up a string into words, where **words** are defined as the characters separated by a set of specified delimiters, and to return the starting position and the length of the *n*th word.

Syntax: `CALL SCAN(character-value, n-word, position, length <, 'delimiter-list'>)`

character-value is any SAS character expression.

n-word is the nth "word" in the string. If *n* is greater than the number of words, the SCAN call routine returns a value of 0 for *position* and *length*. If *n* is negative, the scan proceeds from right to left.

position is the name of the numeric variable to which the starting position in the *character-value* of the *n*th word is returned.

length is the name of a numeric variable to which the length of the *n*th word is returned.

delimiter-list is an optional argument. If it is omitted, the default set of delimiters are (for ASCII environments):

blank . < (+ & ! $ *) ; ^ - / , % |

For EBCDIC environments, the default delimiters are:

blank . < (+ | & ! $ *) ; ¬ - / , % | ¢

If you specify any delimiters, only those delimiters will be active. Delimiters are slightly different in ASCII and EBCDIC systems.

Examples

For these examples STRING1 = "ABC DEF" and STRING2 = "ONE?TWO THREE+FOUR|FIVE"

Function	Position	Length
CALL SCAN(STRING1,2,POSITION,LENGTH)	5	3
CALL SCAN(STRING1,-1,POSITION,LENGTH)	5	3
CALL SCAN(STRING1,3,POSITION,LENGTH)	0	0
CALL SCAN(STRING2,1,POSITION,LENGTH)	1	7
CALL SCAN(STRING2,4,POSITION,LENGTH)	20	4
CALL SCAN(STRING2,2,POSITION,LENGTH," ")	9	15
CALL SCAN(STRING1,0,POSITION,LENGTH)	missing	missing

Program 1.43: Demonstrating the SCAN call routine

```
***Primary function: CALL SCAN;

DATA WORDS;
   INPUT STRING $40.;
   DELIM = 'Default';
   N = 2;
   CALL SCAN(STRING,N,POSITION,LENGTH);
   OUTPUT;
   N = -1;
   CALL SCAN(STRING,N,POSITION,LENGTH);
   OUTPUT;
   DELIM = '#';
   N = 2;
   CALL SCAN(STRING,N,POSITION,LENGTH,'#');
   OUTPUT;
DATALINES;
ONE TWO THREE
One*#Two Three*Four
;
PROC PRINT DATA=WORDS NOOBS;
   TITLE "Listing of Data Set WORDS";
RUN;
```

Explanation

The SCAN routine is called three times in this program, twice with default delimiters and once with the pound sign (#) as the delimiter. Notice that using a negative argument results in a scan from right to left. The output from this program is shown next:

STRING	DELIM	N	POSITION	LENGTH
ONE TWO THREE	Default	2	5	3
ONE TWO THREE	Default	-1	9	5
ONE TWO THREE	#	2	0	0
One*#Two Three*Four	Default	2	5	4
One*#Two Three*Four	Default	-1	16	4
One*#Two Three*Four	#	2	6	35

Listing of Data Set WORDS

SAS9.1 Function: CALL SCANQ

Purpose: To break up a string into words, where *words* are defined to be the characters separated by a set of specified delimiters, and to return the starting position and the length of the *n*th word. The basic differences between this call routine and CALL SCAN is that CALL SCANQ uses white space characters as default delimiters and it can accept a value of 0 for the *n*-word argument. In addition, the SCANQ call routine ignores delimiters within quotation marks.

Syntax: CALL SCAN(*character-value, n-word, position, length <,'delimiter-list'>*)

character-value is any SAS character expression.

n-word is the *n*th "word" in the string. If *n* is zero, or if the absolute value of *n* is greater than the number of words, the SCANQ call routine returns values of 0 for *position* and *length*.

position is the name of the numeric variable to which the starting position in the *character-value* of the *n*th word is returned.

length is the name of a numeric variable to which the length of the *n*th word is returned.

delimiter-list is an optional argument. If it is omitted, the default set of delimiters are white space characters (blank, horizontal and vertical tab, carriage return, line feed, and form feed). Also, the beginning or end of a line also delimits a word. **Note: this is a different set of default delimiters from the SCAN call routine.** If you specify any delimiters, only those delimiters will be active. Also note that in the last example (STRING3), *position* and *length* include single quotation marks.

If you specify any delimiters, only those delimiters will be active.

Examples

For these examples STRING1 = "ABC DEF" and STRING2 = "ONE TWO THREE FOUR FIVE", and STRING3 = "'AB CD' 'X Y'"

Function	Position	Length
CALL SCANQ(STRING1,2,POSITION,LENGTH)	5	3
CALL SCANQ(STRING1,-1,POSITION,LENGTH)	5	3
CALL SCANQ(STRING1,3,POSITION,LENGTH)	0	0
CALL SCANQ(STRING2,4,POSITION,LENGTH)	5	3
CALL SCANQ(STRING2,2,POSITION,LENGTH," ")	9	15
CALL SCANQ(STRING1,0,POSITION,LENGTH)	0	0
CALL SCANQ(STRING3,2,POSITION,LENGTH)	9	5

Program 1.44: Using CALL SCANQ to count the words in a string

```
***Primary function: CALL SCANQ;

DATA COUNT;
   INPUT STRING $40.;
   DO I = 1 TO 99 UNTIL (LENGTH EQ 0);
      CALL SCANQ(STRING,I,POSITION,LENGTH);
   END;
   NUM_WORDS = I-1;
   DROP POSITION LENGTH I;
DATALINES;
ONE TWO THREE
ONE TWO
ONE
;
PROC PRINT DATA=COUNT NOOBS;
   TITLE "Listing of Data Set COUNT";
RUN;
```

Explanation

When the value of the second argument in the CALL SCANQ routine is greater than the number of words in a string, both the position and length values are set to 0. Here, the call routine is placed in a DO loop, which iterates until the routine returns a value of 0 for the length. The number of words is, therefore, one fewer than this number. The listing is shown below:

```
                    Listing of Data Set COUNT

                                 NUM_
              STRING             WORDS

              ONE TWO THREE        3
              ONE TWO             2
              ONE                 1
```

Functions That Substitute Letters or Words in Strings

TRANSLATE can substitute one character for another in a string. TRANWRD is more flexible—it can substitute a word or several words for one or more words.

Function: TRANSLATE

Purpose   To exchange one character value for another. For example, you might want to change values 1–5 to the values A–E.

Syntax: TRANSLATE(*character-value, to-1, from-1 <,… to-n, from-n>*)

character-value is any SAS character expression.

to-n is a single character or a list of character values.

from-n is a single character or a list of characters.

Each character listed in *from-n* is changed to the corresponding value in *to-n*. If a character value is not listed in *from-n*, it will be unaffected.

Examples

In these examples, CHAR = "12X45", ANS = "Y"

Function	Returns
TRANSLATE(CHAR,"ABCDE","12345")	"ABXDE"
TRANSLATE(CHAR,'A','1','B','2','C','3','D','4','E','5')	"ABXDE"
TRANSLATE(ANS,"10","YN")	"1"

Program 1.45: Converting values of '1','2','3','4', and '5' to 'A','B','C','D', and 'E' respectively

```
***Primary function: TRANSLATE;

DATA MULTIPLE;
   INPUT QUES : $1. @@;
   QUES = TRANSLATE(QUES,'ABCDE','12345');
DATALINES;
1 4 3 2 5
5 3 4 2 1
;
PROC PRINT DATA=MULTIPLE NOOBS;
   TITLE "Listing of Data Set MULTIPLE";
RUN;
```

Explanation

In this example, you want to convert the character values of 1–5 to the letters A–E. The two arguments in this function seem backwards to this author. You would expect the order to be "from–to" rather than the other way around. I suppose others at SAS felt the same way, since a more recent function, TRANWRD (next example), uses the "from – to" order for its arguments. While you could use a format, along with a PUT function to do this translation,

the TRANSLATE function is more compact and easier to use in cases like this. A listing of
data set MULTIPLE follows:

```
                    Listing of Data Set MULTIPLE

                    QUES

                      A
                      D
                      C
                      B
                      E
                      E
                      C
                      D
                      B
                      A
```

Program 1.46: Converting the values "Y" and "N" to 1's and 0's

```
***Primary functions: TRANSLATE, UPCASE
***Other functions: INPUT;

DATA YES_NO;
   LENGTH CHAR $ 1;
   INPUT CHAR @@;
   X = INPUT(
       TRANSLATE(
       UPCASE(CHAR),'01','NY'),1.);
DATALINES;
N Y n y A B 0 1
;
PROC PRINT DATA=YES_NO NOOBS;
   TITLE "Listing of Data Set YES_NO";
RUN;
```

Explanation

This rather silly program was written mainly to demonstrate the TRANSLATE and
UPCASE functions. A couple of IF statements, combined with the UPCASE function in the
DATA step would probably be more straightforward. In this program, the UPCASE
function converts lowercase values of "n" and "y" to their uppercase equivalents. The

TRANSLATE function then converts the Ns and Ys to the characters "0" and "1," respectively. Finally, the INPUT function does the character to numeric conversion. Note that the data values of "1" and "0" do not get translated, but do get converted to numeric values. As you can see in the listing below, the program does get the job done.

```
                  Listing of Data Set YES_NO


                     CHAR    X

                      N      0
                      Y      1
                      n      0
                      y      1
                      A      .
                      B      .
                      0      0
                      1
```

Function: **TRANWRD**

Purpose: To substitute one or more words in a string with a replacement word or words. It works like the find and replace feature of most word processors.

Syntax: TRANWRD(*character-value, from-string, to-string*)

character-value is any SAS character expression.

from-string is one or more characters that you want to replace with the character or characters in the to-string.

to-string is one or more characters that replace the entire *from-string*.

Making the analogy to the find and replace feature of most word processors here, *from-string* represents the string to find and *to-string* represents the string to replace. Notice that the order of *from-* and *to-string* in this function is opposite (and more logical to this author) from the order in the TRANSLATE function.

Examples

For these examples STRING = "123 Elm Road", FROM = "Road" and TO = "Rd."

Function	Returns
TRANWRD(STRING,FROM,TO)	"123 Elm Rd."
TRANWRD("Now is the time","is","is not")	"Now is not the time"
TRANWRD("one two three","four","4")	"one two three"
TRANWRD("Mr. Rogers","Mr."," ")	" Rogers"
TRANWRD("ONE TWO THREE","ONE TWO","A B")	"A B THREE"

Program 1.47: Converting words such as Street to their abbreviations such as St. in an address

```
***Primary function: TRANWRD;

DATA CONVERT;
   INPUT @1 ADDRESS $20. ;
   *** Convert Street, Avenue and Road to their abbreviations;
   ADDRESS = TRANWRD(ADDRESS,'Street','St.');
   ADDRESS = TRANWRD (ADDRESS,'Avenue','Ave.');
   ADDRESS = TRANWRD (ADDRESS,'Road','Rd.');
DATALINES;
89 Lazy Brook Road
123 River Rd.
12 Main Street
;
PROC PRINT DATA=CONVERT;
   TITLE 'Listing of Data Set CONVERT';
RUN;
```

Explanation

TRANWRD is one of the relatively new SAS functions—and it is enormously useful. This example uses it to help standardize a mailing list, substituting abbreviations for full words. Another use for this function is to make *to-string* a blank, thus allowing you to remove words such as Jr. or Mr. from an address. The converted addresses are shown in the listing below:

```
                    Listing of Data Set CONVERT

            Obs     ADDRESS

             1      89 Lazy Brook Rd.
             2      123 River Rd.
             3      12 Main St.
```

Functions That Compute the Length of Strings

These four functions compute the length of character values. The LENGTH function (the oldest of the lot) does not count trailing blanks in its calculation. The LENGTHN function is identical to the LENGTH function with one exception: If there is a null string (technically speaking, a string consisting of all blanks), the LENGTH function returns a value of 1 while the LENGTHN function returns a value of 0. I would recommend using the LENGTHN function as your general purpose length function in place of the older LENGTH function (unless, of course, you used the fact that the length of a null string is 1 instead of 0 in your program). The LENGTHC function operates like the LENGTH function except it counts trailing blanks in its computation. Finally, LENGTHM computes the length used to store this variable in memory. In most applications, the LENGTHM and LENGTHC functions return the same value. You may see some differences when working with macro variables. The LENGTHM function is a useful way to determine the storage length of a character variable (instead of using PROC CONTENTS, for example).

Function: **LENGTH**

Purpose: To determine the length of a character value, not counting trailing blanks. A null argument returns a value of 1.

Syntax: LENGTH(*character-value*)

character-value is any SAS character expression.

Examples

For these examples CHAR = "ABC   "

Function	Returns
LENGTH("ABC")	3
LENGTH(CHAR)	3
LENGTH(" ")	1

SAS9.1 Function: LENGTHC

Purpose: To determine the length of a character value, including trailing blanks.

Syntax: LENGTHC(*character-value*)

character-value is any SAS character expression.

Examples

For these examples CHAR = "ABC   "

Function	Returns
LENGTH("ABC")	3
LENGTH(CHAR)	6
LENGTH(" ")	1

SAS9.1 Function: LENGTHM

Purpose: To determine the length of a character variable in memory.

Syntax: LENGTHM(*character-value*)

character-value is any SAS character expression.

Examples

For these examples CHAR = "ABC   "

Function	Returns
LENGTHM("ABC")	3
LENGTHM(CHAR)	6
LENGTHM(" ")	1

SAS9.1 **Function: LENGTHN**

Purpose: To determine the length of a character value, not counting trailing blanks. A null argument returns a value of 0.

Syntax: **LENGTHN(*character-value*)**

character-value is any SAS character expression.

Examples

For these examples CHAR = "ABC   "

Function	Returns
LENGTH("ABC")	3
LENGTH(CHAR)	3
LENGTH(" ")	0

Program 1.48: Demonstrating the LENGTH, LENGTHC, LENGTHM, and LENGTHN functions

```
***Primary functions: LENGTH, LENGTHC, LENGTHM, LENGTHN;

DATA LENGTH_FUNC;
   NOTRAIL = "ABC";
   TRAIL   = "DEF   "; * Three trailing blanks;
   NULL    = " ";      * Null string;
   LENGTH_NOTRAIL = LENGTH(NOTRAIL);
   LENGTH_TRAIL   = LENGTH(TRAIL);
```

```
     LENGTH_NULL      = LENGTH(NULL);
     LENGTHC_NOTRAIL = LENGTHC(NOTRAIL);
     LENGTHC_TRAIL   = LENGTHC(TRAIL);
     LENGTHC_NULL    = LENGTHC(NULL);
     LENGTHM_NOTRAIL = LENGTHM(NOTRAIL);
     LENGTHM_TRAIL   = LENGTHM(TRAIL);
     LENGTHM_NULL    = LENGTHM(NULL);
     LENGTHN_NOTRAIL = LENGTHN(NOTRAIL);
     LENGTHN_TRAIL   = LENGTHN(TRAIL);
     LENGTHN_NULL    = LENGTHN(NULL);
RUN;

PROC PRINT DATA=LENGTH_FUNC NOOBS HEADING=H;
   TITLE "Listing of Data Set LENGTH_FUNC";
RUN;
```

Explanation

The LENGTH and LENGTHN functions return the length of a character variable, **not counting trailing blanks**. The only difference between the LENGTH and LENGTHN functions is that the LENGTH function returns a value of 1 for a null string while the LENGTHN function returns a 0. The LENGTHC function **does count trailing blanks** in its calculations. Finally, the LENGTHM function returns the number of bytes of memory used to store the variable. Notice in this program that the LENGTHM and LENGTHC functions yield the same value. Look over the listing below to be sure you understand the differences among these functions:

```
                       Listing of Data Set LENGTH_FUNC


                      LENGTH_  LENGTH_  LENGTH_  LENGTHC_  LENGTHC_  LENGTHC_
        NOTRAIL TRAIL  NULL   NOTRAIL   TRAIL    NULL     NOTRAIL    TRAIL     NULL

          ABC    DEF          3        3        1        3         6         1


        LENGTHM_       LENGTHM_         LENGTHM_         LENGTHN_         LENGTHN_         LENGTHN_
        NOTRAIL         TRAIL            NULL            NOTRAIL          TRAIL            NULL

           3             6               1               3                3                0
```

Functions That Count the Number of Letters or Substrings in a String

The COUNT function counts the number of times a given substring appears in a string. The COUNTC function counts the number of times specific characters occur in a string.

SAS9.1 Function: COUNT

Purpose: To count the number of times a given substring appears in a string. With the use of a modifier, case can be ignored. If no occurrences of the substring are found, the function returns a 0.

Syntax: COUNT(*character-value*, *find-string* <,*'modifiers'*>)

character-value is any SAS character expression.

find-string is a character variable or SAS string literal to be counted.

The following modifiers, placed in single or double quotation marks, may be used with COUNT:

i or I ignore case.

t or T ignore trailing blanks in both the character value and the *find-string*.

Examples

For these examples, STRING1 = "How Now Brown COW" and STRING2 = "ow"

Function	Returns
COUNT(STRING1, STRING2)	3
COUNT(STRING1,STRING2,'I')	4
COUNT(STRING1, "XX")	0
COUNT("ding and dong","g ")	1
COUNT("ding and dong","g ","T")	2

Program 1.49: Using the COUNT function to count the number of times the word "the" appears in a string

```
***Primary Function: COUNT;

DATA DRACULA;
   INPUT STRING $CHAR60.;
   NUM = COUNT(STRING,"the");
   NUM_NO_CASE = COUNT(STRING,"the",'I');
DATALINES;
The number of times "the" appears is the question
THE the
None on this line!
There is the map
;
PROC PRINT DATA=DRACULA NOOB;
   TITLE "Listing of Data Set Dracula";
RUN;
```

Explanation

In this program, the COUNT function is used with and without the I (ignore case) modifier. In the first observation, the first "The" has an uppercase T, so it does not match the substring and is not counted for the variable NUM. But when the I modifier is used, it does count. The same holds for the second observation. When there are no occurrences of the substring, as in the third observation, the function returns a 0. The fourth line of data demonstrates that COUNT ignores word boundaries when searching for strings. A listing of data set DRACULA is displayed below:

```
                        Listing of Data Set DRACULA


                                                         NUM_NO_
       STRING                                     NUM     CASE

       The number of times "the" appears is the question   2       3
       THE the                                     1       2
       None on this line!                          0       0
       There is the map                            1       2
```

SAS9.1 Function: COUNTC

Purpose: To count the number of individual characters that appear or do not appear in a string. With the use of a modifier, case can be ignored. Another modifier allows you to count characters that do not appear in the string. If no specified characters are found, the function returns a 0.

Syntax: COUNTC(*character-value, characters <,'modifiers'>*)

character-value is any SAS character expression.

characters is one or more characters to be counted. It may be a string literal (letters in quotation marks) or a character variable.

The following modifiers, placed in quotation marks, may be used with COUNTC:

  i or I   ignore case.

  o or O   If this modifier is used, COUNTC processes the character or characters and modifiers only once. If the COUNTC function is used in the same DATA step, the previous character and modifier values are used and the current values are ignored.

  t or T   ignore trailing blanks in the *character-value* or the characters. Note, this modifier is especially important when looking for blanks or when you are using the v modifier (below).

  v or V   count only the characters that do **not** appear in the character-value. Remember that this count will include trailing blanks unless the t modifier is used.

Examples

For these examples, STRING1 = "How Now Brown COW" and STRING2 = "wo"

Function	Returns
COUNTC("AaBbbCDE","CBA")	3
COUNTC("AaBbbCDE","CBA",'I')	7
COUNTC(STRING1, STRING2)	6
COUNTC(STRING1,STRING2,'I')	8
COUNTC(STRING1, "XX")	0
COUNTC("ding and dong","g ")	4 (2 g's and 2 blanks)
COUNTC("ding and dong","g ","T")	2 (blanks trimmed)
COUNTC("ABCDEabcde","BCD",'VI')	4 (A, E, a, and e)

Program 1.50: Demonstrating the COUNTC function to find one or more characters or to check if characters are not present in a string

```
***Primary Function: COUNTC;

DATA COUNT_CHAR;
   INPUT STRING $20.;
   NUM_A = COUNTC(STRING,'A');
   NUM_Aa = COUNTC(STRING,'a','i');
   NUM_A_OR_B = COUNTC(STRING,'AB');
   NOT_A = COUNTC(STRING,'A','v');
   NOT_A_TRIM = COUNTC(STRING,'A','vt');
   NOT_Aa = COUNTC(STRING,'A','iv');
DATALINES;
UPPER A AND LOWER a
abAB
BBBbbb
;
PROC PRINT DATA=COUNT_CHAR;
   TITLE "Listing of Data Set COUNT_CHAR";
RUN;
```

Explanation

This program demonstrates several features of the COUNTC function. The first use of the function simply looks for the number of times the uppercase letter A appears in the string. Next, by adding the i modifier, the number of upper- or lowercase A's is counted. Next, when you place more than one character in the list, the function returns the total number of the listed characters. The v modifier is interesting. The first time it is used, COUNTC is counting the number of characters in the string that are not uppercase A's. Notice in the listing below, that this count includes the trailing blanks. However, in the next statement of the program, when the v and t modifiers are used together, the trailing blanks are not counted.

```
                    Listing of Data Set COUNT_CHAR


                                       NUM_A_          NOT_A_
     Obs   STRING           NUM_A  NUM_Aa  OR_B   NOT_A   TRIM   NOT_Aa

      1    UPPER A AND LOWER a   2     3      2      18     17     17
      2    abAB                  1     2      2      19      3     18
      3    BBBbbb                0     0      3      20      6     20
```

Miscellaneous String Functions

Don't be put off by the "miscellaneous" in this heading. Many of these functions are extremely useful—they just didn't fit neatly into categories.

Function: MISSING

Purpose: To determine if the argument is a missing (character or numeric) value. This is a handy function to use since you don't have to know if the variable you are testing is character or numeric. The function returns a 1 (true) if the value is a missing value, a 0 (false) otherwise.

Syntax: MISSING(*variable*)

variable is a character or numeric variable or expression.

Examples:

For these examples, NUM1 = 5, NUM2 = ., CHAR1 = "ABC", and CHAR2 = " "

Function	Returns
MISSING(NUM1)	0
MISSING(NUM2)	1
MISSING(CHAR1)	0
MISSING(CHAR2)	1

Program 1.51: Determining if there are any missing values for all variables in a data set

```
***Primary function: MISSING
***Other function: DIM;

***First, create a data set for testing;
DATA TEST_MISS;
   INPUT @1 (X Y Z)(1.)
         @4 (A B C D)($1.);
DATALINES;
123ABCD
..7 FFF
987RONC
;
DATA FIND_MISS;
   SET TEST_MISS END=LAST;
   ARRAY NUMS[*] _NUMERIC_;
   ARRAY CHARS[*] _CHARACTER_;
   DO I = 1 TO DIM(NUMS);
      IF MISSING(NUMS[I]) THEN NN + 1;
   END;
   DO I = 1 TO DIM(CHARS);
      IF MISSING(CHARS[I]) THEN NC + 1;
   END;
   FILE PRINT;
   TITLE "Count of Missing Values";
   IF LAST THEN PUT NN "Numeric and " NC "Character values missing";
RUN;
```

Explanation

Notice that the MISSING function can take either a numeric or a character argument. In this program, since you need to have separate arrays for the character and numeric variables, you could have just as easily used the standard period and blank to represent missing values. Because of the END= option in the SET statement, the program outputs the counts when the last observation is processed from the data set TEST_MISS. Output from this program is shown below:

```
            Count of Missing Values

            2 Numeric and 1 Character values missing
```

Function: **RANK**

Purpose: To obtain the relative position of the ASCII (or EBCDIC) characters. This can be useful if you want to associate each character with a number so that an ARRAY subscript can point to a specific character.

Syntax: RANK(*letter*)

letter can be a string literal or a SAS character variable. If the literal or variable contains more than one character, the RANK function returns the collating sequence of the first character in the string.

Examples

For these examples, STRING1 = "A" and STRING2 = "XYZ"

Function	Returns
RANK(STRING1)	65
RANK(STRING2)	88
RANK("X")	88
RANK("a")	97

Program 1.52: Using the collating sequence to convert plain text to Morse Code

```
***Primary function: RANK
***Other functions: LENGTH, UPCASE, SUBSTR;

DATA _NULL_;
  ARRAY DOT_DASH[26] $ 4 _TEMPORARY_ ('.-' '-...' '-.-.' '-..' '.'
                                      '..-.' '-.' '....' '..' '.---'
                                      '-.-' '.-..' '--' '-.' '---' '.--'
                                      '--.-' '.-.' '...' '-' '..-'
                                      '...-' '.--' '-..-' '-.--' '--..');
    INPUT @1 STRING $80.;
    FILE PRINT;
       TITLE "Morse Code Conversion Using the RANK Function";
    DO I = 1 TO LENGTH(STRING);
       LETTER = UPCASE(SUBSTR(STRING,I,1));
       IF LETTER = ' ' THEN PUT LETTER @;
       ELSE  DO;
          NUM = RANK(LETTER) - 64;
          PUT DOT_DASH[NUM] ' ' @;
       END;
    END;
    PUT;
DATALINES;
This is a test SOS
Now is the time for all good men
;
```

Explanation

The RANK function returns a value of 65 for an uppercase A, a value of 66 for a B, and so forth (in the ASCII character set). If you subtract 64 from the RANK value of the letters A to Z, you will get the numbers 1 to 26. Each element in the temporary array is the Morse code equivalent of the 26 letters of the alphabet.

The DO loop starts from 1 to the LENGTH of STRING. Each letter is converted to uppercase and its order in the alphabet is returned by the expression RANK(LETTER) – 64. This value is then used as the subscript in the DOT_DASH array and the appropriate series of dots and dashes is written to the output screen. As an "exercise for the reader," this problem can also be solved in an elegant manner using a user-defined format mapping the letters of the alphabet to the Morse equivalents. The output from this program is shown below:

```
Morse Code Conversion Using the RANK Function
-    ....  ..  ...     ..  ...       .-    -   .  ...   -   .  ...   ---  ...
-.   ---  .--    ..  ...      -   ....  .     -   ..  --   .     ..-.  ---  .-.
     .-  .-..  .-..      -..  ---  ---  -..     --   .   -.
```

Function: **REPEAT**

Purpose: To make multiple copies of a string.

Syntax: REPEAT(*character-value, n*)

character-value is any SAS character expression.

n is the number of repetitions. The result of this function is the original string plus *n* repetitions. Thus if *n* equals 1, the result will be two copies of the original string in the result. If you do not declare the length of the character variable holding the result of the REPEAT function, it will default to 200.

Examples

For these examples, STRING = "ABC"

Function	Returns
REPEAT(STRING,1)	"ABCABC"
REPEAT("HELLO ",3)	"HELLO HELLO HELLO HELLO"
REPEAT("*",5)	"******"

Program 1.53: Using the REPEAT function to underline output values

```
***Featured Function: REPEAT;

DATA _NULL_;
   FILE PRINT;
   TITLE "Demonstrating the REPEAT Function";
   LENGTH DASH $ 50;
   INPUT STRING $50.;
   IF _N_ = 1 THEN PUT 50*"*";
   DASH = REPEAT("-",LENGTH(STRING) - 1);
   PUT STRING / DASH;
DATALINES;
Short line
This is a longer line
Bye
;
```

Explanation

I must admit, I had a hard time coming up with a reasonable program to demonstrate the REPEAT function. The program above underlines each string with the same number of dashes as there are characters in the string. Since you want the line of dashes to be the same length as the string, you subtract one from the length, remembering that the REPEAT function results in $n + 1$ copies of the original string (the original plus n repetitions).

The two important points to remember when using the REPEAT function are: always make sure you have defined a length for the resulting character variable, and the result of the REPEAT function is $n + 1$ repetitions of the original string. The output from the program above is shown below:

```
Demonstrating the REPEAT Function
**************************************************
Short line
----------
This is a longer line
--------------------
Bye
---
```

Function: REVERSE

Purpose: To reverse the order of text of a character value.

Syntax: REVERSE(*character-value*)

character-value is any SAS character expression.

Examples

For these examples STRING1 = "ABCDE" and STRING2 = "XYZ   "

Function	Returns
REVERSE(STRING1)	"EDCBA"
REVERSE(STRING2)	" ZYX"
REVERSE("1234")	"4321"

Program 1.54: Using the REVERSE function to create backwards writing

```
***Primary function: REVERSE;

DATA BACKWARDS;
   INPUT @1 STRING $CHAR10.;
   GNIRTS = REVERSE(STRING);
DATALINES;
Ron Cody
   XYZ
ABCDEFG
        X
1234567890
;
PROC PRINT DATA=BACKWARDS NOOBS;
   TITLE "Listing of Data Set BACKWARDS";
RUN;
```

Explanation

It is important to realize that if you don't specify the length of the result, it will be the same length as the argument of the REVERSE function. Also, if there were trailing blanks in the original string, there will be leading blanks in the reversed string. Look specifically at the last two observations in the listing below to see that this is the case.

```
          Listing of Data Set BACKWARDS

          STRING          GNIRTS

        Ron Cody          ydoC noR
          XYZ               ZYX
        ABCDEFG           GFEDCBA
                     X    X
        1234567890    0987654321
```

Chapter 2

Perl Regular Expressions

Introduction

Perl regular expressions were added in SAS 9. SAS regular expressions (similar to Perl regular expressions but using a different syntax to indicate text patterns) have actually been around since Release 6.12, but many SAS users are unfamiliar with either SAS or Perl regular expressions. Both SAS regular expressions (the RX functions) and Perl regular expressions (the PRX functions) allow you to locate patterns in text strings. For example, you could write a regular expression to look for three digits, a dash, two digits, a dash, followed by four digits (the general form of a social security number). The syntax of both SAS and Perl regular expressions allows you to search for classes of characters (digits, letters, non-digits, etc.) as well as specific character values.

Since SAS already has such a powerful set of string functions, you may wonder why you need regular expressions. Many of the string processing tasks can be performed either with the traditional character functions or regular expressions. However, regular expressions can sometimes provide a much more compact solution to a complicated string manipulation task. Regular expressions are especially useful for reading highly unstructured data streams. For example, you may have text and numbers all jumbled up in a data file and you want to extract all of the numbers on each line that contains numbers.

Once a pattern is found, you can obtain the position of the pattern, extract a substring, or substitute a string. This book describes both the Perl and SAS regular expressions, but for several reasons, a much more extensive treatment is given to the Perl regular expression functions. First, more people may already be familiar with Perl regular expressions. Second, the implementation of the Perl regular expression in SAS is said to be more efficient. Finally, there is a more extensive set of Perl regular expression functions compared to the SAS regular expressions. The syntax and usage of these two sets of functions is different and it is confusing to use both. If you are new to regular expressions, I suggest that you stick to the Perl regular expressions exclusively.

I have not attempted to provide a complete description of Perl regular expressions in this book. Hopefully, it will be a good start, but to become an expert, you will need to obtain a book on Perl or some other documentation on regular expressions.

A Brief Tutorial on Perl Regular Expressions

I have heard it said that Perl regular expressions are "write only." That means, with some practice, you can become fairly accomplished at writing regular expressions, but reading them, even the ones you wrote yourself, is quite difficult. I strongly suggest that you **comment** any regular expressions you write so that you will be able to change or correct your program at a future time.

The PRXPARSE function is used to create a regular expression. Since this expression is compiled, it is usually placed in the DATA step following a statement such as IF _N_ = 1 then .... Since this statement is executed only once, you also need to retain the value returned by the PRXPARSE function. It is good programming practice to use the RETAIN statement with _N_ when you use the PRXPARSE function since you avoid executing the function for each iteration of the DATA step. So, to get started, let's take a look at the simplest type of regular expression, an exact text match. Note: each of these functions will be described in detail in the appropriate section of this chapter following this tutorial.

Program 2.1: Using a Perl regular expression to locate lines with an exact text match

```
***Primary functions: PRXPARSE, PRXMATCH;

DATA _NULL_;
    TITLE "Perl Regular Expression Tutorial - Program 1";

    IF _N_ = 1 THEN PATTERN_NUM = PRXPARSE("/cat/");
    *Exact match for the letters 'cat' anywhere in the string;
    RETAIN PATTERN_NUM;

    INPUT STRING $30.;
    POSITION = PRXMATCH(PATTERN_NUM,STRING);
    FILE PRINT;
    PUT PATTERN_NUM= STRING= POSITION=;
DATALINES;
There is a cat in this line.
Does not match CAT
cat in the beginning
At the end, a cat
cat
;
```

Explanation

You write your Perl regular expression as the argument of the PRXPARSE function. The single or double quotes inside the parentheses are part of the SAS syntax. Everything else is a standard Perl regular expression. In this example, we are using the forward slashes (/) as the default Perl delimiters. Each time you compile a regular expression, SAS assigns sequential numbers to the resulting expression. This number is needed to perform searches by the other PRX functions such as PRXMATCH, PRXCHANGE, PRXNEXT, PRXSUBSTR, PRXPAREN, or PRXPOSN. Thus, the value of PATTERN_NUM in this program is 1. In this simple example, the PRXMATCH function is used to return the position of the word "cat" in each of the strings. The two arguments in the PRXMATCH function are the return code from the PRXPARSE function and the string to be searched. The result is the first position where the word "cat" is found in each string. If there is no match, the PRXMATCH function returns a 0. Let's look at the output below.

```
Perl Regular Expression Tutorial - Program 1
PATTERN_NUM=1 STRING=There is a cat in this line. POSITION=12
PATTERN_NUM=1 STRING=Does not match CAT POSITION=0
PATTERN_NUM=1 STRING=cat in the beginning POSITION=1
PATTERN_NUM=1 STRING=At the end, a cat POSITION=15
PATTERN_NUM=1 STRING=cat POSITION=1
```

Notice that the value of PATTERN_NUM is 1 in each observation and the value of POSITION is the location of the letter "c" in "cat" in each of the strings. In the second line of output, the value of POSITION is 0 since the word "cat" (lowercase) was not present in that string.

Be careful. Spaces count. For example, if you change the PRXPARSE line to read:

```
IF _N_ = 1 THEN PATTERN_NUM = PRXPARSE("/ cat /");
```

then the output will be:

```
PATTERN_NUM=1 STRING=There is a cat in this line. POSITION=11
PATTERN_NUM=1 STRING=Does not match CAT POSITION=0
PATTERN_NUM=1 STRING=cat in the beginning POSITION=0
PATTERN_NUM=1 STRING=At the end, a cat POSITION=14
PATTERN_NUM=1 STRING=cat POSITION=0
```

Notice that the string in lines 3 and 5 no longer match because the regular expression has a space before and after the word "cat." (The reason there is a match in the fourth observation is that the length of STRING is 30 and there are trailing blanks after the word "cat.")

Perl regular expressions use special characters (called metacharacters) to represent classes of characters. (Named in honor of Will Rogers: "I never meta character I didn't like. ") Before we present a table of Perl regular expression metacharacters, it is instructive to introduce a few of the more useful ones. The expression \d refers to any digit (0–9), \D to any non-digit, and \w to any word character (A–Z, a–z, 0–9, and _). The three metacharacters, *, +, and ? are particularly useful because they add quantity to a regular expression. For example, the * matches the preceding subexpression zero or more times; the + matches the previous subexpression one or more times, and the ? matches the previous expression zero or one times. So, here are a few examples using these characters:

`PRXPARSE("/\d\d\d/")`	matches any three digits in a row.
`PRXPARSE("/\d+/")`	matches one or more digits.
`PRXPARSE("/\w\w\w* /")`	matches any word with two or more characters followed by a space.
`PRXPARSE("/\w\w? +/")`	matches one- or two-word characters such as x, xy, or _X followed by one or more spaces.
`PRXPARSE("/(\w\w) +(\d) +/")`	matches two-word characters, followed by one or more spaces, followed by a single digit, followed by one or more spaces. Note that the expression for the two-word characters (\w\w) is placed in parentheses. Using the parentheses in this way creates what is called a **capture** buffer. The second set of parentheses (around the \d) represents the second capture buffer. Several of the Perl regular expression functions can make use of these capture buffers to extract and/or replace specific portions of a string. For example, the location of the two-word characters or the single digit can be obtained using the PRXPOSN function.

Remember that the quotes are needed by the PRXPARSE function and the outer slashes are used to delimit the regular expression. Since the backslash, forward slash, parentheses, and several other characters have special meaning in a regular expression, you may wonder, how do you search a string that contains characters such as \, (,)? You do this by preceding any of these special characters with a \ character (in Perl jargon called an escape character). So, to match a \ in a string, you code two backslashes like this: \\. To match an open parenthesis, you use \(.

The table below describes several of the wild cards and metacharacters used with regular expressions:

Metacharacter	Description	Examples
*	Matches the previous subexpression zero or more times	cat* matches "cat", "cats", "catanddog" c(at)* matches "c", "cat", and "catatat"
+	Matches the previous subexpression one or more times	\d+ matches one or more digits
?	Matches the previous subexpression zero or one times	hello? matches "hell" and "hello"
. (period)	Matches exactly one character	r.n matches "ron", "run", and "ran"
\d	Matches a digit 0 to 9	\d\d\d matches any three-digit number
\D	Matches a non-digit	\D\D matches "xx", "ab" and "%%"
^	Matches the beginning of the string	^cat matches "cat" and "cats" but not "the cat"
$	Matches the end of a string	cat$ matches "the cat" but not "cat in the hat"
[xyz]	Matches any one of the characters in the square brackets	ca[tr] matches "cat" and "car"
[a-e]	Matches the letters a to e	[a-e]\D+ matches "adam", "edam", and "car"
[a-eA-E]	Matches the letter a to e or A to E	[a-eA-E]\w+ matches "Adam", "edam," and "B13"
{n}	Matches the previous subexpression *n* times	\d{5} matches any 5-digit number and is equivalent to \d\d\d\d\d
{n,}	Matches the previous subexpression *n* or more times	\w{3,} matches "cat" "_NULL_" and is equivalent to \w\w\w+

Table (*continued*)

Metacharacter	Description	Examples
{n,m}	Matches the previous subexpression *n* or more times, but no more than *m*	\w{3,5} matches "abc" "abcd" and "abcde"
[^abcxyz]	Matches any characters except abcxyz	[^8]\d\d matches "123" and "999" but not "800"
x|y	Matches x or y	c(a|o)t matches "cat" and "cot"
\s	Matches a white space character, including a space or a tab,	\d+\s+\d+ matches one or more digits followed by one or more spaces, followed by one or more digits such as "123•••4" Note: •=space
\w	Matches any word character (upper- and lowercase letters, blank and underscore)	\w\w\w matches any three-word characters
\(	Matches the character (	\(\d\d\d\) matches three digits in parentheses such as "(123)"
\)	Matches the character)	\(\d\d\d\) matches three digits in parentheses such as "(123)"
\\	Matches the character \	\D•\\•\D matches "the \ character" Note: •=space
\1	Matches the previous capture buffer and is called a back reference.	(\d\D\d)\1 matches "9a99a9" but not "9a97b7" (.)\1 matches any two repeated characters

This is not a complete list of Perl metacharacters, but it's enough to get you started. The *SAS OnlineDoc 9.1* or any book on Perl programming will provide you with more details. Examples of each of the PRX functions in this chapter will also help you understand how to write these expressions. Note: The wording of arguments in this book might differ from the wording of arguments in *SAS OnlineDoc. 9.1*.

Function That Defines a Regular Expression

SAS9.1 Function: PRXPARSE

Purpose: To define a Perl regular expression to be used later by the other Perl regular expression functions.

Syntax: PRXPARSE(*Perl-regular-expression*)

Perl-regular-expression is a Perl regular expression. See examples in the brief tutorial and in the sample programs in this chapter. The PRXPARSE function is usually executed only once in a DATA step and the return value is retained.

The forward slash (/) is the default delimiter. However, you may use any non-alphanumeric character instead of /. Matching brackets can also be used as delimiters. Look at the last few examples below to see how other delimiters may be used.

If you want the search to be case-insensitive, you can follow the final delimiter with the letter i. For example, PRXPARSE("/cat/I") will match Cat, CAT, or cat (see the fourth example below).

Examples

Function	Matches	Does Not Match
PRXPARSE("/cat/")	"The cat is black"	"cots"
PRXPARSE("/^cat/")	"cat on the roof"	"The cat"
PRXPARSE("/cat$/")	"There is a cat"	"cat in the house"
PRXPARSE("/cat/i")	"The CaT"	"no dogs allowed"
PRXPARSE("/r[aeiou]t/")	"rat", "rot, "rut	"rt" and "rxt"
PRXPARSE("/\d\d\d /")	"345" and "999" (three digits followed by a space)	"1234" and "99"
PRXPARSE("/\d\d\d?/")	"123" and "12" (any two or three digits)	"1", "1AB", "1 9"
PRXPARSE("/\d\d\d+/")	"123" and "12345" (three or more digits)	"12X"
PRXPARSE("/\d\d\d*/")	"123", "12", "12345" (two or more digits)	"1" and "xyz"
PRXPARSE("/(\d|x)\d/")	"56" and "x9"	"9x" and "xx"
PRXPARSE("/[^a-e]\D/")	"fX", "9 ", "AA"	"aa", "99", "b%"
PRXPARSE("/^\/\//")	"//sysin dd *"	"the // is here"
PRXPARSE("/^\/(\/|*)/")	a "//" or "/*" in cols 1 and 2	"123 /*"
PRXPARSE("#//#")	"//"	"/*"
PRXPARSE("/\/\//")	"//" (equivalent to previous expression)	"/*"
PRXPARSE("[\d\d]")	any two digits	"ab"
PRXPARSE("<cat>")	"the cat is black"	"cots"

See examples of the PRXPARSE function in all the examples in this chapter.

Functions That Locate Text Patterns

SAS9.1 Function: PRXMATCH

Purpose: To locate the position in a string, where a regular expression match is found. This function returns the first position in a string expression of the pattern described by the regular expression. If this pattern is not found, the function returns a 0.

Syntax: PRXMATCH(*pattern-id* or *regular-expression*, *string*)

pattern-id is the value returned from the PRXPARSE function.

regular-expression is a Perl regular expression, placed in quotation marks (SAS 9.1 and higher). Note: If you use *pattern-id*, you must use the PRXPARSE function first. If you place the regular expression (in quotation marks) directly in the PRXMATCH function, you do not use the PRXPARSE function.

string is a character variable or a string literal.

Examples

Regular Expression	String	Returns	Does Not Match (Returns 0)
/cat/	"The cat is black"	5	"cots"
/^cat/	"cat on the roof"	1	"The cat"
/cat$/	"There is a cat"	12	"cat in the house"
/cat/I	"The CaT"	5	"no dogs allowed"
/r[aeiou]t/	"rat", "rot, "rut	1	"rt" and "rxt"
/\d\d\d /	"345" and "999"	1	"1234" and "99"
/\d\d\d?/	"123" and "12"	1	"1", "1AB", "1 9"
/\d\d\d+/	"123" and "12345"	1	"12"
/\d\d\d*/	"123", "12", "12345"	1	"1" and "xyz"
/r.n/	"ron", "ronny", "r9n", "r n"	1	"rn"

Table (*continued*)

Regular Expression	String	Returns	Does Not Match (Returns 0)
`/[1-5]\d[6-9]/`	`"299"`, `"106"`, `"337"`	1	`"666"`, `"919"`, `"11"`
`/(\d|x)\d/`	`"56"` and `"x9"`	1	`"9x"` and `"xx"`
`/[^a-e]\D/`	`"fX"`, `"9 "`, `"AA"`	1	`"aa"`, `"99"`, `"b%"`
`/^\/\//`	`"//sysin dd *"`	1	`"the // is here"`
`/^\/(\/|\*)/`	a `"//"` or `"/*"` in cols 1 and 2	1	`"123 /*"`

Examples of PRXMATCH without using PRXPARSE: `STRING = "The cat in the hat"`

Function	Returns
`PRXMATCH("/cat/",STRING)`	4
`PRXMATCH("/\d\d+/","AB123")`	3

Program 2.2: Using a regular expression to search for phone numbers in a string

---

```
***Primary functions: PRXPARSE, PRXMATCH;

DATA PHONE;
   IF _N_ = 1 THEN PATTERN = PRXPARSE("/\(\d\d\d\) ?\d\d\d-\d{4}/");
   ***Regular expression will match any phone number in the form:
      (nnn)nnn-nnnn or (nnn) nnn-nnnn.;
   /*
      \(       matches a left parenthesis
      \d\d\d   matches any three digits
      (blank)? matches zero or one blank
      \d\d\d   matches any three digits
      -        matches a dash
      \d{4}    matches any four digits
   */
   RETAIN PATTERN;
```

```
    INPUT STRING $CHAR40.;
    IF PRXMATCH(PATTERN,STRING) GT 0 THEN OUTPUT;
DATALINES;
One number (123)333-4444
Two here:(800)234-2222 and (908) 444-2344
None here
;
PROC PRINT DATA=PHONE NOOBS;
    TITLE "Listing of Data Set Phone";
RUN;
```

Explanation

To search for an open parenthesis, you use a '\('. The three \d's specify any three digits. The closed parenthesis is written as '\)'. The space followed by the '?' means zero or one space. This is followed by any three digits and a dash. Following the dash are any four digits. The notation: \d{4} is a short way of writing \d\d\d\d. The number in the braces indicates how may times to repeat the previous subexpression. Since you execute the PRXPARSE function only once, remember to use the RETAIN statement to retain the value returned by the function.

Since the PRXMATCH function returns the first position of a match, any line containing one or more valid phone numbers will return a value greater than zero. Output from PROC PRINT is shown next:

```
                    Listing of Data Set Phone

            RETURN    STRING

              1       One number (123)333-4444
              1       Two here:(800)234-2222 and (908) 444-234
```

Program 2.3: Modifying Program 2.2 to search for toll-free phone numbers

```
***Primary functions: PRXPARSE, PRXMATCH
***Other function: MISSING;

DATA TOLL_FREE;
    IF _N_ = 1 THEN DO
        RE = PRXPARSE("/\(8(00|77|87)\) ?\d\d\d-\d{4}\b/");
        ***Regular expression looks for phone numbers of the form:
            (nnn)nnn-nnnn or (nnn) nnn-nnnn.  In addition the first
            digit of the area code must be an 8 and the next two
            digits must be either a 00, 77, or 87.;
        IF MISSING(RE) THEN DO;
            PUT "ERROR IN COMPILING REGULAR EXPRESSION";
            STOP;
        END;
    END;
    RETAIN RE;
    INPUT STRING $CHAR80.;
    POSITION = PRXMATCH(RE,STRING);
    IF POSITION GT 0 THEN OUTPUT;
DATALINES;
One number on this line (877)234-8765
No numbers here
One toll free, one not:(908)782-6354 and (800)876-3333 xxx
Two toll free:(800)282-3454 and (887) 858-1234
No toll free here (609)848-9999 and (908) 345-2222
;
PROC PRINT DATA=TOLL_FREE NOOBS;
    TITLE "Listing of Data Set TOLL_FREE";
RUN;
```

Explanation

Several things have been added to this program compared to the previous one. First, the regular expression now searches for numbers that begin with either (800), (877), or (887). This is accomplished by placing an "8" in the first position and then using the OR operator (the |) to select either 00, 77, or 87 as the next two digits. One other difference between this expression and the one used in the previous program is that the number is followed by a word boundary (a space or end-of-line: \b). Hopefully, you're starting to see the impressive power of regular expressions by now. The MISSING function tests if its argument is missing or not. If you have an invalid regular expression, the value of the regular expression

RE will be missing, and the MISSING function will return a true value. See the listing of data set TOLL_FREE below:

```
                    Listing of Data Set TOLL_FREE

  RE  STRING                                                      POSITION

   1  One number on this line (877)234-8765                          25
   1  One toll free, one not:(908)782-6354 and (800)876-3333 xxx     42
   1  Two toll free:(800)282-3454 and (887) 858-1234                 15
```

Program 2.4: Using PRXMATCH without PRXPARSE (entering the regular expression directly in the function)

```
***Primary function: PRXMATCH;

DATA MATCH_IT;
   INPUT @1 STRING $20.;
   POSITION = PRXMATCH("/\d\d\d/",STRING);
DATALINES;
LINE 345 IS HERE
NONE HERE
ABC1234567
;
PROC PRINT DATA=MATCH_IT NOOBS;
   TITLE "Listing of Data Set MATCH_IT";
RUN;
```

Explanation

In this program, the regular expression to search for three digits is placed directly in the PRXMATCH function instead of in a return code from PRXPARSE. The output is:

```
                 Listing of Data Set MATCH_IT

              STRING              POSITION

              LINE 345 IS HERE        6
              NONE HERE               0
              ABC1234567              4
```

SAS9.1 **Function:** **CALL PRXSUBSTR**

Purpose: Used with the PRXPARSE function to locate the starting position and length of a pattern within a string. The PRXSUBSTR call routine serves much the same purpose as the PRXMATCH function, plus it returns the length of the match as well as the starting position.

Syntax: CALL PRXSUBSTR(*pattern-id*, *string*, *start* <,*length*>)

pattern-id is the return code from the PRXPARSE function.

string is the string to be searched.

start is the name of the variable that is assigned the starting position of the pattern.

length is the name of a variable, if specified, that is assigned the length of the substring. If no substring is found, the value of length is zero.

Note: It is especially useful to use the SUBSTRN function (instead of the SUBSTR function) following the call to PRXSUBSTR, since using a zero length as an argument of the SUBSTRN function results in a character missing value.

Examples

For these examples, RE = PRXPARSE("/\d+/");

Function	String	Start	Length
CALL PRXSUBSTR(RE,STRING,START,LENGTH)	"ABC 1234 XYZ"	5	4
CALL PRXSUBSTR(RE,STRING,START,LENGTH)	"NO NUMBERS HERE"	0	0
CALL PRXSUBSTR(RE,STRING,START,LENGTH)	"123 456 789"	1	3

Program 2.5: Locating all 5- or 9-digit zip codes in a list of addresses

Here is an interesting problem that shows the power of regular expressions. You have a list of mailing addresses. Some addresses have three lines, some four, others, possibly more or less. Some of the addresses have zip codes, some do not. The zip codes are either 5- or 9-digits in length. Go through the file and extract all the valid zip codes.

```
***Primary functions: PRXPARSE and CALL PRXSUBSTR
***Other function: SUBSTRN;

DATA ZIPCODE;
   IF _N_ = 1 THEN RE = PRXPARSE("/ \d{5}(-\d{4})?/");
   RETAIN RE;
   /*
      Match a blank followed by 5 digits followed by
      either nothing or a dash and 4 digits

      \d{5}     matches 5 digits
      -         matches a dash
      \d{4}     matches 4 digits
      ?         matches zero or one of the preceding subexpression

   */

   INPUT STRING $80.;
   LENGTH ZIP_CODE $ 10;
   CALL PRXSUBSTR(RE,STRING,START,LENGTH);
   IF START GT 0 THEN DO;
      ZIP_CODE = SUBSTRN(STRING,START + 1,LENGTH - 1);
      OUTPUT;
   END;
   KEEP ZIP_CODE;
DATALINES;
John Smith
```

```
12 Broad Street
Flemington, NJ 08822
Philip Judson
Apt #1, Building 7
777 Route 730
Kerrville, TX 78028
Dr. Roger Alan
44 Commonwealth Ave.
Boston, MA 02116-7364
;
PROC PRINT DATA=ZIPCODE NOOBS;
    TITLE "Listing of Data Set ZIPCODE";
RUN;
```

Explanation

The regular expression is looking for a blank, followed by five digits, followed by zero or one occurrences of a dash and four digits. The PRXSUBSTR call routine checks if this pattern is found in the string. If it is found (START greater than zero), the SUBSTRN function extracts the zip code from the string. Note that the starting position in this function is START + 1 since the pattern starts with a blank. Also, since the SUBSTRN function is conditionally executed only when START is greater than zero, the SUBSTR function would be equivalent. A listing of the zip codes is shown below:

```
            Listing of Data Set ZIPCODE

                ZIP_CODE

                08822
                78028
                02116-7364
```

Program 2.6: Extracting a phone number from a text string

```
***Primary functions: PRXPARSE, CALL PRXSUBSTR
***Other functions: SUBSTR, COMPRESS, and MISSING;

DATA EXTRACT;
   IF _N_ = 1 THEN DO;
      PATTERN = PRXPARSE("/\(\d\d\d\) ?\d\d\d-\d{4}/");
      IF MISSING(PATTERN) THEN DO;
         PUT "ERROR IN COMPILING REGULAR EXPRESSION";
         STOP;
      END;
   END;
   RETAIN PATTERN;

   LENGTH NUMBER $ 15;
   INPUT STRING $CHAR80.;
   CALL PRXSUBSTR(PATTERN,STRING,START,LENGTH);
      IF START GT 0 THEN DO;
      NUMBER = SUBSTR(STRING,START,LENGTH);
      NUMBER = COMPRESS(NUMBER," ");
      OUTPUT;
   END;
   KEEP NUMBER;
DATALINES;
THIS LINE DOES NOT HAVE ANY PHONE NUMBERS ON IT
THIS LINE DOES: (123)345-4567 LA DI LA DI LA
ALSO VALID (123) 999-9999
TWO NUMBERS HERE (333)444-5555 AND (800)123-4567
;
PROC PRINT DATA=EXTRACT NOOBS;
   TITLE "Extracted Phone Numbers";
RUN;
```

Explanation

This program is similar to Program 2.2. You use the same regular expression to test if a phone number has been found, using the PRXMATCH function. The call to PRXSUBSTR gives you the starting position of the phone number and its length (remember, the length can vary because of the possibility of a space following the area code). The values obtained from the PRXSUBSTR function are then used in the SUBSTR function to extract the actual number from the text string. Finally, the COMPRESS function removes any blanks from the string. See the listing below for the results.

```
                        Extracted Phone Numbers

                             NUMBER

                           (123)345-4567
                           (123)999-9999
                           (333)444-5555
```

SAS9.1 **Function:** **CALL PRXPOSN**

Purpose: To return the position and length for a capture buffer (a subexpression defined in the regular expression). Used in conjunction with the PRXPARSE and one of the PRX search functions (such as PRXMATCH).

Syntax: CALL PRXPOSN(*pattern-id, capture-buffer-number, start <,length>*)

pattern-id is the return value from the PRXPARSE function.

capture-buffer-number is a number indicating which capture buffer is to be evaluated.

start is the name of the variable that is assigned the value of the first position in the string where the pattern from the *n*th capture buffer is found.

length is the name of the variable, if specified, that is assigned the length of the found pattern.

Before we get to the examples and sample programs, let's spend a moment discussing capture buffers. When you write a Perl regular expression, you can make pattern groupings using parentheses. For example, the pattern: /(\d+) *([a-zA-Z]+)/ has two capture buffers. The first matches one or more digits; the second matches one or more upper- or lowercase letters. These two patterns are separated by zero or more blanks.

Example

For these examples the following lines of SAS code were submitted:
```
PATTERN = PRXPARSE("/(\d+) *([a-zA-Z]+)/");
MATCH = PRXMATCH(PATTERN,STRING);
```

Function	String	Start	Length
CALL PRXPOSN(PATTERN,1,START,LENGTH)	"abc123 xyz4567"	4	3
CALL PRXPOSN(PATTERN,2,START,LENGTH)	"abc123 xyz4567"	8	3
CALL PRXPOSN(PATTERN,1,START,LENGTH)	"XXXYYYZZZ"	0	0

Program 2.7: Using the PRXPOSN function to extract the area code and exchange from a phone number

```
***Primary functions: PRXPARSE, PRXMATCH, CALL PRXPOSN
***Other function: SUBSTR;
RUN;
DATA PIECES;
   IF _N_ THEN RE = PRXPARSE("/\(((\d\d\d)\) ?(\d\d\d)-\d{4}/");
   /*
      \(        matches an open parenthesis
      \d\d\d    matches three digits
      \)        matches a closed parenthesis
      b?        matches zero or more blanks (b = blank)
      \d\d\d    matches three digits
      -         matches a dash
      \d{4}     matches four digits
   */
   RETAIN RE;

   INPUT NUMBER $CHAR80.;
   MATCH = PRXMATCH(RE,NUMBER);
   IF MATCH GT 0 THEN DO;
      CALL PRXPOSN(RE,1,AREA_START);
      CALL PRXPOSN(RE,2,EX_START,EX_LENGTH);
      AREA_CODE = SUBSTR(NUMBER,AREA_START,3);
      EXCHANGE = SUBSTR(NUMBER,EX_START,EX_LENGTH);
   END;
   DROP RE;
DATALINES;
```

```
THIS LINE DOES NOT HAVE ANY PHONE NUMBERS ON IT
THIS LINE DOES: (123)345-4567 LA DI LA DI LA
ALSO VALID (609) 999-9999
TWO NUMBERS HERE (333)444-5555 AND (800)123-4567
;
PROC PRINT DATA=PIECES NOOBS HEADING=H;
   TITLE "Listing of Data Set PIECES";
RUN;
```

Explanation

The regular expression in this program looks similar to the one in Program 2.2. Here we have added a set of parentheses around the expression that identifies the area code '\d\d\d' and the expression that identifies the exchange '\d\d\d'. The PRXMATCH function returns the starting position if the match is successful, 0 otherwise. The first call to PRXPOSN requests the position of the start of the first capture buffer. Since we know that the length is 3, we do not need to include a length argument in the calling sequence. The next function call asks for the starting position and length (although we don't need the length) of the starting position of the exchange (the first three digits following the area code or the blank after the area code). Note: We don't need the length of the exchange either, but it was included to illustrate how lengths are obtained. The SUBSTR function then extracts the substrings. A listing of the resulting data set is shown below:

```
                    Listing of Data Set PIECES


       NUMBER

       THIS LINE DOES NOT HAVE ANY PHONE NUMBERS ON IT
       THIS LINE DOES: (123)345-4567 LA DI LA DI LA
       ALSO VALID (609) 999-9999
       TWO NUMBERS HERE (333)444-5555 AND (800)123-4567
```

MATCH	AREA_ START	EX_START	EX_LENGTH	AREA_ CODE	EXCHANGE
0	.	.	.		
17	18	22	3	123	345
12	13	18	3	609	999
18	19	23	3	333	444

Program 2.8: Using regular expressions to read very unstructured data

```
***Primary functions: PRSPARSE, PRXMATCH, CALL PRXPOSN
***Other functions: SUBSTR, INPUT;

***This program will read every line of data and, for any line
   that contains two or more numbers, will assign the first
   number to X and the second number to Y;

DATA READ_NUM;
***Read the first number and second numbers on line;
   IF _N_ = 1 THEN RET = PRXPARSE("/(\d+) +\D*(\d+)/");
   /*
      \d+      matches one or more digits
      b+       matches one or more blanks (b = blank)
      \D*      matches zero or more non-digits
      \d+      matches one or more digits
   */
   RETAIN RET;

   INPUT STRING $CHAR40.;
   POS = PRXMATCH(RET,STRING);
   IF POS GT 0 THEN DO;
      CALL PRXPOSN(RET,1,START1,LENGTH1);
      IF START1 GT 0 THEN X = INPUT(SUBSTR(STRING,START1,LENGTH1),9.);
      CALL PRXPOSN(RET,2,START2,LENGTH2);
      IF START2 GT 0 THEN Y = INPUT(SUBSTR(STRING,START2,LENGTH2),9.);
      OUTPUT;
   END;
   KEEP STRING X Y;
DATALINES;
XXXXXXXXXXXXXXXXXX 9 XXXXXXX            123
This line has a 6 and a 123 in it
456 789
None on this line
Only one here: 77
;
PROC PRINT DATA=READ_NUM NOOBS;
   TITLE "Listing of Data Set READ_NUM";
RUN;
```

Explanation

This example shows how powerful regular expressions can be used to read very unstructured data. Here the task was to read every line of data and to locate any line with two or more numbers on it, then, assign the first value to X and the second value to Y. (See the program example under the PRXNEXT function for a more general solution to this problem.) The listing of READ_NUM, below, shows that this program worked as desired. The variable STRING was kept in the data set so you could see the original data and the extracted numbers in the listing.

```
                    Listing of Data Set READ_NUM

     STRING                                      X      Y

     XXXXXXXXXXXXXXXXXX 9 XXXXXXX        123      9    123
     This line has a 6 and a 123 in it            6    123
     456 789                                    456    789
```

SAS9.1 **Function: CALL PRXNEXT**

Purpose: To locate the *n*th occurrence of a pattern defined by the PRXPARSE function in a string. Each time you call the PRXNEXT routine, the next occurrence of the pattern will be identified.

Syntax: CALL PRXNEXT(*pattern-id, start, stop, position, length*)

pattern-id is the value returned by the PRXPARSE function.

start is the starting position to begin the search.

stop is the last position in the string for the search. If stop is set to –1, the position of the last non-blank character in the string is used.

position is the name of the variable that is assigned the starting position of the *n*th occurrence of the pattern or the first occurrence after start.

length is the name of the variable that is assigned the length of the pattern.

Examples

For these examples the following statements were issued:
```
RE = PRXPARSE("/\d+/");
***Look for 1 or more digits;
STRING = "12 345 ab 6 cd";
START = 1;
STOP = LENGTH(STRING);
```

Function	Returns (1st call)	Returns (2nd call)	Returns (3rd call)
CALL PRXNEXT(RE, START, STOP, POS, LENGTH)	START = 3 STOP = 14 POS = 1 LENGTH = 2	START = 7 STOP = 14 POS = 4 LENGTH = 3	START = 12 STOP = 14 POS = 11 LENGTH = 1

Program 2.9: Finding digits in random positions in an input string using CALL PRXNEXT

```
***Primary functions: PRXPARSE, CALL PRXNEXT
***Other functions: LENGTH, INPUT;

DATA FIND_NUM;
   IF _N_ = 1 THEN RET = PRXPARSE("/\d+/");
   *Look for one or more digits in a row;
   RETAIN RET;

   INPUT STRING $40.;
   START = 1;
   STOP = LENGTH(STRING);
   CALL PRXNEXT(RET,START,STOP,STRING,POSITION,LENGTH);
   ARRAY X[5];
   DO I = 1 TO 5 WHILE (POSITION GT 0);
      X[I] = INPUT(SUBSTR(STRING,POSITION,LENGTH),9.);
      CALL PRXNEXT(RET,START,STOP,STRING,POSITION,LENGTH);
   END;
   KEEP X1-X5 STRING;
DATALINES;
THIS 45 LINE 98 HAS 3 NUMBERS
NONE HERE
12 34 78 90
;
```

```
PROC PRINT DATA=FIND_NUM NOOBS;
   TITLE "Listing of Data Set FIND_NUM";
RUN;
```

Explanation

The regular expression /\d+/ says to look for one or more digits in a string. The initial value of START is set to 1 and STOP to the length of the string (not counting trailing blanks). The PRXNEXT function is called, the value of START is set to the position of the blank after the first number, and the value of STOP is set to the length of the string. POSITION is the starting position of the first digit, and LENGTH is the number of digits in the number. The SUBSTR function extracts the digits and the INPUT function does the character-to-numeric conversion. This continues until no more digits are found (POSITION = 0). See the listing below to confirm that the program worked as expected.

```
                    Listing of Data Set FIND_NUM

   STRING                          X1    X2    X3    X4    X5

   THIS 45 LINE 98 HAS 3 NUMBERS   45    98     3     .     .
   NONE HERE                        .     .     .     .     .
   12 34 78 90                     12    34    78    90     .
```

SAS9.1 Function: PRXPAREN

Purpose: To return a value indicating the largest capture buffer number that found a match. Use PRXPAREN when a Perl regular expression contains several alternative matches. You may want to use this function with the PRXPOSN function. This function is used in conjunction with PRXPARSE and PRXMATCH.

Syntax: PRXPAREN(*pattern-id*)

pattern-id is the value returned by the PRXPARSE function.

Examples

For this example,
RETURN = PRXPARSE(/"(one)|(two)|(three)/") and POSITION = PRXMATCH(RETURN,STRING);

Function	String	Returns
PRXPAREN(RETURN)	"three two one"	3
PRXPAREN(RETURN)	"only one here:	1
PRXPAREN(RETURN)	"two one three"	2

Program 2.10: Demonstrating the PRXPAREN function

```
***Primary functions: PRXPARSE, PRXMATCH, PRXPAREN;

DATA PAREN;
   IF _N_ = 1 THEN PATTERN = PRXPARSE("/(\d )|(\d\d )|(\d\d\d )/");
   ***One or two or three digit number followed by a blank;
   RETAIN PATTERN;

   INPUT STRING $CHAR30.;
   POSITION = PRXMATCH(PATTERN,STRING);
   IF POSITION GT 0 THEN WHICH_PAREN = PRXPAREN(PATTERN);
DATALINES;
one single digit 8 here
two 888 77
12345 1234 123 12 1
;
PROC PRINT DATA=PAREN NOOBS;
   TITLE "Listing of Data Set PAREN";
RUN;
```

Explanation

The Perl regular expression in the PRXPARSE function matches a one-, two-, or three-digit number followed by a blank. In the first observation, the single digit matches the first capture buffer so the PRXPAREN function returns a 1. In the second observation, the 888 is matched by the third capture buffer, and a 3 is returned. Finally, the first match in the third string is the three digit number which, again, is matched by capture buffer 3.

```
                    Listing of Data Set PAREN

                                                      WHICH_
          PATTERN   STRING                  POSITION   PAREN

             1      one single digit 8 here    18        1
             1      two 888 77                  5        3
             1      12345 1234 123 12 1         3        3
```

Function That Substitutes One String for Another

SAS9.1 Function: CALL PRXCHANGE

Purpose: To substitute one string for another. One advantage of using PRXCHANGE over TRANWRD is that you can search for strings using wild cards. Note that you need to use the substitution (s) operator in the regular expression to specify the search and replacement expression (see the explanation following the program).

Syntax: CALL PRXCHANGE(*pattern-id* or *regular-expression*, *times*, *old-string* <, *new-string* <, *result-length* <, *truncation-value* <, *number-of-changes*>>>>);

pattern-id is the value returned from the PRXPARSE function.

regular-expression is a Perl regular expression, placed in quotation marks (SAS 9.1 and higher).

times is the number of times to search for and replace a string. A value of −1 will replace all matching patterns.

old-string is the string that you want to replace. If you do not specify *new-string*, the replacement will take place in *old-string*.

new-string, if specified, names the variable to hold the text after replacement. If *new-string* is not specified, the changes are made to *old-string*.

result-length is the name of the variable that, if specified, is assigned a value representing the length of the string after replacement. Note that trailing blanks in *old-string* are not copied to *new-string*.

truncation-value is the name of the variable that, if specified, is assigned a value of 0 or 1. If the resulting string is longer than the length of *new-string*, the value is 1; otherwise it is a 0. This value is useful to test if your string was truncated because the replacements resulted in a length longer than the original specified length.

number-of-changes is the name of the variable that, if specified, is assigned a value representing the total number of replacements that were made.

Program 2.11: Demonstrating the CALL PRXCHANGE function

```
***Primary functions: PRXPARSE, CALL PRXCHANGE;

DATA CAT_AND_MOUSE;
   INPUT TEXT $CHAR40.;
   LENGTH NEW_TEXT $ 80;

   IF _N_ = 1 THEN MATCH = PRXPARSE("s/[Cc]at/Mouse/");
   *Replace "Cat" or "cat" with Mouse;
   RETAIN MATCH;

   CALL PRXCHANGE(MATCH,-1,TEXT,NEW_TEXT,R_LENGTH,TRUNC,N_OF_CHANGES);
   IF TRUNC THEN PUT "Note: NEW_TEXT was truncated";
DATALINES;
The Cat in the hat
There are two cat cats in this line
;
PROC PRINT DATA=CAT_AND_MOUSE NOOBS;
   TITLE "Listing of CAT_AND_MOUSE";
RUN;
```

Explanation

The regular expression and the replacement string is specified in the PRXPARSE function, using the substitution operator (the "s" before the first /). In this example, the regular expression to be searched for is /[Cc]at/. This matches either "Cat" or "cat" anywhere in the string. The replacement string is "Mouse." Since the length of NEW_TEXT was set to 80, even though the replacement of cat (or Cat) with Mouse results in a longer string, the new length does not exceed 80. Therefore, no truncation occurs. The –1 indicates that you want to replace every occurrence of "Cat" or "cat" with "Mouse." If you did not supply a NEW_TEXT variable, the replacement would be made to the original string. The output from PROC PRINT is shown below:

```
                         Listing of CAT_AND_MOUSE

    TEXT

    The Cat in the hat
    There are two cat cats in this line


                                                             N_OF_
    NEW_TEXT                          MATCH  R_LENGTH  TRUNC  CHANGES

    The Mouse in the hat                1       42       0       1
    There are two Mouse Mouses in this line  1   44      0       2
```

Program 2.12: Demonstrating the use of capture buffers with PRXCHANGE

```
***Primary functions: PRXPARSE, CALL PRXCHANGE;

DATA CAPTURE;
   IF _N_ = 1 THEN RETURN = PRXPARSE("S/(\w+ +)(\w+)/$2 $1/");
   RETAIN RETURN;

   INPUT STRING $20.;
   CALL PRXCHANGE(RETURN,-1,STRING);
DATALINES;
Ron Cody
Russell Lynn
;
PROC PRINT DATA=CAPTURE NOOBS;
   TITLE "Listing of Data Set CAPTURE");
RUN;
```

Explanation

The regular expression specifies one or more word characters, followed by one or more blanks (the first capture buffer), followed by one or more word characters (the second capture buffer). In the substitute portion of the regular expression, the $1 and $2 expressions refer to the first and second capture buffer, respectively. So, by placing the $2 before the $1, the two words are reversed, as shown below.

```
                Listing of Data Set CAPTURE

            RETURN    STRING

                 1       Cody Ron
                 1       Lynn Russell
```

Function That Releases Memory Used by a Regular Expression

SAS9.1 **Function: CALL PRXFREE**

Purpose: To free resources that were allocated to a Perl regular expression (usually used with a test for end-of-file). If you do not call PRXFREE, the resources used will be freed when the DATA step ends.

Syntax: CALL PRXFREE(*pattern-id*)

pattern-id is the value returned from the PRXPARSE function

Examples

For this example, the statement:
PATTERN = PRXPARSE("/\d/") preceded the call to PRXFREE

Function	Returns
PRXFREE(PATTERN)	Sets the value returned by PRXPARSE to missing

Program 2.13: Data cleaning example using PRXPARSE and CALL PRXFREE

```
***Primary functions: PRXPARSE, RXMATCH, CALL PRXFREE;

DATA INVALID;
   ***Valid ID's are 1 to 3 digits with leading blanks;
   INFILE 'C:\BOOKS\FUNCTIONS\IDNUMS.DAT' END=LAST;
   IF _N_ = 1 THEN VALID = PRXPARSE("/\d\d\d| \d\d|  \d/");
   /*
      \d\d\d                matches three digits
      (single blank)\d\d    matches a blank followed by two digits
      (two blanks)\d        matches two blanks followed by one digit
   */

   RETAIN VALID;
   INPUT @1 ID $CHAR3.;
   POS = PRXMATCH(VALID,ID);
   IF POS EQ 0 THEN OUTPUT INVALID;
   IF LAST THEN CALL PRXFREE(VALID);
   DROP VALID;
RUN;
```

Explanation

In this example, valid IDs are character values of either three digits, a blank followed by two digits, or two blanks followed by one digit. The INFILE statement option END=LAST creates the logical variable (LAST), which is true when the last record is being read from the file. So, when LAST is true, a call is made to PRXFREE to release resources used by the regular expression. Note that the $CHAR3. informat is used to read the ID variable since you want to maintain any leading blanks.

C h a p t e r   3

SAS Regular Expressions

Introduction

As mentioned in Chapter 2, "Perl Regular Expressions," SAS also has a set of regular expression functions of its own. These have been available since Release 6.12. However, more people may already be familiar with the Perl expressions, and the Perl expressions are said to be more efficient in SAS. However, the differences in syntax between the two sets of functions can make it difficult to use both. For example, spaces are critical in Perl regular expressions but not in SAS regular expressions. Therefore, this chapter will be very brief as I encourage you to use Perl regular expressions in your programs.

Function That Defines a Regular Expression

Function: RXPARSE

Purpose: To define a SAS regular expression to be used later by the other SAS regular expression (RX) functions.

Syntax: RXPARSE(*SAS-regular-expression*)

SAS-regular-expression is a SAS regular expression. The RXPARSE function is usually executed only once in a DATA step and the return value is retained.

The table below describes several of the wild cards and metacharacters used with regular expressions:

Metacharacter	Description	Examples
*	Matches the previous pattern zero or more times	cat* matches "cat", "cats", "catanddog" c(at)* matches "c", "cat", and "catatat"
+	Matches the previous pattern one or more times	$d+ matches one or more digits
?	Matches exactly one character	r?n matches "ron", "run", and "ran"
:	Matches zero or more characters	a:b matches "axb" and "ab"
$d or $D	Matches a digit 0 to 9	dd$d matches any three-digit number
$a or $A	Matches an upper- or lowercase letter	aa matches "xx", "ab" and "XX"
^	Non-pattern match	^d matches "x" and "%" but not "7"
$'xyz'	Matches any one of the characters in quotation marks	ca$'tr' matches "cat" and "car"
$'a-e'	Matches the letters a to e	$'a-e'$a+ matches "adam", "edam" and "car"

Table (*continued*)

Metacharacter	Description	Examples
$'a-eA-E'	Matches the letter a to e or A to E	$'a-eA-E'$a+ matches "Adam", "edam", and "B13"
x|y	Matches x or y	c(a|o)t matches "cat" and "cot"
$w	Matches a white space character, including a space or a tab	$d+$w+$d+ matches one or more digits followed by one or more spaces, followed by one or more digits such as "123•••4" Note: •=space
'('	Matches the character (	'('dd$d')' matches three digits in parentheses such as "(123)"
')'	Matches the character)	'('dd$d')' matches three digits in parentheses such as "(123)"
$u or $U	Matches any uppercase letter	uu$u matches "ABC"
$l or $L	Matches any lowercase letter	ll matches "ab"

Program 3.1: Using a SAS regular expression to locate data lines containing telephone numbers

```
***Primary functions: RXPARSE, RXMATCH
***Other function: MISSING;

DATA LOCATE;
   IF _N_ = 1 THEN DO;
      PHONE = RXPARSE("'('$D$D$D')''(' ')*$D$D$D'-'$D$D$D$D");
      RETAIN PHONE;
      IF MISSING(PHONE) THEN DO;
         PUT "Bad parsing of regular expression";
         STOP;
      END;
   END;

   INPUT STRING $CHAR80.;
   IF RXMATCH(PHONE,STRING) THEN OUTPUT;
DATALINES;
```

```
THIS LINE DOES NOT HAVE ANY PHONE NUMBERS ON IT
THIS LINE DOES: (123)345-4567 LA DI LA DI LA
(800)    123-1234 NOTE: MULTIPLE SPACES
TWO NUMBERS HERE (333)444-5555 AND (800)123-4567
;
PROC PRINT DATA=LOCATE NOOBS;
   TITLE "Lines Containing Phone Numbers";
RUN;
```

Explanation

The regular expression defined in the argument of the RXPARSE function is looking for a left parenthesis, three digits and a right parenthesis, followed by zero or more spaces, followed by three digits, a dash, followed by four digits. If the pattern is found, the RXMATCH function will return a value greater than 0. A listing of data set LOCATE is shown next:

```
                    Lines Containing Phone Numbers

         PHONE                        STRING

           1       THIS LINE DOES: (123)345-4567 LA DI LA DI LA
           1       (800)    123-1234 NOTE: MULTIPLE SPACES
           1       TWO NUMBERS HERE (333)444-5555 AND (800)123-4567
```

Functions That Locate Text Patterns

Function: RXMATCH

Purpose: To return the first position in a string matched by the regular expression pattern. This function is used with the RXPARSE function to match a pattern in a text string. Look under RXPARSE for a list of SAS regular expression descriptions.

Syntax: RXMATCH(*pattern-id, string*)

pattern-id is the value returned from the RXPARSE function.

string is a character variable or a string literal.

Examples

Regular Expression	String	Returns	Does Not Match (Returns 0)
$cat	"The cat is black"	5	"cots"
r$'aeiou't	"rat", "rot, "rut	1	"rt" and "rxt"
dd$d	"345" and "999"	1	"1234" and "99"
dd+	"123" and "12""	1	"1", "1AB", "1 9"
dddd*	"123" and "12345"	1	"12"
aa	"123abc", "yy", "1a2bc3"	4,1,4	"123" and "x"
r?n	"ron", "ronny", "r9n", "r n"	1	"rn"
r:n	"ron", "rn"	1	"123", "xyz"

Function: **CALL RXSUBSTR**

Purpose: To locate the starting position and length of a substring identified by a SAS regular expression. This call routine is always used in conjunction with the RXPARSE function.

Syntax: CALL RXSUBSTR(*pattern-id, string, start, length*)

pattern-id is the value returned from the PRXPARSE function.

string is the string to be processed.

start is the name of the variable that is assigned the starting position of the pattern. If no pattern is found, start is set to 0.

length is the name of the variable that is assigned the length of the located pattern. If no pattern is found, length is set to 0.

Program 3.2: Extracting a phone number from a string, using a SAS regular expression

```
***Primary functions: RXPARSE and CALL RXSUBSTR
***Other functions: SUBSTR, COMPRESS, MISSING;

DATA EXTRACT;
    IF _N_ = 1 THEN DO;
        PHONE = RXPARSE("'('$D$D$D')'('  ')*$D$D$D'-'$D$D$D$D");
        RETAIN PHONE;
        IF MISSING(PHONE) THEN DO;
            PUT "Bad parsing of regular expression";
            STOP;
        END;
    END;
    LENGTH PHONE_NUMBER $ 13;
    INPUT STRING $CHAR80.;
    CALL RXSUBSTR(PHONE,STRING,START,LENGTH);
    IF START GT 0; ***Only valid numbers beyond this point;
    TEMP = SUBSTR(STRING,START,LENGTH);
    PHONE_NUMBER = COMPRESS(TEMP,' ');
    KEEP PHONE_NUMBER;
DATALINES;
THIS LINE DOES NOT HAVE ANY PHONE NUMBERS ON IT
THIS LINE DOES: (123)345-4567 LA DI LA DI LA
(800)    123-1234 NOTE: MULTIPLE SPACES
TWO NUMBERS HERE (333)444-5555 AND (800)123-4567
;
PROC PRINT DATA=EXTRACT NOOBS;
    TITLE "Lines Containing Phone Numbers";
RUN;
```

Explanation

This program is similar to Program 3.1 except that once a match is found, the RXSUBSTR call routine is used to find the starting location of the number and its length. These values are then used in the SUBSTR function to extract the number. Finally, since some of the numbers contain spaces after the area code, the COMPRESS function removes any spaces from the string. A listing of the data set EXTRACT, below, lists all the valid phone numbers:

```
                          Lines Containing Phone Numbers

                  PHONE_NUMBER

                     (123)345-4567
                     (800)123-1234
                     (333)444-5555
```

Function That Substitutes One String for Another

Function: CALL RXCHANGE

Purpose: To exchange a string for a pattern matched by a regular expression.

Syntax: `CALL RXCHANGE(return, times, old-string`
`<, new-string>)`

`return` is the value returned from the RXPARSE function.

`times` is the number of times to make the substitution in a string.

`old-string` is the original string to be changed. If `new-string` is not specified, the change is made to `old-string`.

`new-string`, if specified, is the name of the character variable which will hold the changed values. Hint: Use a LENGTH statement to set the length of `new-string` and define it as a character variable before calling the RXCHANGE function.

The RXCHANGE function works in concert with the RXPARSE function. The original pattern and the changed value are specified in the RXPARSE function, separated by the word 'TO'. Some examples of using RXPARSE expressions to make changes are:

RXPARSE ("cat TO dog")   Changes the word "cat" to "dog"

RXPARSE ("Street TO St., Road TO Rd.")   Changes "Street" to "St." and
                                                                        "Road" to "Rd."

RXPARSE ("<$a+> ', ' <$a+> TO =2 ' ' =1");   Changes last-name, first-name
                                                                        to first-name last-name when the
                                                                        name is originally written as
                                                                        last-name, first-name

In the last example above, the patterns in angle brackets ('<>') are called **tag sets**. The first tag set is referenced as '=1' in the TO portion of the expression, the second tag set as '=2', etc. So, in this example, you are looking for one or more letters, followed by a comma and a space, followed by two or more letters. Imagine that you are reading the string "Cody, Ronald." This matches the pattern, and the changed string will be the second tag set (which matches "Ronald") a space, followed by the first tag set ("Cody"). The resulting string will be "Ronald Cody."

Examples

For these examples, RET = RXPARSE ("cat TO dog") and STRING="The cat is white".

Function	Returns
CALL RXCHANGE(RET,99,STRING)	STRING="The dog is white"
CALL RXCHANGE(RET,99,STRING,NEW)	STRING="The cat is white" NEW="The dog is white"

Program 3.3: Using RXCHANGE to place two asterisks around every number

```
***Primary functions: RXPARSE, RXMATCH, CALL RXCHANGE;

DATA EXCHANGE;
    INPUT STRING $CHAR80.;
    LENGTH NEW_STRING $ 80;
    IF _N_ = 1 THEN
        RETURN = RXPARSE("<$d+> TO '**' =1 '**'");
    RETAIN RETURN;
    POS = RXMATCH(RETURN,STRING);
    IF POS GT 0 THEN CALL RXCHANGE(RETURN,99,STRING,NEW_STRING);
DATALINES;
89 Lazy Brook Road
123 Sesame street
none here
;
PROC PRINT DATA=EXCHANGE NOOBS;
    TITLE "Listing of Data Set EXCHANGE";
RUN;
```

Explanation

The regular expression in this program looks for one or more digits as the find pattern. The <> brackets around this expression creates a **tag**. This tag can be used in the replace part of the expression by using an equals sign (=) followed by a number. The number 1 refers to the first tag, the number 2 to the second tag, and so forth. These tags references can then be used, along with quoted strings, to make up the replacement set. In this program, the digits are surrounded by two asterisks. The listing is shown below:

```
                       Listing of Data Set EXCHANGE

    STRING                   NEW_STRING            RETURN    POS

    89 Lazy Brook Road    **89** Lazy Brook Road      1       1
    123 Sesame street     **123** Sesame street       1       1
    none here                                         1       0
```

Function That Releases Memory Used by a Regular Expression

Function: CALL RXFREE

Purpose: To free resources that were allocated to a SAS regular expression (usually used with a test for end-of-file). Note that resources are automatically released when a DATA step ends.

Syntax: CALL RXFREE(*return*)

return is the value returned from the RXPARSE function.

Examples

For this example, the statement: RETURN = RXPARSE("$d") preceded the call to PXFREE.

Function	Returns
RXFREE(RETURN)	Does not return any value

Program 3.4: Data cleaning example using RXPARSE and CALL RXFREE

```
***Primary functions: RXPARSE, RXMATCH, CALL RXFREE;

DATA INVALID;
   ***Valid ID's are 1 to 3 digits with leading blanks;
   INFILE 'C:\BOOKS\FUNCTIONS\IDNUMS.DAT' END=LAST;
   IF _N_ = 1 THEN VALID = RXPARSE("$d$d$d | ' ' $d$d | ' '$d");
   RETAIN VALID;
   INPUT @1 ID $CHAR3.;
   POS = RXMATCH(VALID,ID);
   IF POS EQ 0 THEN OUTPUT INVALID;
   IF LAST THEN CALL RXFREE(VALID);
   DROP VALID;
RUN;
PROC PRINT DATA=INVALID NOOBS;
   TITLE "Listing of Data Set INVALID";
RUN;
```

Explanation

In this example, valid IDs are character values of either three digits, a blank followed by two digits, or two blanks followed by one digit. (See the tutorial, PRXPARSE, and PRXMATCH for explanations of the Perl regular expressions.) The INFILE statement option END=LAST creates the logical variable (LAST), which is true when the last record is being read from the file. So, when LAST is true, a call is made to RXFREE to release resources used by the regular expression. The listing of data set INVALID is:

```
               Listing of Data Set INVALID

         ID     POS

         ABC     0
                 0
         1 4     0
         8       0
         9X9     0
```

Chapter 4
Date and Time Functions

Introduction

Before you start working with SAS date and time functions, remember that **SAS date values** are the number of days between January 1, 1960, and a specified date. Dates after January 1, 1960, are stored as positive numbers; dates before January 1, 1960, are stored as negative numbers. **SAS datetime values** are the number of seconds between midnight, January 1, 1960, and the specified date and time. **SAS time values** are the number of seconds between midnight of the current day and another time value. Some of the more commonly used date functions extract the day of the week, the month, or the year from a SAS date value. Other functions deal with intervals, either the number of intervals between two dates or the date after a given number of intervals have passed. One very useful function (MDY) can create a SAS date value, given a value for the month, day, and year. Now let's get started.

Functions That Create SAS Date, Datetime, and Time Values

The first three functions in this group of functions create SAS date values, datetime values, and time values from the constituent parts (month, day, year, hour, minute, second). The DATE and TODAY functions are equivalent and they both return the current date. The DATETIME and TIME functions are used to create SAS datetime and time values, respectively.

Function: MDY

Purpose: To create a SAS date from the month, day, and year.

Syntax: `MDY(month, day, year)`

> `month` is a numeric variable or constant representing the month of the year (a number from 1 to 12).
>
> `day` is a numeric variable or constant representing the day of the month (a number from 1 to 31).
>
> `year` is a numeric variable or constant representing the year.
>
> Values of month, day, and time that do not define a valid date result in a missing value, and an error message is written to the SAS log.

Examples

For these examples, M = 11, D = 15, Y = 2003

Function	Returns
MDY(M,D,Y)	16024 (15NOV2003 – formatted value)
MDY(10,21,1980)	7599 (21OCT1980 – formatted value)
MDY(1,1,1950)	-3652 (01JAN1950 – formatted value)
MDY(13,01,2003)	numeric missing value

Program 4.1: Creating a SAS date value from separate variables representing the day, month, and year of the date

```
***Primary function: MDY;

DATA FUNNYDATE;
    INPUT @1  MONTH  2.
          @7  YEAR   4.
          @13 DAY    2.;
    DATE = MDY(MONTH,DAY,YEAR);
    FORMAT DATE MMDDYY10.;
DATALINES;
05    2000  25
11    2001  02
;
PROC PRINT DATA=FUNNYDATE NOOBS;
    TITLE "Listing of FUNNYDATE";
RUN;
```

Explanation

Here the values for month, day, and year were not in a form where any of the standard date informats could be used. Therefore, the day, month, and year values were read into separate variables and the MDY function was used to create a SAS date. See the listing below:

```
                        Listing of FUNNYDATE

          MONTH    YEAR    DAY         DATE

              5    2000     25      05/25/2000
             11    2001      2      11/02/2001
```

Program 4.2: Program to read in dates and set the day of the month to 15 if the day is missing from the date

```
***Primary function: MDY
   Other functions:  SCAN, INPUT;

DATA MISSING;
   INPUT @1 DUMMY $10.;
   DAY = SCAN(DUMMY,2,'/');
   IF DAY NE ' ' THEN DATE = INPUT(DUMMY,MMDDYY10.);
   ELSE DATE = MDY(INPUT(SCAN(DUMMY,1,'/'),2.),
               15,
               INPUT(SCAN(DUMMY,3,'/'),4.));
   FORMAT DATE DATE9.;
DATALINES;
10/21/1946
1/  /2000
01/  /2002
;
PROC PRINT DATA=MISSING NOOBS;
   TITLE "Listing of MISSING";
RUN;
```

Explanation

This program reads in a date and, when the day of the month is missing, it uses the 15th of the month. If the date was already stored as a character string in a SAS data set, this approach would work well.

The entire date is first read as a character string as the variable DUMMY. Next, the SCAN function is called with the slash character (/) as the "word" delimiter. The second word is the month. If this is not missing, the INPUT function is used to convert the character string into a SAS date.

If DAY is missing, the MDY function is used to create the SAS date, with the value of 15 representing the day of the month. The listing follows:

```
                          Listing of MISSING

                   DUMMY        DAY        DATE

                10/21/1946      21      21OCT1946
                1/  /2000               15JAN2000
                01/  /2002              15JAN2002
```

Function: **DHMS**

Purpose: To create a SAS datetime value from a SAS date value and a value for the hour, minute, and second.

Syntax: DHMS(*date, hour, minute, second*)

date is a SAS date value, either a variable or a date constant.

hour is a numerical value for the hour of the day. If hour is greater than 24, the function will return the appropriate datetime value.

minute is a numerical value for the number of minutes.

second is a numerical value for the number of seconds.

Values of the date value that are invalid result in a missing value, and an error message is written to the SAS log.

Examples

For these examples, DATE = '02JAN1960'D, H = 23, M = 15, S = 30

Function	Returns
DHMS(DATE,H,M,S)	170130 (02JAN60:23:15:30 – formatted)
DHMS('04JUN2003'd,25,12,12)	1370394732 (05JUN03:01:12:12 – formatted)
DHMS('01JAN1960'd,0,70,0)	4200 (01JAN60:01:10:00 – formatted)

See Program 4.3.

Function: HMS

Purpose: To create a SAS time value from the hour, minute, and second.

Syntax: HMS(*hour, minute, second*)

hour is the value corresponding to the number of hours.

minute is the value corresponding to the number of minutes.

second is the value corresponding to the number of seconds.

Examples

For these examples, H = 1, M = 30, S = 15

Function	Returns
HMS(H, M, S)	5415 (1:30:15 – formatted value)
HMS(0, 0, 23)	23 (0:00:23 – formatted value)

See Program 4.3.

Function: DATE and TODAY (equivalent functions)

Purpose: To return the current date.

Syntax: DATE() or TODAY()

Note that the parentheses are needed even though these functions do not take any arguments. (What did the TODAY function say to the MEAN function? "Don't give me any arguments!")

Examples

Note: This function was run on June 4, 2003.

Function	Returns
DATE()	15860 (04JUN2003 – formatted)
TODAY()	15860 (04JUN2003 – formatted)

See Program 4.3.

Function: DATETIME

Purpose: To return the datetime value for the current date and time.

Syntax: DATETIME()

Examples

Note: This function was run at 8:10 PM on June 4, 2004.

Function	Returns
DATETIME()	1370376600 (04JUN03:20:10:00– formatted)

See Program 4.3.

Function: TIME

Purpose: To return the time of day when the program was run.

Syntax: TIME()

Examples

Note: This function was run at 8:10 PM.

Function	Returns
TIME()	72600 (20:10:00 – formatted)

Program 4.3: Determining the date, datetime value, and time of day

```
***Primary functions: DHMS, HMS, TODAY, DATETIME, and TIME
***Other functions: YRDIF, INT;

DATA TEST;
   DATE = TODAY();
   DT = DATETIME();
   TIME = TIME();
   DT2 = DHMS(DATE,8,15,30);
   TIME2 = HMS(8,15,30);
   DOB = '01JAN1960'D;
   AGE = INT(YRDIF(DOB, TODAY(), 'ACTUAL'));
   FORMAT DATE DOB DATE9. DT DT2 DATETIME. TIME TIME2 TIME.;
RUN;

PROC PRINT DATA=TEST NOOBS;
   TITLE "Listing of Data Set TEST";
RUN;
```

Explanation

Since this program was run in the evening of June 22, 2003, the values for the date, datetime, and time values correspond to that date and time.

The variable DT2 is a SAS datetime value created from the current date and specified values for the hour, minute, and second. TIME2 is a SAS time value created from three values for hour, minute, and second.

Finally, the age was computed using the YRDIF function (computes the number of years from the first date to the second) and this value was truncated using the INT function. See the listing below:

```
                    Listing of Data Set TEST

        DATE            DT              TIME            DT2

      22JUN2003    22JUN03:18:58:48    18:58:48    22JUN03:08:15:30


        TIME2         DOB      AGE

       8:15:30    01JAN1960     43
```

Creating a Data Set to Demonstrate Other Date Functions

Run Program 4.4 to create a SAS data set called DATES. A listing of this data set follows:

Program 4.4:   Program to create the DATES data set

```
DATA DATES;
   INFORMAT DATE1 DATE2 DATE9.;
   INPUT DATE1 DATE2;
   FORMAT DATE1 DATE2 DATE9.;
DATALINES;
01JAN1960 15JAN1960
02MAR1961 18FEB1962
25DEC2000 03JAN2001
01FEB2002 31MAR2002
;
PROC PRINT DATA=DATES NOOBS;
   TITLE "Listing of Data Set DATES";
RUN;
```

Explanation

Although this is not a function example program, one feature should be explained: Since the INPUT statement is reading list input (i.e., one or more spaces between the data values) and since you need to supply an informat so that the values will be read as SAS date values, an INFORMAT statement precedes the INPUT statement, indicating that both variables, DATE1 and DATE2, should be read with the DATE9. informat.

```
                    Listing of Data Set DATES

                    DATE1        DATE2

                 01JAN1960     15JAN1960
                 02MAR1961     18FEB1962
                 25DEC2000     03JAN2001
                 01FEB2002     31MAR2002
```

Functions That Extract the Year, Month, Day, Etc., from a SAS Date

This group of functions takes a SAS date value and returns parts of the date, such as the year, the month, or the day of the week. Since these functions are demonstrated in a single program, let's supply the syntax and examples.

Function: YEAR

Purpose: To extract the year from a SAS date.

Syntax: YEAR(*date*)

date is a SAS date value.

Examples

Function	Returns
YEAR('16AUG2002'd)	2002
YEAR('16AUG02'd)	2002

See Program 4.5.

Function: **QTR**

Purpose: To extract the quarter (January–March = 1, April–June = 2, etc.) from a SAS date.

Syntax: QTR(*date*)

   date is a SAS date value.

Examples

Function	Returns
QTR('05FEB2003'd)	1
QTR('01DEC2003'd)	4

See Program 4.5.

Function: **MONTH**

Purpose: To extract the month of the year from a SAS date, 1 = January, 2=February, etc.

Syntax: MONTH(*date*)

   date is a SAS date value.

Examples

Function	Returns
MONTH('16AUG2002'd)	8

See Program 4.5.

SAS9.1 Function: WEEK

Purpose: To extract the week number of the year from a SAS date (the week-number value is a number from 0 to 53 or 1 to 53, depending on the optional modifier).

Syntax: `WEEK(<date> <,'modifier'>))`

date is a SAS date value. If *date* is omitted, the WEEK function returns the week number of the current date.

modifier is an optional argument that determines how the week-number value is determined. If *modifier* is omitted, the first Sunday of the year is week 1. For dates prior to this date, the WEEK function returns a 0. The various modifiers provide several different methods for computing the value returned by the WEEK function. Most users will probably want to use this function without any modifiers. For details about the modifiers, see the SAS OnlineDoc.

Examples

Function	Returns
WEEK('16AUG2002'd)	32
WEEK('01JAN1960'd)	0
WEEK('03JAN1960'd)	1
WEEK('01JAN1960'd,'V')	53

See Program 4.5 for an example.

Function: **WEEKDAY**

Purpose: To extract the day of the week from a SAS date, 1 = Sunday, 2=Monday, etc.

Syntax: `WEEKDAY(date)`

`date` is a SAS date value.

Examples

Function	Returns
`WEEKDAY('16AUG2002'd)`	5 (Thursday)

Function: **DAY**

Purpose: To extract the day of the month from a SAS date, a number from 1 to 31.

Syntax: `DAY(date)`

`date` is a SAS date value.

Examples

Function	Returns
`DAY('16AUG2002'd)`	16

See Program 4.5.

Program 4.5 : Demonstrating the functions YEAR, QTR, MONTH, WEEK, DAY, and WEEKDAY

```
***Primary functions: YEAR, QTR, MONTH, WEEK, DAY, and WEEKDAY;

DATA DATE_FUNCTIONS;
   SET DATES(DROP=DATE2);
   YEAR = YEAR(DATE1);
   QUARTER = QTR(DATE1);
   MONTH = MONTH(DATE1);
```

```
    WEEK = WEEK(DATE1);
    DAY_OF_MONTH = DAY(DATE1);
    DAY_OF_WEEK = WEEKDAY(DATE1);
RUN;
PROC PRINT DATA=DATE_FUNCTIONS NOOBS;
    TITLE "Listing of Data Set DATE_FUNCTIONS";
RUN;
```

Explanation

These basic date functions are straightforward. They all take a SAS date as the single
argument and return the year, the quarter, the month, the week, the day of the month, or the
day of the week. Remember that the WEEKDAY function returns the day of the **week**,
while the DAY function returns the day of the **month** (it's easy to confuse these two
functions). A listing of DATE_FUNCTIONS follows:

```
                    Listing of Data Set DATE_FUNCTIONS


                                                      DAY_OF_    DAY_OF_
          DATE1     YEAR    QUARTER    MONTH   WEEK    MONTH       WEEK

        01JAN1960   1960       1         1      0        1          6
        02MAR1961   1961       1         3      9        2          5
        25DEC2000   2000       4        12     52       25          2
        01FEB2002   2002       1         2      4        1          6
```

Functions That Extract Hours, Minutes, and Seconds from SAS Datetime and Time Values

The HOUR, MINUTE, and SECOND functions work with SAS datetime or time values in
much the same way as the MONTH, YEAR, and WEEKDAY functions work with SAS date
values.

Function: **HOUR**

Purpose: To extract the hour from a SAS datetime or time value.

Syntax: HOUR(*time* or *dt*)

time or *dt* is a SAS time or datetime value.

Examples

For these examples, DT = '02JAN1960:5:10:15'dt, T = '5:8:10'T

Function	Returns
HOUR(DT)	5
HOUR(T)	5
HOUR(HMS(5,8,9))	5

See Program 4.6.

Function: **MINUTE**

Purpose: To extract the minute value from a SAS datetime or time value.

Syntax: MINUTE(*time* or *dt*)

time or *dt* is a SAS time or datetime value.

Examples

For these examples, DT = '02JAN1960:5:10:15'dt, T = '5:8:10'T

Function	Returns
MINUTE(DT)	5
MINUTE(T)	5
MINUTE(HMS(5,8,9))	5

See Program 4.6.

Function: **SECOND**

Purpose: To extract the second value from a SAS datetime or time value.

Syntax: SECOND(*time* or *dt*)

time or *dt* is a SAS time or datetime value.

Examples

For these examples, DT = '02JAN1960:5:10:15'dt, T = '5:8:10'T

Function	Returns
SECOND(DT)	15
SECOND(T)	10
SECOND(HMS(5,8,9))	9

Program 4.6: Demonstrating the HOUR, MINUTE, and SECOND functions

```
***Primary functions: HOUR, MINUTE, and SECOND;

DATA TIME;
   DT = '01JAN1960:5:15:30'DT;
   T = '10:05:23'T;
   HOUR_DT = HOUR(DT);
   HOUR_TIME = HOUR(T);
   MINUTE_DT = MINUTE(DT);
   MINUTE_TIME = MINUTE(T);
   SECOND_DT = SECOND(DT);
   SECOND_TIME = SECOND(T);
   FORMAT DT DATETIME.;
RUN;

PROC PRINT DATA=TIME NOOBS HEADING=H;
   TITLE "Listing of Data Set TIME";
RUN;
```

Explanation

The variable DT is a SAS datetime value (computed as a SAS datetime constant), and T is a SAS time value (computed as a SAS time constant). The program demonstrates that the HOUR, MINUTE, and SECOND functions can take either SAS datetime or time values as arguments. The listing follows:

```
                       Listing of Data Set TIME


                           HOUR_ MINUTE_ MINUTE_ SECOND_ SECOND_
        DT          T  HOUR_DT TIME   DT    TIME    DT    TIME

   01JAN60:05:15:30 36323   5    10    15     5     30     23
```

Functions That Extract the Date or Time from SAS Datetime Values

The DATEPART and TIMEPART functions extract either the date or the time from a SAS datetime value (the number of seconds from January 1, 1960).

Function: DATEPART

Purpose: To compute a SAS date from a SAS datetime value.

Syntax: DATEPART(*date-time-value*)

date-time-value is a SAS datetime value.

Examples

For these examples, DT = '02JAN1960:5:10:15'dt

Function	Returns
DATETIME(DT)	1 (01JAN1960 – formatted)
DATETIME('4JUN2003:20:48:15'DT)	15860 (04JUN2003 – formatted)

See Program 4.7.

Function: **TIMEPART**

Purpose: To extract the time part of a SAS datetime value.

Syntax: TIMEPART(*date-time-value*)

Date-time-value is a SAS datetime value.

Examples

For these examples, DT = '02JAN1960:5:10:15'dt

Function	Returns
TIMEPART(DT)	18615 (5:10:15 – formatted)
TIMEPART('4JUN2003:20:48:15'DT)	74895 (20:48:15 – formatted)

Program 4.7: Extracting the date part and time part of a SAS datetime value

```
***Primary functions: DATEPART and TIMEPART;

DATA PIECES_PARTS;
   DT = '01JAN1960:5:15:30'DT;
   DATE = DATEPART(DT);
   TIME = TIMEPART(DT);
   FORMAT DT DATETIME. TIME TIME. DATE DATE9.;
RUN;

PROC PRINT DATA=PIECES_PARTS NOOBS;
   TITLE "Listing of Data Set PIECES_PARTS";
RUN;
```

Explanation

The DATEPART and TIMEPART functions extract the date and the time from the datetime value, respectively. These two functions are especially useful when you import data from other sources, such as Excel, using the Import Wizard. There, spreadsheet columns that were formatted as dates in Excel wind up as datetime values in the SAS data set. You can use these two functions to separate the date and time from that value. See the listing below:

```
┌─────────────────────────────────────────────────────────┐
│              Listing of Data Set PIECES_PARTS            │
│                                                          │
│         DT                      DATE      TIME           │
│                                                          │
│    01JAN60:05:15:30        01JAN1960    5:15:30          │
└─────────────────────────────────────────────────────────┘
```

Functions That Work with Date, Datetime, and Time Intervals

Functions in this group work with date or time intervals. The INTCK function, when used with date or datetime values, can determine the number of interval boundaries crossed between two dates. When used with SAS time values, it can determine the number of hour, minute, or second boundaries between two time values.

The INTNX function, when used with SAS date or datetime values, is used to determine the date after a given number of intervals have passed. When used with SAS time values, it computes the time after a given number of time interval units have passed.

You will find an excellent description of these two functions in *SAS Language Reference: Concepts* or in the following technical note:

`http://ftp.sas.com/techsup/download/technote/ts668.html.`

Note: The wording of arguments in this book might differ from the wording of arguments in the *SAS OnlineDoc 9.1*.

YRDIF makes it much easier to compute the number of years between two dates. Thus, it can be used to compute a person's age.

Function: INTCK

Purpose: To return the number of intervals between two dates, two times, or two datetime values. To be more accurate, the INTCK function counts the number of times a boundary has been crossed going from the first value to the second.

For example, if the interval is YEAR and the starting date is January 1, 2002, and the ending date is December 31, 2002, the function returns a 0. The reason for this is that the boundary for YEAR is January 1 and, even though the starting date is on a boundary, no boundaries are crossed in going from the first date to the second. Using the same logic, going from December 31, 2002, to January 1, 2003, *does* cross a year boundary and returns a 1. This is true even though, in the first case, there are 364 days between the dates and, in the latter case, only one day.

These intervals can be used "as is" or with multipliers such as two-year intervals, and they can be shifted so that the boundary is, for example, the seventh month of the year (July) instead of January 1.

When used with multi-intervals and shifted intervals, the INTCK function can become very complicated. A limited discussion of the finer points of the INTCK function follows the syntax and examples below.

Syntax:
```
INTCK('interval<Multiple><.shift>', start-value,
end-value)
```

Intervals can be date units:

Interval	Description
DAY	Day
WEEK	Week
WEEKDAY	Each weekday (Monday to Friday, or any set of days you choose)
TENDAY	Ten-day period
SEMIMONTH	Two-week period
MONTH	Month
QTR	Quarter (Jan–Mar = 1, Apr–Jun = 2, etc.)
SEMIYEAR	Half year
YEAR	Year

Intervals can be time units:

Interval	Description
SECOND	Seconds
MINUTE	Minutes
HOUR	Hours

Intervals can be datetime units:

Interval	Description
DTDAY	Day
DTWEEK	Week
DTWEEKDAY	Each weekday (Monday to Friday)
DTTENDAY	Ten-day period
DTSEMIMONTH	Two-week period
DTMONTH	Month
DTQTR	Quarter (Jan–Mar = 1, Apr–Jun = 2, etc.)
DTSEMIYEAR	Half year
DTYEAR	Year

interval is one item from the list above, placed in quotation marks.

multiple is an optional modifier in the interval. You can specify multiples of an interval. For example, MONTH2 specifies two-month intervals; DAY50 specifies 50-day intervals.

.shift is an optional parameter that determines the starting point in an interval. For example, YEAR.4 specifies yearly intervals, starting from April 1. The shift value for single intervals is shown in the table below:

Shift value for SAS date and datetime values:

Interval	Shift Value
YEAR	Month
SEMIYEAR	Month
QTR	Month
MONTH	Month
SEMIMONTH	Semimonth*
TENDAY	Tenday
WEEKDAY	Day
WEEK	Day
DAY	Day

Shift value for SAS time intervals:

Interval	Shift Value
HOUR	Hour*
MINUTE	Minute*
SECOND	Second*

*Only multi-intervals of these intervals can be shifted.

For all multi-unit intervals except WEEK, SAS creates an interval starting from January 1, 1960. Multiple intervals are all shifted by the same unit as the non-multiple intervals (see lists above). So, YEAR4.24 specifies four-year intervals with the interval boundary at the beginning of the second year (January 1, 1962, January 1, 1966, etc.). MONTH4.2 indicates four-month intervals, with the boundary being the first day of the second month. See the discussion on interval multipliers and shifted intervals below.

Some example of intervals are:

Interval	Interpretation
YEAR	Each year
YEAR2	Every two years
YEAR.4	Each April
YEAR4.11	November, every four years

Table (*continued*)

Interval	Interpretation
MONTH	Every month
MONTH4	Every four months
MONTH6.3	Every six months with boundaries at March and September
WEEK	Each week
WEEK2	Every two weeks
WEEK.4	Every week starting with Wednesday
WEEK2.4	Every two weeks starting with Wednesday
WEEKDAY	Five-day weeks with weekend days, Saturday and Sunday
WEEKDAY1W	Six-day weeks with weekend day, Sunday
WEEKDAY12W	Five-day weeks with weekend days, Sunday and Monday
HOUR	Every hour
HOUR4	Every four hours
HOUR8.7	Every eight hours with boundaries 6 AM, 2 PM, and 10 PM
DTMONTH	Every month (used with datetime values)

start-value is a SAS date, time, or datetime value.

end-value is a SAS date, time, or datetime value.

Examples

Function	Returns
INTCK('WEEK','16AUG2002'd,'24AUG2002'd)	1
INTCK('YEAR', '01JAN2002'd,'31DEC2002'd)	0
INTCK('YEAR', '01JAN2002'd,'02JAN2003'd)	1
INTCK('YEAR', '31DEC2002'd,'01JAN2003'd)	1
INTCK('QTR','01JAN2002'd,'01AUG2002'd)	2
INTCK('MONTH3','01JAN2002'd,'15APR2002'd)	1
INTCK('YEAR.7','05MAY2002'd,'15JUL2002'd)	1
INTCK('HOUR','06:01:00't,'07:23:15't)	1

See Program 4.8.

A Discussion of Interval Multipliers and Shifted Intervals

Some applications of interval multipliers are quite straightforward. For example, if you use YEAR2 as your interval, the intervals will be every two years. The value of

```
INTCK('YEAR2','15JAN2000'd,'21JAN2003'd)
```

is equal to 1 (one boundary, January 1, 2002, was crossed in going from January 15, 2000, to January 21, 2002). The reason that January 1, 2002, is a boundary is that the counting of boundaries goes back to January 1, 1960, which was an even number. Therefore, the boundaries will be even-numbered years.

You can shift some single intervals. For example, YEAR.7 indicates yearly intervals with the boundary being July 1 of every year. For the intervals of YEAR, SEMIYEAR, and QTR, the shift amount is months. For example, the value of

```
INTCK('YEAR.7','01JUN2000'd,'03JUL2002'd)
```

is equal to 3 (crossing boundaries at July 1, 2000, July 1, 2001, and July 1, 2002).

Shifting intervals that use multipliers is similar. For example, YEAR2.12 indicates two-year intervals, with boundaries at the second year of each interval: January 1, 1961, January 1, 1963, etc. That is, every odd year. For example, the value of

```
INTCK('YEAR2.12','15JAN2000'd,'21JAN2003'd)
```

is equal to 2 (crossing the boundaries at January 1, 2001, and January 1, 2003).

Multi-month intervals are shifted by months, not weeks (since there is not an even number of weeks in a month). MONTH4.2 means four-month intervals with the boundary being the second month of each four-month period. By the way, the .2 does not mean "shift the boundary by 2 months." It means the boundary is the second month of each interval. As Charley Mullin says in his technical note: "The boundary is shifted TO an interval, not BY the interval."

The value of

```
INTCK('MONTH4.2','28JAN2003'd,'03JUL2003'd)
```

is equal to 2 (crossing the boundaries at February 1, 2003, and June 1, 2003).

WEEK and multi-week intervals present a special problem. For example, you might expect the value of

```
INTCK(WEEK,'01JAN1960'd,'04JAN1960'd)
```

to equal 0. However, it is equal to 1. The problem is that weekly intervals are counted every time a Sunday is crossed and January 1, 1960, is a Friday. The way that SAS decided to solve this problem was to start counting from Sunday in the same week of January 1, 1960, which is December 27, 1959. Going from January 1, 1960, to January 4, 1960, crosses a boundary (Sunday, January 3). This gets even more complicated when you are dealing with multi-week intervals.

As the default, the interval of WEEKDAY treats Saturday and Sunday as part of the preceding day. For example, the value of

```
INTCK('WEEKDAY','01JUN2003'd,'30JUN2003'd)
```

is equal to 21. June 1, 2003, is a Sunday, and June 30 falls on a Monday. The number of weekdays that have occurred between them is 21.

You can specify days other than Saturday and Sunday to be treated as weekend days. For example, if you had a six-day work week, with Sunday as the day off, you could indicate the interval as WEEKDAY1W. So, the value of

```
INTCK('WEEKDAY1W','01JUN2003'd,'30JUN2003'd)
```

is equal to 25 (Monday through Saturday for four weeks plus Monday, June 30).

If you were in the restaurant business and your restaurant was closed on Sunday and Monday, you would use the interval: WEEKDAY12W to compute the number of work days between two dates.

Function: **INTNX**

Purpose: To return the date after a specified number of intervals have passed.

Syntax: **INTNX('*interval*', *start-date*, *increment* <,'*alignment*'>)**

interval the same values that are used with the INTCK function (placed in quotation marks).

start-date is a SAS date.

increment is the number of intervals between the start date and the date returned by the function.

alignment is an optional argument and has a value of BEGINNING (B), MIDDLE (M), or END (E). The default is BEGINNING. For example, if the interval is WEEK, an increment of 1 from January 1, 1960, with the default returns the date January 3, 1960 (a Sunday, the beginning of a boundary). The same date and interval with an alignment of MIDDLE returns the date January 6, 1960 (a Wednesday, the middle of the interval).

Examples

For these examples, DT1 = '01JAN1960:7:5:12'DT

Note: Values in parentheses in the Returns column are the formatted values.

Function	Returns
`INTNX('WEEK','01JAN1960'd,1)`	`2` (Sunday, Jan 3, 1960)
`INTNX('WEEK','01JAN1960'd,1,'MIDDLE')`	`5` (Wednesday, Jan 6, 1960)
`INTNX('WEEK.4','01JAN1960'd,1)`	`5` (Wednesday, Jan 6, 1960)
`INTNX('WEEK2','01JAN1960'd,1)`	`9` (Sunday, Jan 10, 1960)
`INTNX('QTR','01JAN2003'd,1)`	`15796` (Tuesday, April 1, 2003)
`INTNX('YEAR.3','01JAN2003'd,1)`	`15765` (Saturday, March 1, 2003)
`INTNX('YEAR.3','01JAN2003'd,2)`	`16131` (Monday, March 1, 2004)
`INTNX('YEAR','01JUN2003'd,1)`	`16071` (Thursday, January 1, 2004)
`INTNX('YEAR','01JUN2003'd,2)`	`16437` (Saturday, January 1, 2005)
`INTNX('YEAR4.11','01JAN2003'd,1)`	`16376` (Monday, November 1, 2004)
`INTNX('DTMONTH',DT1,3)`	`7862400` (01APR60:00:00:00)
`INTNX('HOUR','9:15:09'T,2)`	`39600` (11:00:00)
`INTNX('YEAR','15JAN1960'D,-1)`	`-365` (January 1, 1959)

See Program 4.8.

Using the INTNX Function to Determine Starting Boundaries for Multi-Day Intervals

Interval boundaries are straightforward for intervals such as years, quarters, and months. However, suppose you want to create 12-day intervals. How many 12-day intervals are there from January 1, 2004, to January 11, 2004? How many boundaries have you crossed? The problem here is that you have to realize that you start counting 12-day intervals from January 1, 1960, to determine where the boundaries are. Here's an easy way to see what date the counting starts on: use the INTNX function like this:

```
START_INTERVAL = INTNX('DAY12','01JAN2004'd,1)
```

The value is Saturday, January 10, 2004. So, in going from January 1, 2004, to January 11, 2004, you cross one boundary (January 10, 2004). To check, note that

```
INTCK('DAY12','01JAN2004'd, '11JAN2004'd)
```

is equal to 1.

Function: **YRDIF**

Purpose: To return the difference in years between two dates (includes fractional parts of a year).

Syntax: YRDIF(*start-date, end-date, 'basis'*)

start-date is a SAS date value.

end-date is a SAS date value.

basis is an argument that controls how SAS computes the result. A value of 'ACT/ACT' (alias 'ACTUAL') is probably the best choice. It uses the actual number of days between the dates, using either 365 or 366 days, depending on whether there are leap years involved. Other choices sometimes used in accounting or interest calculations are:

'30/360'	Uses 30-day months and 360-day years in the calculation.
'ACT/365'	Uses the actual number of days between the two dates, but uses 365-day years, even if a leap year is in the interval.
'ACT/360'	Uses the actual number of days between the two dates, but uses 360-day years.

Examples

Function	Returns
YRDIF('01JAN2002'd,'01JAN2003'd,'ACTUAL')	1
YRDIF('01JAN2002'd,01FEB2002'd,'ACT/ACT')	.0849
YRDIF('01FEB2002'd,01MAR2003'd,'ACTUAL')	1.9767
YRDIF('01JAN2002'd,'01JAN2003'd,'ACT/365')	1.0139

Program 4.8:   Program to demonstrate the date interval functions

```
***Primary functions: INTCK, INTNX, YRDIF;

DATA PERIOD;
   SET DATES;
   INTERVAL_MONTH = INTCK('MONTH',DATE1,DATE2);
   INTERVAL_YEAR  = INTCK('YEAR',DATE1,DATE2);
   YEAR_DIFF      = YRDIF(DATE1,DATE2,'ACTUAL');
   INTERVAL_QTR   = INTCK('QTR',DATE1,DATE2);
   NEXT_MONTH     = INTNX('MONTH',DATE1,1);
   NEXT_YEAR      = INTNX('YEAR',DATE1,1);
   NEXT_QTR       = INTNX('QTR',DATE1,1);
   SIX_MONTH      = INTNX('MONTH',DATE1,6);
   FORMAT NEXT: SIX_MONTH DATE9.;
RUN;
PROC PRINT DATA=PERIOD HEADING=H;
   ID DATE1 DATE2;
   TITLE "Listing of Data Set PERIOD";
RUN;
```

Explanation

Before we discuss the date functions in this program, let me point out that the ID statement of PROC PRINT lists both DATE1 and DATE2 as ID variables. This allows the values to be repeated on the lower portion of the listing.

The interval functions can be somewhat confusing. It helps to keep in mind that the INTCK function counts how many times you cross a "boundary" going from the start date to the end date. The listing follows:

```
                    Listing of Data Set PERIOD

              INTERVAL_  INTERVAL_   YEAR_  INTERVAL_     NEXT_
   DATE1    DATE2  MONTH     YEAR    DIFF     QTR        MONTH

 01JAN1960 15JAN1960    0        0   0.03825     0     01FEB1960
 02MAR1961 18FEB1962   11        1   0.96712     4     01APR1961
 25DEC2000 03JAN2001    1        1   0.02461     1     01JAN2001
 01FEB2002 31MAR2002    1        0   0.15890     0     01MAR2002


    DATE1       DATE2  NEXT_YEAR     NEXT_QTR    SIX_MONTH

 01JAN1960 15JAN1960 01JAN1961     01APR1960    01JUL1960
 02MAR1961 18FEB1962 01JAN1962     01APR1961    01SEP1961
 25DEC2000 03JAN2001 01JAN2001     01JAN2001    01JUN2001
 01FEB2002 31MAR2002 01JAN2003     01APR2002    01AUG2002
```

Functions That Work with Julian Dates

This group of functions involves Julian dates. Julian dates are commonly used in computer applications and represent a date as a two- or four-digit year followed by a three-digit day of the year (1 to 365 or 366, if it is a leap year). For example, January 3, 2003, in Julian notation would be either 2003003 or 03003. December 31, 2003 (a non-leap year) would be either 2003365 or 03365.

Function: DATEJUL

Purpose: To convert a Julian date into a SAS date.

Syntax: DATEJUL(*jul-date*)

jul-date is a numerical value representing the Julian date in the form *dddyy* or *dddyyyy*.

Examples

For these examples JDATE = 1960123

Function	Returns
DATEJUL(1960001)	0 (01JAN1960 formatted)
DATEJUL(2003365)	16070 (31DEC2003 formatted)
DATEJUL(JDATE)	122 (02MAY1960 formatted)

See Program 4.9.

Function: JULDATE

Purpose: To convert a SAS date into a Julian date.

Syntax: JULDATE(*date*)

date is a SAS date.

Examples

For these examples, DATE = '31DEC2003'D

Function	Returns
JULDATE(DATE)	3365
JULDATE('01JAN1960'D)	60001
JULDATE(122)	60123

See Program 4.9.

Function: JULDATE7

Purpose: To convert a SAS date into seven-digit Julian date.

Syntax: JULDATE7(*date*)

date is a SAS date.

Examples

For these examples, DATE = '31DEC2003'D

Function	Returns
JULDATE7(DATE)	2003365
JULDATE7('01JAN1960'D)	1960001
JULDATE7(122)	1960123

Program 4.9: Demonstrating the three Julian date functions

```
   ***Primary functions: DATEJUL, JULDATE, and JULDATE7.;

   ***Note: option YEARCUTOFF set to 1920;
OPTIONS YEARCUTOFF = 1920;
DATA JULIAN;
   INPUT DATE : DATE9. JDATE;
   JDATE_TO_SAS = DATEJUL(JDATE);
   SAS_TO_JDATE = JULDATE(DATE);
   SAS_TO_JDATE7 = JULDATE7(DATE);
   FORMAT DATE JDATE_TO_SAS MMDDYY10.;
DATALINES;
01JAN1960 2003365
15MAY1901 1905001
21OCT1946 5001
;

PROC PRINT DATA=JULIAN NOOBS;
   TITLE "Listing of Data Set JULIAN";
   VAR DATE SAS_TO_JDATE SAS_TO_JDATE7 JDATE JDATE_TO_SAS;
RUN;
```

Explanation

It is important to realize that Julian dates without four-digit years will be converted to SAS dates, based on the value of the YEARCUTOFF system option. To avoid any problems, it is best to use seven-digit Julian dates. The listing is shown next:

```
                          Listing of Data Set JULIAN


                  SAS_TO_    SAS_TO_                   JDATE_
          DATE     JDATE      JDATE7      JDATE        TO_SAS

        01/01/1960   60001    1960001    2003365    12/31/2003
        05/15/1901  1901135   1901135    1905001    01/01/1905
        10/21/1946   46294    1946294       5001    01/01/2005
```

C h a p t e r   5

Array Functions

Introduction

Although there are only three array functions, chances are, you will need to use some or all of them if you use arrays in your programs. They are all used either to determine the number of elements in, or the upper and lower bounds of, a SAS array.

Function: DIM

When you define an array, you can either enter the number of elements in the array in parentheses (or square or curly brackets) following the array name or you can use an asterisk (*) to indicate that you don't care to count the number of elements (perhaps you are "counting challenged"). SAS programmers often use an asterisk in place of the number of array elements when the list of variables is very long or where they are using keywords such as _CHARACTER_ or _NUMERIC_ in place of the list of variables. However, when you want to use a DO loop to process all the elements of the array, you need to know the number of elements. Here is where the DIM function comes in handy. It returns the number of elements in an array, given the array name as its argument.

Purpose: To determine the number of elements in an array.

Syntax: DIM(*array-name*)

array-name is the name of the SAS array for which you want to determine the number of elements.

Examples

For these examples, three arrays are defined as:

```
ARRAY ONE[*] X1-X3;
ARRAY TWO[3:6] A1 A2 A3 A4;
ARRAY THREE[2,3] X1-X6;
```

Function	Returns
DIM(ONE)	3
DIM(TWO)	4
DIM(THREE)	2 (number of elements in the 1st dimension)

Program 5.1: Setting all numeric values of 999 to missing and all character values of 'NA' to missing

```
***Primary function: DIM
***Other function: UPCASE;

DATA MIXED;
   INPUT X1-X5 A $ B $ Y Z;
DATALINES;
1 2 3 4 5 A b 6 7
2 999 6 5 3 NA C 999 10
5 4 3 2 1 na B 999 999
;
DATA ARRAY_1;
   SET MIXED;
   ARRAY NUMS[*] _NUMERIC_;
   ARRAY CHARS[*] _CHARACTER_;
   DO I = 1 TO DIM(NUMS);
      IF NUMS[I] = 999 THEN NUMS[I] = .;
   END;
```

```
   DO I = 1 TO DIM(CHARS);
        CHARS[I] = UPCASE(CHARS[I]);
        IF CHARS[I] = 'NA' THEN CHARS[I] = ' ';
     END;
     DROP I;
RUN;
PROC PRINT DATA=ARRAY_1 NOOBS;
   TITLE "Listing of Data Set ARRAY_1";
RUN;
```

Explanation

The keys to this program are the two keywords _NUMERIC_ and _CHARACTER_. These refer to all numeric and character variables defined at that point in the DATA step. Since the two array statements follow a SET statement, the _NUMERIC_ keyword will represent all the numeric variables in the MIXED data set. In a similar manner, _CHARACTER_ will represent all the character variables in the MIXED data set. (Remember that an array must consist of all character or all numeric variables.) Note that if these two array statements were placed before the SET statement, the two arrays would have no elements. Since the asterisk (*) is used to represent the number of elements in the two arrays (since it could be inconvenient to obtain these numbers or because these numbers might change), it is convenient to use the DIM function to determine this number.

The first DO loop starts from the number one and ends with the number of numeric variables in the MIXED data set. Inside the loop, you check to see if the value is equal to 999, in which case you then set the value to a SAS missing value. In a similar manner, the next DO loop starts from the number one and ends with the number of character variables in the data set MIXED. Notice the use of the UPCASE function to convert any lowercase values to uppercase. Since all the character values are now uppercase, to change values of 'NA' to a SAS missing value, all you need to do is check for uppercase values of 'NA'. This results in any upper- or lowercase values of 'NA' being set to missing values. A listing of data set ARRAY_1 is shown below:

```
                 Listing of Data Set ARRAY_1

        X1    X2    X3    X4    X5    A    B    Y    Z

         1     2     3     4     5    A    B    6    7
         2     .     6     5     3         C    .   10
         5     4     3     2     1         B    .    .
```

Program 5.2: Creating a macro to compute and print out the number of numeric and character variables in a SAS data set

```
***Primary function: DIM;

%MACRO COUNT(DSN);
   DATA _NULL_;
      IF 0 THEN SET &DSN;
      ARRAY NUMS[*] _NUMERIC_;
      ARRAY CHARS[*] _CHARACTER_;
      N_NUMS = DIM(NUMS);
      N_CHARS = DIM(CHARS);
      FILE PRINT;
      TITLE1 "*** Statistics for Data Set &DSN ***";
      PUT / "There are " N_NUMS "numeric variables and "
          N_CHARS "character variables";
   RUN;
%MEND COUNT;
```

Explanation

This macro uses an interesting trick to determine the number of numeric and character variables in a SAS data set; that is, the strange-looking conditional SET statement. The SET statement follows an IF statement (IF 0) that is never true, so the data values are never read. You would think that nothing useful could come from such a statement. However, during the compile stage, SAS performs certain operations, one being the evaluation of the list of numeric and character variables in the data set listed in the SET statement. (Veteran SAS programmers often use the trick of a conditional SET statement to determine the number of observations in a SAS data set by using the NOBS= option in the SET statement.) So, even though the SET statement is never executed in the execution stage, the two arrays defined by the _NUMERIC_ and _CHARACTER_ keywords are properly assigned, and the DIM function determines the number of elements in each of the two arrays. To test this macro, we can call it like this:

```
%COUNT(MIXED);
```

with the result listed next:

```
*** Statistics for Data Set MIXED ***

There are 7 numeric variables and 2 character variables
```

Functions: **HBOUND and LBOUND**

Purpose: To determine the lower and upper bounds of the array when the array bounds do not run from 1 to *n*.

Syntax: HBOUND(*array-name*)   or   BOUND(*array-name*)

array-name is the name of any previously defined SAS array.

When you index your array starting from the number one (the default), the DIM function works just fine. However, if you explicitly set your subscripts to start from a number other than one (using a colon between the lower and upper bounds of the array in the parentheses following the array name), the HBOUND and LBOUND functions become useful. Remember that the DIM function returns the number of variables, not the upper bound.

Program 5.3: Determining the lower and upper bounds of an array where the array bounds do not start from one

---

```
***Primary functions: LBOUND and HBOUND;

DATA ARRAY_2;
   ARRAY INCOME[1990:1995] INCOME1990-INCOME1995;
   ARRAY TAX[1990:1995] TAX1990-TAX1995;
   INPUT INCOME1990 - INCOME1995;
   DO YEAR = LBOUND(INCOME) TO HBOUND(INCOME);
      TAX[YEAR] = .25 * INCOME[YEAR];
   END;
   FORMAT INCOME: TAX: DOLLAR8.;
   DROP YEAR;
DATALINES;
50000 55000 57000 66000 65000 68000
;
PROC PRINT DATA=ARRAY_2 NOOBS;
   TITLE "Listing of Data Set ARRAY_2";
RUN;
```

Explanation

This programmer found it convenient to use YEAR as the subscript in the two arrays in the program. Notice the colon separating the lower and upper bounds of these two arrays. In this case, the two bounds are obvious, but we will use the two bound functions anyway to demonstrate them. Here, the expression LBOUND(INCOME) will return the value 1990 and the expression HBOUND(INCOME) will return the value 1995. The FORMAT statements uses a little known, but useful SAS feature. The colon following the two variable names in this statement acts as a "wildcard" character. For example, INCOME: refers to all variables in the data set that begin with the letters 'INCOME'. A listing of data set ARRAY_2 is shown below:

```
                      Listing of Data Set ARRAY_2

  INCOME1990   INCOME1991   INCOME1992   INCOME1993   INCOME1994   INCOME1995

    $50,000      $55,000      $57,000      $66,000      $65,000      $68,000

   TAX1990      TAX1991      TAX1992      TAX1993      TAX1994      TAX1995

    $12,500      $13,750      $14,250      $16,500      $16,250      $17,000
```

Chapter 6

Truncation Functions

Introduction

This chapter covers five functions that involve rounding or truncation. TRUNC allows you to perform logical comparisons on numerical values that were stored with fewer than 8 bytes. There is also a novel use of the ROUND function to place values into groups, such as an age group.

There is a group of functions (CEILZ, FLOORZ, INTZ, and ROUNDZ) similar to the ones in this chapter, that do not "fuzz" the result. Fuzzing the result means to return an integer value if the result is within 10^{-12} of an integer. The "Z" suffix functions do not fuzz the result.

Functions That Round and Truncate Numerical Values

Function: CEIL

Purpose: To "round up" to the next largest integer.

Syntax: CEIL(*numeric-value*)

numeric-value is any SAS numeric variable, expression, or numerical constant. For negative arguments, the returned value is an integer between the number and zero (see examples below). For positive arguments, the function returns just the integer portion of the number (the same as the INT function). Values within 10^{12} of the value of an integer will return the integer.

Examples

Function	Returns
CEIL(1.2)	2
CEIL(1.8)	2
CEIL(-1.2)	-1
CEIL(-1.8)	-1

Program 6.1: Using the CEIL function to round up a value to the next penny

```
***Primary function CEIL;

DATA ROUNDUP;
   INPUT MONEY @@;
   UP = CEIL(100*MONEY)/100;
DATALINES;
123.452 45 1.12345 4.569
;
PROC PRINT DATA=ROUNDUP NOOBS;
   TITLE "Listing of Data Set ROUNDUP";
RUN;
```

Explanation

You can use the CEIL function in cases where you want the next largest integer. Remember that for negative arguments, this function is equivalent to the INT function: the values will be rounded up (i.e., closer to zero). The listing of data set ROUNDUP is shown below:

```
            Listing of Data Set ROUNDUP

             MONEY        UP

            123.452     123.46
             45.000      45.00
              1.123       1.13
              4.569       4.57
```

Function: **FLOOR**

Purpose: To "round down" to the next smallest integer. This is sometimes used for ages, where you want a person's age as of his or her last birthday.

Syntax: FLOOR(*numeric-value*)

numeric-value is any SAS numeric variable, expression, or numerical constant. For positive arguments, this function is equivalent to the INT function. Values within 10^{-12} of an integer will return the value of the integer. For negative arguments, this function returns the next lowest negative number (see examples below):

Examples

Function	Returns
FLOOR(1.2)	1
FLOOR(1.8)	1
FLOOR(-1.2)	-2
FLOOR(-1.8)	-2

Program 6.2: Computing a person's age as of his or her last birthday (rounding down)

```
***Primary function: FLOOR
***Other function: YRDIF;

DATA FLEUR;
    INPUT @1 DOB MMDDYY10.;
    AGE = YRDIF(DOB,'01JAN2003'D,"ACTUAL");
    AGE_FLOOR = FLOOR(AGE);
    ***Note: Since AGE is positive, the INT function is equivalent;
    FORMAT DOB MMDDYY10.;
DATALINES;
10/21/1946
05/25/2000
;
PROC PRINT DATA=FLEUR NOOBS;
    TITLE "Listing of Data Set FLEUR";
RUN;
```

Explanation

AGE is computed by using the YRDIF function (see Chapter 4, "SAS Date and Time Functions"). Since the result may include a fractional part of a year, the FLOOR function is used to return the value of the next smallest integer, the person's age as of his or her last birthday. Note that since AGE will always be a positive number, the INT function would give equivalent results and could be used here. A listing of data set FLEUR is shown below:

```
               Listing of Data Set FLEUR


                                        AGE_
                   DOB        AGE       FLOOR

               10/21/1946   56.1973      56
               05/25/2000    2.6038       2
```

Function: INT

Purpose: To remove the fractional part of a number.

Syntax: INT(*numeric-value*)

numeric-value is any SAS numeric variable, expression, or numerical constant. For positive arguments, this function is equivalent to the FLOOR function. Values within 10^{-12} of the value an integer will return the value of the integer. For negative arguments, this function returns the next highest negative number (see examples below):

Examples

Function	Returns
INT(1.2)	1
INT(1.8)	1
INT(-1.2)	-1
INT(-1.8)	-1

Program 6.3: Using the INT function to compute age as of a person's last birthday

```
***Primary function: INT;

DATA AGES;
   INFORMAT DOB MMDDYY10.;
   INPUT DOB @@;
   AGE = ('01JAN2003'D - DOB) / 365.25;
   AGE_INT = INT(AGE);
   FORMAT DOB MMDDYY10.;
DATALINES;
10/21/1946 11/12/1956 6/7/2002 12/20/1966 3/6/1930 5/8/1980
;
PROC PRINT DATA=AGES NOOBS;
   TITLE "Listing of Data Set AGES";
RUN;
```

Explanation

This program is similar to Program 6.2. In this example, AGE is computed directly, without the use of the YRDIF function, and the INT function is used instead of the FLOOR function to drop the fractional part of the age.

```
              Listing of Data Set AGES

                  DOB      AGE     AGE_INT

              10/21/1946   56.1971     56
              11/12/1956   46.1355     46
              06/07/2002    0.5695      0
              12/20/1966   36.0329     36
              03/06/1930   72.8241     72
              05/08/1980   22.6502     22
```

Function: ROUND

Purpose: To round a numerical value. The rounding can be to the nearest integer or to any desired value such as to the nearest tenth or the nearest 10.

Syntax: ROUND(*numeric-value <, round-off-unit>*)

numeric-value is any SAS variable, numeric expression, or numeric constant.

round-off-unit is a value to determine how the rounding should be done. If *round-off-unit* is omitted, the default round off unit is 1. A value of .1 will round to the nearest tenth. A value of 10 will round to the nearest 10.

Examples

Function	Returns
ROUND(1.2)	1
ROUND(1.8)	2
ROUND(3.14159,.01)	3.14
ROUND(23.1,5)	25
ROUND(-1.2)	-1

Program 6.4: Rounding students' grades several ways

```
***Primary function: ROUND
***Other function: MEAN;

DATA SCORES;
   INPUT ID TEST1-TEST3;
   TEST_AVE = MEAN(OF TEST1-TEST3);
   ROUND_ONE = ROUND(TEST_AVE);
   ROUND_TENTH = ROUND(TEST_AVE,.1);
   ROUND_TWO = ROUND(TEST_AVE,2);
DATALINES;
1   100 95 95
2   78 79 88
;
PROC PRINT DATA=SCORES NOOBS;
   TITLE "Listing of Data Set SCORES";
   ID ID;
   VAR TEST_AVE ROUND:;
RUN;
```

Explanation

This program demonstrates several variations on the ROUND function. The first line using the ROUND function does not include the optional second argument, so the value is rounded to the nearest integer. The next line rounds the test average to the nearest tenth. Finally, the third use of the ROUND function rounds the test average to the nearest two points. The listing below shows the results of the different round-off units:

```
              Listing of Data Set SCORES

                    ROUND_      ROUND_     ROUND_
      ID    TEST_AVE  ONE       TENTH      TWO

       1    96.6667    97        96.7        96
       2    81.6667    82        81.7        82
```

Program 6.5: Using the ROUND function to group ages into 10-year intervals

```
***Primary function: ROUND
***Other function: YRDIF;

DATA DECADES;
   INFORMAT DOB MMDDYY10.;
   INPUT DOB @@;
   AGE = YRDIF(DOB,'01JAN2003'D,"ACTUAL");
   DECADE = ROUND(AGE + 5., 10);
   FORMAT DOB MMDDYY10.;
DATALINES;
10/21/1946 11/12/1956 6/7/2002 12/20/1966 3/6/1930 5/8/1980
11/11/1998 10/21/1990 5/5/1994 10/21/1992
;
PROC PRINT DATA=DECADES NOOBS;
   TITLE "Listing of Data Set DECADES";
RUN;
```

Explanation

This is a somewhat novel use of the ROUND function. You have to take great care when using this function to group values. In this program, the round-off unit is 10. If you didn't add 5 to the AGE, ages from 0 to 5 would be set to 0, greater than 5 to less than 15 would be rounded to 10, and so forth. If, instead, you want the 0–10 group to be set to 10, 10–20 to be set to 20, etc., you can add 5 to the value before you do the rounding. A more direct method, using a user-defined format and a PUT function (or a series of IF and ELSE IF statements) might be less prone to error than the method presented here. But, then again, this method requires only a single line of code. The listing below shows how the rounding was performed:

```
                    Listing of Data Set DECADES

                        DOB        AGE       DECADE

                    10/21/1946   56.1973       60
                    11/12/1956   46.1366       50
                    06/07/2002    0.5699       10
                    12/20/1966   36.0329       40
                    03/06/1930   72.8247       80
                    05/08/1980   22.6503       30
                    11/11/1998    4.1397       10
                    10/21/1990   12.1973       20
                    05/05/1994    8.6603       10
                    10/21/1992   10.1967       20
```

Demonstrating the Difference between Various Truncation Functions

The following program (thanks to Mike Zdeb) demonstrates how the various truncation functions treat positive and negative values:

Program 6.6: Demonstrating the various truncation functions

```
***Primary functions: CEIL, FLOOR, INT, and ROUND;

DATA TRUNCATE;
   INPUT X @@;
   CEIL = CEIL(X);
   FLOOR = FLOOR(X);
   INT = INT(X);
   ROUND = ROUND(X);
DATALINES;
7.2 7.8 -7.2 -7.8
;
PROC PRINT DATA=TRUNCATE NOOBS;
   TITLE "Listing of Data Set TRUNCATE";
RUN;
```

Explanation

The listing below shows how the various truncation functions work with positive and negative numbers:

```
          Listing of Data Set TRUNCATE

       X     CEIL    FLOOR    INT    ROUND

      7.2     8       7        7       7
      7.8     8       7        7       8
     -7.2    -7      -8       -7      -7
     -7.8    -7      -8       -7      -8
```

Function That Returns SAS Numerical Values Stored in Fewer than 8 Bytes

Function: **TRUNC**

Purpose: To allow you to make comparisons between numerical constants and SAS numerical values stored in fewer than 8 bytes. Note that this is necessary only for non-integer values. Be sure to refer to the system companion book for a chart that tells you the largest integer that can be expressed in n bytes of storage.

Syntax: TRUNC(*numeric-value, precision*)

numeric-value is any SAS variable, numeric expression or numeric constant.

precision is an integer between 3 and 8, representing the number of bytes of precision.

Examples

Function	Returns
TRUNC(3.,3)	3.0000000000000
TRUNC(3.,4)	3.0000000000000
TRUNC(3.,8)	3.0000000000000
TRUNC(3.1,3)	3.0996093750000
TRUNC(3.1,4)	3.0999984741211
TRUNC(3.1,8)	3.1000000000000

Program 6.7: Logical comparisons with numbers stored with fewer than 8 bytes of precision

```
***Primary function: TRUNC;

DATA TEST;
   LENGTH X4 4 X8 8;
   INPUT X4 X8;
DATALINES;
1.234 1.234
;
DATA TRUNCTEST;
   SET TEST;
   IF X8 = 1.234 THEN COMPARE_X8 = 'TRUE ';
   ELSE COMPARE_X8 = 'FALSE';
   IF X4 = 1.234 THEN COMPARE_X4 = 'TRUE ';
   ELSE COMPARE_X4 = 'FALSE';
   IF X4 = TRUNC(1.234,4) THEN COMPARE_TRUNC_X4 = 'TRUE ';
   ELSE COMPARE_TRUNC_X4 = 'FALSE';
RUN;

PROC PRINT DATA=TRUNTEST NOOBS;
   TITLE "Listing of Data Set TRUNTEST";
RUN;
```

Explanation

To understand what is going on here, you need to remember that all numerical values, regardless of their storage length, are expanded to 8 bytes when they are brought into the PDV. When this happens, you lose precision of the value (4 bytes are zeros) and if you then try to compare this value to a numerical constant, the values may not agree. In this program, the variables X4 and X8 are read from data set TEST. The value of X8 agrees with the numerical constant and COMPARE_X8 is 'TRUE'. However, when you compare the stored value of X4 against the numerical constant, they do not agree. So, when you check the value of numerical variables stored in fewer than 8 bytes, you should use the TRUNC function to create a numerical constant with the same degree of precision as the stored value. See the listing below to confirm this.

```
                     Listing of Data Set TRUNCTEST


                            COMPARE_     COMPARE_      COMPARE_
           X4       X8         X8           X4        TRUNC_X4

        1.23400   1.234       TRUE        FALSE         TRUE
```

C h a p t e r   7

Descriptive Statistics Functions

Introduction

The name of this chapter, "Descriptive Statistics Functions," is somewhat misleading. Although some of the functions such as MEAN (average) and STD (standard deviation) can be thought of as "statistical," many of these functions have extremely useful, everyday, non-statistical uses. So, don't be scared off. As is true throughout the book, I've used the same function categories as the SAS documentation to avoid confusion. You will find some of these functions indispensable in your SAS programming.

Functions That Determine the Number of Missing and Nonmissing Values in a List of SAS Variables

Function: N

Purpose: To determine the number of non-missing values in a list of numeric values.

Syntax: `N(<of> numeric-values)`

`numeric-values` is either a list of numeric values (numeric variables or numbers), separated by commas, or a list of variables in the form BASEn–BASEm (e.g., X1–X5). If the latter style is used, you must place the word **of** before the list. The reason for this is that without the word **of**, SAS interprets a list such as X1–X5 as the value of X1 minus the value of X5.

Examples

For these examples let: X = 5, Y = ., Z = 7, X1 = 1, X2 = 2, X3 = 3, X4 = .

Function	Returns
N(X,Y,Z)	2
N(OF X1-X4)	3
N(10,20,. ,30,40,50)	5
N(OF X1-X4,Y,Z)	4

Program 7.1: Using the N function to determine the number of non-missing values in a list of variables

```
***Primary functions: N, MEAN;

DATA QUIZ;
   INPUT QUIZ1-QUIZ10;
   ***Compute quiz average if 8 or more quizzes taken;
   IF N(OF QUIZ1-QUIZ10) GE 8 THEN QUIZ_AVE = MEAN(OF QUIZ1-QUIZ10);
DATALINES;
90 88 79 100 97 96 94 95 93 88
60 90 66 77 . . . 88 84 86
90 . . 90 90 90 90 90 90 90
;
PROC PRINT DATA=QUIZ NOOBS HEADING=H;
   TITLE "Listing of Data Set QUIZ";
RUN;
```

Explanation

This program uses the N function to determine the number of non-missing quiz scores. If the number is eight or more, an average is computed. Otherwise, QUIZ_AVE will be a missing value. In the listing below, notice the missing value for QUIZ_AVE in the second observation.

```
                       Listing of Data Set QUIZ

 QUIZ1 QUIZ2 QUIZ3 QUIZ4 QUIZ5 QUIZ6 QUIZ7 QUIZ8 QUIZ9 QUIZ10 QUIZ_AVE

    90    88    79   100    97    96    94    95    93    88     92
    60    90    66    77     .     .     .    88    84    86      .
    90     .     .    90    90    90    90    90    90    90     90
```

Function: **NMISS**

Purpose: To determine the number of missing values in a list of numeric values.

Syntax: `NMISS(<of> numeric-values)`

`numeric-values` is either a list of numeric values (numeric variables or numbers), separated by commas or a list of variables in the form BASE*n*– BASE*m* (e.g., X1–X5). If the latter style is used, you must place the word **of** before the list.

Examples

For these examples let: `X = 5, Y = ., Z = 7, X1 = 1, X2 = 2, X3 = 3, X4 = .`

Function	Returns
`NMISS(X,Y,Z)`	1
`NMISS(OF X1-X4)`	1
`NMISS(10,20,. ,30,40,50)`	1
`NMISS(OF X1-X4,Y,Z)`	2

Program 7.2: Computing a SUM and MEAN of a list of variables, only if there are no missing values

```
***Primary functions: NMISS, MEAN and SUM
***Other function: N;

 DATA NOMISS;
   INPUT X1-X3 Y Z;
   IF NMISS(OF X1-X3,Y,Z) EQ 0 THEN DO;

   ***An alternative statement is:
   IF N(OF X1-X3,Y,Z) EQ 5 THEN DO;

     SUM_VARS = SUM(OF X1-X3,Y,Z);
     AVERAGE  = MEAN(OF X1-X3,Y,Z);
   END;
```

```
DATALINES;
1 2 3 4 5
9 . 8 7 6
8 8 8 8 8
;
PROC PRINT DATA=NOMISS NOOBS;
    TITLE "Listing of Data Set NOMISS";
RUN;
```

Explanation

In this example, you want to compute a SUM and MEAN only if there are no missing values
in the list of variables. If the NMISS function returns a 0, you know that there are no
missing values in your list of numeric values, and you can compute the sum and mean of
these numeric values. If there are any missing values, NMISS will be greater than 0 and the
value of SUM_VARS and AVERAGE will remain missing. You could, alternatively, use a
regular assignment statement to compute the SUM and MEAN, but if there is a long list of
variables, this could get tedious. A listing of data set NOMISS is shown next:

```
                      Listing of Data Set NOMISS


            X1    X2    X3    Y    Z    SUM_VARS    AVERAGE


             1     2     3    4    5       15          3
             9     .     8    7    6        .          .
             8     8     8    8    8       40          8
```

Functions That Compute Sums, Means, and Medians

Function: MEAN

Purpose: To compute the mean (average) of the non-missing values of a list of
numeric values.

Syntax: MEAN(<of> *numeric-values*)

numeric-values is either a list of numeric values (numeric variables or
numbers), separated by commas, or a list of variables in the form BASE*n*–
BASE*m* (e.g., X1–X5). If the latter style is used, you must place the word

of before the list. Note that this function computes the mean only of the non-missing values in the list. If all numeric values in the list have missing values, the result is a missing value.

Examples

For these examples let: X = 5, Y = ., Z = 7, X1 = 1, X2 = 2, X3 = 3, X4 = .

Function	Returns
MEAN(X,Y,Z)	6
MEAN(OF X1-X4)	2
MEAN(10,20,. ,30,40,50)	30
MEAN(OF X1-X4,Y,Z)	3.25

See Program 7.3 for an example.

SAS9.1 Function: MEDIAN

Purpose: To compute the median of the non-missing values of a list of numeric values.

Syntax: MEDIAN(<of> *numeric-values*)

numeric-values is either a list of numeric values (numeric variables or numbers), separated by commas, or a list of variables in the form BASE*n*–BASE*m* (e.g., X1–X5). If the latter style is used, you must place the word **of** before the list. Note that this function computes the median only of the non-missing values in the list. If all numeric values in the list have missing values, the result is a missing value.

Examples

For these examples let: X = 5, Y = ., Z = 7, X1 = 1, X2 = 2, X3 = 3, X4 = .

Function	Returns
MEDIAN(X,Y,Z)	6
MEDIAN(OF X1-X4)	2
MEDIAN(10,20,. ,30,40,50)	30
MEDIAN(OF X1-X4,Y,Z)	2.5

See Program 7.3 for an example.

Function: SUM

Purpose: To compute the sum of the non-missing values in a list of numeric values.

Syntax: SUM(<of> *numeric-values*)

numeric-values is either a list of numeric values (numeric variables or numbers), separated by commas, or a list of variables in the form BASE*n*–BASE*m* (e.g., X1–X5). If the latter style is used, you must place the word **of** before the list. Note that this function computes the sum only of the non-missing values in the list. If all numeric values in the list have missing values, the result is a missing value. A useful trick is to add a 0 in the list of numeric values if you want the function to return a 0 if all the values are missing. For example: TOTAL = SUM(0, OF COST1-COST5).

Examples

For these examples let: X = 5, Y = ., Z = 7, X1 = 1, X2 = 2, X3 = 3, X4 = .

Function	Returns
SUM(X,Y,Z)	12
SUM(OF X1-X4)	6
SUM(10,20,. ,30,40,50)	150
SUM(0,Y,X4)	0

Program 7.3: Computing a mean, median, and sum of eight variables, only if there are at least six non-missing values

---

```
***Primary functions: N, MEAN, MEDIAN, SUM;

DATA SCORE;
   INPUT @1 (ITEM1-ITEM8)(1.);
   IF N(OF ITEM1-ITEM8) GE 6 THEN DO;
      MEAN = MEAN(OF ITEM1-ITEM8);
      MEDIAN = MEDIAN(OF ITEM1-ITEM8);
      SUM = SUM(OF ITEM1-ITEM8);
   END;
DATALINES;
12345678
1.3.5678
1...5678
;
PROC PRINT DATA=SCORE NOOBS;
   TITLE "Listing of SCORE";
RUN;
```

Explanation

The combination of the N with several of the descriptive statistics functions is particularly useful. Since the MEAN, MEDIAN, and SUM functions ignore missing values, you may want to use the N function to determine if there are a minimum number of values before you do your calculations. In the program above, the mean, median, and sum are computed only if the number of non-missing values is six or more. A listing of the resulting data set is shown below. Notice that the mean, median, and sum have missing values in the third observation.

```
                          Listing of SCORE

  ITEM1 ITEM2 ITEM3 ITEM4 ITEM5 ITEM6 ITEM7 ITEM8 MEAN MEDIAN SUM

    1     2     3     4     5     6     7     8    4.5   4.5    36
    1     .     3     .     5     6     7     8    5.0   5.5    30
    1     .     .     .     5     6     7     8    .     .      .
```

Functions That Compute the Spread or Dispersion of Data Values

Function: RANGE

Purpose: To compute the range (distance between the highest and lowest value) in a list of numeric values.

Syntax: `RANGE(<of> numeric-values)`

numeric-values is either a list of numeric values (numeric variables or numbers), separated by commas, or a list of variables in the form BASE*n*–BASE*m* (e.g., X1–X5). If the latter style is used, you must place the word **of** before the list. The reason for this is that without the word **of**, SAS interprets a list such as X1–X5 as the value of X1 minus the value of X5.

Examples

For these examples let X = 5, Y = ., Z = 7, X1 = 1, X2 = 2, X3 = 3, X4 = .

Function	Returns
`RANGE(X,Y,Z)`	2
`RANGE(OF X1-X4)`	2
`RANGE(10,20,. ,30,40,50)`	40
`RANGE(OF X1-X4,Y,Z)`	6

See Program 7.4 for an example.

SAS9.1 Function: IQR

Purpose: To compute the interquartile range (distance between the 25th percentile and the 75th percentile) in a list of numeric values.

Syntax: `IQR(<of> numeric-values)`

numeric-values is either a list of numeric values (numeric variables or numbers), separated by commas, or a list of variables in the form BASE*n*–BASE*m* (e.g., X1–X5). If the latter style is used, you must place the word

of before the list. The reason for this is that without the word **of**, SAS interprets a list such as X1–X5 as the value of X1 minus the value of X5.

Examples

For these examples let X = 5, Y = ., Z = 7, X1 = 1, X2 = 2, X3 = 3, X4 = .

Function	Returns
IQR(X,Y,Z)	2
IQR(OF X1-X4)	2
IQR(10,20,. ,30,40,50)	20
IQR(OF X1-X4,Y,Z)	3.5

See Program 7.4 for an example.

Function: STD

Purpose: To compute the standard deviation of a series of variables in a single observation.

Syntax: STD(<of> *numeric-values*)

numeric-values is either a list of numeric values (numeric variables or numbers), separated by commas, or a list of variables in the form BASE*n*– BASE*m* (e.g., X1–X5). If the latter style is used, you must place the word **of** before the list. Note that this function computes the standard deviation using only the non-missing values in the list. If there are fewer than two non-missing values in the list, the result is a missing value.

Examples

For these examples let: X = 5, Y = ., Z = 7, X1 = 1, X2 = 2, X3 = 3, X4 = .

Function	Returns
STD(X,Y,Z)	1.414
STD(OF X1-X4)	1
STD(10,20,. ,30,40,50)	15.811
STD(OF X1-X4,Y,Z)	2.630

Program 7.4: Computing a range, interquartile range, and standard deviation for each subject

```
***Primary functions: RANGE, IQR, and STD;

DATA HOME_ON_THE_RANGE;
    INPUT SUBJECT X1-X10;
    RANGE = RANGE(OF X1-X10);
    IQR = IQR(OF X1-X10);
    SD = STD(OF X1-X10);
DATALINES;
1  1 2 3 4 5 6 7 8 9 10
2  9 7 4 1 15 0 . 2 7 4
3  1 3 5 7 9 11 13 15 20 100
;
PROC PRINT DATA=HOME_ON_THE_RANGE;
    TITLE "Listing of Data Set HOME_ON_THE_RANGE";
    ID SUBJECT;
RUN;
```

Explanation

This program computes the range (RANGE), interquartile range (IQR), and sample standard deviation (STD) for each subject. Notice that the differences among the three measures of range vary widely, especially when there is an outlier in the data, as with subject three (value of 100). In this case, the inclusion of the outlier greatly inflates the range and standard deviation but has no effect on the IQR. Note: if you replaced the value of 100 with a value of 1000, the IQR would not change.

```
                 Listing of Data Set HOME_ON_THE_RANGE

SUBJECT  X1  X2  X3  X4  X5  X6  X7  X8  X9  X10  RANGE  IQR    SD

   1      1   2   3   4   5   6   7   8   9   10     9     5   3.0277
   2      9   7   4   1  15   0   .   2   7    4    15     5   4.6667
   3      1   3   5   7   9  11  13  15  20  100    99    10  29.2392
```

Functions That Determine the Ordering of Data Values

Function: MIN

Purpose: To determine the smallest non-missing value in a list of numeric values.

Syntax: `MIN(<of> numeric-values)`

numeric-values is either a list of numeric values (numeric variables or numbers), separated by commas, or a list of variables in the form BASE*n*– BASE*m* (e.g., X1–X5). If the latter style is used, you must place the word **of** before the list.

If all of the arguments are missing, this function will return a missing value.

Examples

For these examples let: `X = 5, Y = ., Z = 7, X1 = 1, X2 = 2, X3 = 3, X4 = .`

Function	Returns
`MIN(X,Y,Z)`	5
`MIN(OF X1-X4)`	1
`MIN(10,20,. ,30,40,50)`	10
`MIN(OF X1-X4,Y,Z)`	1

See Program 7.5 for an example.

Function: **MAX**

Purpose: To determine the largest non-missing value in a list of numeric values.

Syntax: `MAX(<of> numeric-values)`

`numeric-values` is either a list of numeric values (numeric variables or numbers), separated by commas, or a list of variables in the form BASE*n*–BASE*m* (e.g., X1–X5). If the latter style is used, you must place the word **of** before the list.

If all of the arguments are missing, this function will return a missing value.

Examples

For these examples let: X = 5, Y = ., Z = 7, X1 = 1, X2 = 2, X3 = 3, X4 = .

Function	Returns
`MAX(X,Y,Z)`	7
`MAX(OF X1-X4)`	3
`MAX(10,20,. ,30,40,50)`	50
`MAX(OF X1-X4,Y,Z)`	7

Program 7.5: Program to read hourly temperatures and determine the daily minimum and maximum temperature

```
***Primary functions: MIN and MAX;

DATA MIN_MAX_TEMP;
   INFORMAT DATE MMDDYY10.;
   INPUT DATE;
   INPUT TEMP1-TEMP24;
   MIN_TEMP = MIN(OF TEMP1-TEMP24);
   MAX_TEMP = MAX(OF TEMP1-TEMP24);
   KEEP MIN_TEMP MAX_TEMP DATE;
   FORMAT DATE MMDDYY10.;
DATALINES;
05/1/2002
```

```
38 38 39 40 41 42 55 58 60 60 59 62 66 70 75 77 60 59 58 57 54 52 51 50
05/02/2002
36 41 39 40 41 46 57 59 63 . 59 62 64 72 79 80 78 62 62 62 60 50 55 55
;
PROC PRINT DATA=MIN_MAX_TEMP NOOBS;
   TITLE "Listing of Data Set MIN_MAX_TEMP";
RUN;
```

Explanation

Here, you have the temperature for each hour of the day and want to determine the minimum and maximum values for the day. Note that the one missing value for the second date does not result in a missing value for the minimum or maximum value. The output listing is:

```
              Listing of Data Set MIN_MAX_TEMP

              DATE       MIN_TEMP      MAX_TEMP

            05/01/2002      38            77
            05/02/2002      36            80
```

A Word about the SMALLEST and LARGEST Functions

These functions are somewhat different from the functions described in this chapter. Given a list of variables, these functions can return the value of the *n*th largest or *n*th smallest value in a list of variables. These functions can be thought of as generalized versions of MIN and MAX. Both of these functions ignore missing values in their calculations (as do MIN and MAX).

SAS9.1 **Function:** **SMALLEST**

Purpose: To determine the value of the *n*th smallest value in a list of numeric values. This ordering ignores missing values.

Syntax: `SMALLEST(N, <of> numeric-values)`

N is a number from 1 to the maximum number of numeric values in the list. If N is larger than the number of values, the function returns a missing value and an error is written to the SAS log. If N is smaller than the number of values but greater than the number of non-missing values, the function returns a missing value, but no error is written to the SAS log.

numeric-values is either a list of numeric values (numeric variables or numbers), separated by commas, or a list of variables in the form BASE*n*–BASE*m* (e.g., X1–X5). If the latter style is used, you must place the word **of** before the list.

Note: SMALLEST(1, *numeric-values*) is equivalent to MIN(*numeric-values*).

Examples

For these examples let: X = 5, Y = ., Z = 7, X1 = 1, X2 = 2, X3 = 3, X4 = .

Function	Returns
SMALLEST(1,X,Y,Z)	5
SMALLEST(2, X,Y,Z)	7
SMALLEST(3, X,Y,Z)	. (missing)
SMALLEST(3, OF X1-X4)	3
SMALLEST(1, 10,20,. ,30,40,50)	10

Program 7.6: Computing the three lowest golf scores for each player (using the SMALLEST function)

```
***Primary function: SMALLEST;

DATA GOLF;
   INFILE DATALINES MISSOVER;
   INPUT ID $ SCORE1-SCORE8;
   LOWEST = SMALLEST(1 ,OF SCORE1-SCORE8);
   NEXT_LOWEST = SMALLEST(2, OF SCORE1-SCORE8);
   THIRD_LOWEST = SMALLEST(3, OF SCORE1-SCORE8);
DATALINES;
001 100 98 . . 96 93
002 90 05 07 99 103 106 110
003 110 120
;
```

```
PROC PRINT DATA=GOLF NOOBS HEADING=H;
   TITLE "Listing of Data Set GOLF";
RUN;
```

Explanation

First, a brief word on the INFILE statement. Since the data values follow a DATALINES statement, the special fileref DATALINES is used in an INFILE statement so that you can use the MISSOVER option. That option is needed because some of the lines of data contain fewer than eight scores.

Next, the SMALLEST function is used to extract the three lowest non-missing scores. The listing follows:

```
                  Listing of Data Set GOLF

    ID     SCORE1    SCORE2    SCORE3    SCORE4    SCORE5    SCORE6

   001      100        98        .         .         96        93
   002       90         5        7        99        103       106
   003      110       120        .         .          .         .

                                NEXT_     THIRD_
    SCORE7    SCORE8   LOWEST   LOWEST    LOWEST

      .         .        93        96        98
    110         .         5         7        90
      .         .       110       120         .
```

SAS9.1 Function: LARGEST

Purpose: To determine the value of the *n*th highest value in a list of numeric values. This ordering ignores missing values.

Syntax: `LARGEST(N, <of> numeric-values)`

N is a number from 1 to the maximum number of numeric values in the list. If N is larger than the number of values, the function returns a missing value and an error is written to the SAS log. If N is smaller than the number of values but greater than the number of non-missing values, the function returns a missing value, but no error is written to the SAS log.

numeric-values is either a list of numeric values (numeric variables or numbers), separated by commas, or a list of variables in the form BASE*n*–BASE*m* (e.g., X1–X5). If the latter style is used, you must place the word **of** before the list.

Note: LARGEST(1, *numeric-values*) is equivalent to MAX(*numeric-values*).

Examples

For these examples let: X = 5, Y = ., Z = 7, X1 = 1, X2 = 2,
X3 = 3, X4 = .

Function	Returns
LARGEST(1,X,Y,Z)	7
LARGEST(2, X,Y,Z)	5
LARGEST(3, X,Y,Z)	. (missing)
LARGEST(3, OF X1-X4)	1
LARGEST(1, 10,20,. ,30,40,50)	50

Program 7.7: Computing a grade based on the five highest scores

```
***Primary function: LARGEST, N;

***This program will compute a grade based on the 5 highest
   (out of 9) scores.  If there are fewer than 5 non-missing scores,
   a missing value will be returned;

DATA HIGH_5;
   INPUT SCORE1-SCORE9;
   ARRAY SCORE[9];
   IF N(OF SCORE1-SCORE9) LT 5 THEN RETURN;
   SUM = 0;
   DO I = 1 TO 5;
      SUM = SUM + LARGEST(I,OF SCORE1-SCORE9);
   END;
   GRADE = SUM / 5;
   DROP I;
DATALINES;
90 100 89 88 10 . . 29 77
. . . . . 100 99 98 97
10 20 30 40 50 60 70 80 90
;
```

```
PROC PRINT DATA=HIGH_5 NOOBS;
   TITLE "Listing of Data Set HIGH_5";
RUN;
```

Explanation

The LARGEST function is used here to select the five highest scores. In case there are fewer than five non-missing scores, GRADE will be missing. The listing of HIGH_5 below shows that this program worked as desired:

				Listing of Data Set HIGH_5						
SCORE1	SCORE2	SCORE3	SCORE4	SCORE5	SCORE6	SCORE7	SCORE8	SCORE9	SUM	GRADE
90	100	89	88	10	.	.	29	77	444	88.8
.	.	.	.	.	100	99	98	97	.	.
10	20	30	40	50	60	70	80	90	350	70.0

A Macro to Average Test Scores Where One or More of the Lowest Scores Are Dropped

For any teachers reading this book, I have included a macro of my own to average any number of test scores where you drop the lowest grade or grades from the calculation. This program does not give students zeros when they take fewer than the minimum number of quizzes. Rather, it computes the average of the actual number of quizzes taken. You may want to modify this program to penalize students taking fewer than the minimum number of quizzes. I think that the practice of dropping lowest grades helps keep students motivated if they score poorly on one or two tests.

Program 7.8: Macro to compute an average of *n* scores where the lowest *m* scores are dropped

```
***Primary functions: N, MIN, LARGEST;
*--------------------------------------------------------------*
| Macro: DROP_N                                                 |
| Purpose: Takes the average of "n" scores by dropping the      |
|          lowest "m" scores from the calculation.              |
| Arguments: DSN       Data set name                            |
|            BASE      Base of variable name holding scores     |
|            N         Total number of scores                   |
|            N_DROP    Number of scores to drop                 |
|            VARNAME   The name of the variable to hold the     |
|                      average                                  |
|            Note: The average variable is added to the original|
|                  data set.                                    |
| Example: %MACRO DROP_N(ROSTER,QUIZ,12,2,AVERAGE);             |
*--------------------------------------------------------------*;

%MACRO DROP_N(DSN, BASE, N, N_DROP, VARNAME);
   DATA &DSN;
      SET &DSN;
      N_OF_SCORES = N(OF &BASE.1-&BASE&N);
      MIN = MIN(N_OF_SCORES,%EVAL(&N - &N_DROP));
      SUM = 0;
      DO I = 1 TO MIN;
         SUM + LARGEST(I,OF &BASE.1-&BASE&N);
      END;
      &VARNAME = SUM / MIN;
      ***Replace MIN with %EVAL(&N - &N_DROP) to penalize
         students taking fewer than the minimum number of quizzes;
      DROP I N_OF_SCORES SUM MIN;
   RUN;
%MEND DROP_N;
```

Explanation

As with other macros in this book, only a brief explanation will be provided. The N function is used to determine the number of non-missing quiz scores. The MIN function finds the number of quizzes to include in the averaging process: either the total number of quizzes minus the number to be dropped or the number of non-missing quiz scores, whichever is smaller. The first argument in the LARGEST function is the *n*th largest value. Suppose there were 9 quizzes, and you want to drop the two lowest scores. If the student took all 9, the minimum of 9 and 7 is 7, and the DO loop adds up the 7 highest scores. If the student took 8 quizzes, the DO loop also adds up the 7 highest (thus only one score being dropped).

Finally, for any student taking 7 or fewer quizzes, the average is simply the average of all quizzes taken.

Note: To give students zeros when they take fewer than the minimum number of quizzes, you just have to replace the denominator of the VARNAME statement with %EVAL(&N - &N_DROP) instead of MIN.

To test this macro, use the short DATA step below to create a SAS data set (ROSTER). The macro is then invoked, using the 9 quiz grades in the computation. In this example, the lowest 2 quiz grades are to be dropped.

```
***Data set to test the macro;
DATA ROSTER;
   INPUT ID QUIZ1-QUIZ9;
DATALINES;
1 6 7 8 9 8 7 6 7 8
2 6 8 8 8 8 8 8 8 .
3 7 8 9 . . . . . .
4 9 9 1 9 9 9 9 . .
;
```

The calling sequence to compute a quiz average, dropping the lowest 2 scores is:

```
%DROP_N(ROSTER,QUIZ,9,2,QUIZ_AVE);
```

Finally, the PRINT procedure is used to list the contents of the ROSTER data set, now with the new variable QUIZ_AVE included.

```
PROC PRINT DATA=ROSTER NOOBS;
   TITLE1 "Listing of Data Set QUIZ";
   TITLE2 "After running macro DROP_N";
RUN;
```

```
                   Listing of Data Set QUIZ
                   After running macro DROP_N


  ID QUIZ1 QUIZ2 QUIZ3 QUIZ4 QUIZ5 QUIZ6 QUIZ7 QUIZ8 QUIZ9 QUIZ_AVE

   1   6     7     8     9     8     7     6     7     8    7.71429
   2   6     8     8     8     8     8     8     8     .    8.00000
   3   7     8     9     .     .     .     .     .     .    8.00000
   4   9     9     1     9     9     9     9     .     .    7.85714
```

SAS9.1 **Function:**   **PCTL**

Purpose: To determine the value, in a list of variables, corresponding to a given percentile. For example, at the 25th percentile, one quarter of the scores would be below this value. This ordering ignores missing values. The PCTLn function uses the standard five SAS definitions for computing percentiles. The default (PCTL) is definition five. In practice, the differences in the definitions are more apparent when there are fewer values in the list and if there are tied values.

Syntax: `PCTL<n>(percentile, <of> numeric-values)`

n is the percentile definition (1 to 5). If n is omitted, definition five is used.

`percentile` is a number from 0 to 100, specifying the percentile to be returned.

`numeric-values` is either a list of numeric values (numeric variables or numbers), separated by commas or a list of variables in the form BASEn–BASEm (e.g., X1–X5). If the latter style is used, you must place the word **of** before the list.

Examples

For these examples, `X1=10, X2=12, X3=15, X4=17, X5=20, and X6=.`

Function	Returns
`PCTL(20, OF X1-X6)`	11
`PCTL2(20, OF X1-X6)`	10
`PCTL(75, 3,5,4,6,5,7,6,8,7,8,.,.)`	7

Program 7.9: Using the PCTL function to determine 25th, 50th, and 75th percentile in a list of values

```
***Primary function: PCTL
***Other functions: RANNOR;

***Generate data set for testing;
DATA TEMPERATURE;
   ARRAY T[24]; ***Temperature for each hour;
   DO DAY = 1 TO 5;
      ***T values normally distributed with mean = 70 and
         standard deviation = 10;
      DO HOUR = 1 TO 24;
         T[HOUR] = 10*RANNOR(0) + 70;
      END;
      OUTPUT;
   END;
   KEEP T1-T24 DAY;
RUN;

DATA PERCENTILE;
   SET TEMPERATURE;
   P25 = PCTL(25, OF T1-T24);
   P50 = PCTL(50, OF T1-T24);
   P75 = PCTL(75, OF T1-T24);
   IQR = P75 - P25;
   LABEL P25 = "25th Percentile"
         P50 = "Median"
         P75 = "75th Percentile"
         IQR = "Inter-quartile Range";
RUN;

PROC PRINT DATA=PERCENTILE NOOBS LABEL;
   TITLE "Listing of Data Set PERCENTILE";
   ID DAY;
   VAR P25 P50 P75 IQR;
RUN;
```

Explanation

The first DATA step creates a test data set of 24 temperatures for each of five days. The next DATA step computes the 25th, 50th (median), and 75th percentile as well as the difference between the 25th and 75th percentile, called the interquartile range (IQR).

```
            Listing of Data Set PERCENTILE

                                              Inter-
                 25th                  75th   quartile
         DAY   Percentile   Median   Percentile   Range

          1     62.0569    72.6482    80.9969    18.9400
          2     59.6860    72.9270    80.6775    20.9915
          3     65.0972    69.3539    74.1094     9.0122
          4     63.3234    70.3072    77.7218    14.3984
          5     63.0695    68.6146    72.1049     9.0354
```

Function: ORDINAL

This function is somewhat different from the functions described previously in this chapter. Given a list of numeric values, this function can return the value of the nth lowest value. Unlike the MIN, MAX, LARGEST, and SMALLEST functions, the ORDINAL function **includes** missing values in its calculations.

Purpose: To determine the value of the nth lowest value in a list of numeric values. This ordering includes missing values.

Syntax: ORDINAL(ordinality, <of> numeric-values)

ordinality is a number from 1 to the maximum number of numeric values in the list.

numeric-values is either a list of numeric values (numeric variables or numbers), separated by commas, or a list of variables in the form BASEn–BASEm (e.g., X1–X5). If the latter style is used, you must place the word **of** before the list.

Examples

For these examples let: X = 5, Y = ., Z = 7, X1 = 1, X2 = 2, X3 = 3, X4 = .

Function	Returns
ORDINAL(1,X,Y,Z)	. (missing value)
ORDINAL(2, X,Y,Z)	5
ORDINAL(3, X,Y,Z)	7
ORDINAL(3, OF X1-X4)	2
ORDINAL(1, 10,20,. ,30,40,50)	. (missing value)

Program 7.10: Program to compute a quiz grade by dropping none, one, or two of the lowest quiz scores, depending on how many quizzes were taken

```
***Primary function: ORDINAL
***Other functions: N, MEAN, and SUM;

DATA QUIZ_AVE;
   INPUT ID $ QUIZ1-QUIZ9;
   N_OF_QUIZZES = N(OF QUIZ1-QUIZ9);
   IF N_OF_QUIZZES  = 9 THEN
      QUIZ_AVE = (SUM(OF QUIZ1-QUIZ9) -
                 ORDINAL(1,OF QUIZ1-QUIZ9) -
                 ORDINAL(2,OF QUIZ1-QUIZ9))/7;
   ELSE IF N_OF_QUIZZES = 8 THEN
      QUIZ_AVE = (SUM(OF QUIZ1-QUIZ9) - ORDINAL(2,OF QUIZ1-QUIZ9))/7;
   ELSE QUIZ_AVE = MEAN(OF QUIZ1-QUIZ9);
DATALINES;
001 6 7 8 9 8 7 6 7 8
002 6 8 8 8 8 8 8 8 .
003 7 8 9 . . . . . .
004 9 9 1 9 9 9 9 . .
;
PROC PRINT DATA=QUIZ_AVE NOOBS;
   TITLE "Listing of Data Set QUIZ_AVE";
RUN;
```

Explanation

Before we discuss this program, I should point out that the LARGEST function would make for a much simpler solution. However, I have decided to include this more complicated program as a demonstration of how to use the ORDINAL function.

This example was developed to compute grades for a course that I teach at the University of Medicine and Dentistry at the New Jersey School of Public Health. Students in my biostatistics course take weekly quizzes. If they take all the quizzes, I drop the two lowest scores. If they miss one quiz, they get to drop the lowest score. If two or more quizzes are missed, no scores are dropped. Using the ORDINAL function is a great help with this problem. The term ORDINAL(1,OF QUIZ1-QUIZ9) returns the lowest quiz score and the statement ORDINAL(2,OF QUIZ1-QUIZ9) returns the second lowest quiz score (including missing values).

Therefore, if all 9 quizzes were taken, the quiz average is the total of all 9 scores, minus the two lowest scores, divided by 7. If only 8 quizzes were taken, you subtract the second lowest quiz score (remember, the value of ORDINAL(1,OF QUIZ1-QUIZ9) will be a missing value in this situation) from the total and divide by 7. Finally, if the number of non-missing quiz scores is not 8 or 9, you compute the mean of the non-missing quiz scores using the MEAN function. You can inspect the listing below to see that this program works as desired:

```
                    Listing of Data Set QUIZ_AVE


     ID    QUIZ1    QUIZ2    QUIZ3    QUIZ4    QUIZ5    QUIZ6

    001      6        7        8        9        8        7
    002      6        8        8        8        8        8
    003      7        8        9        .        .        .
    004      9        9        1        9        9        9

                                      N_OF_
   QUIZ7    QUIZ8    QUIZ9    QUIZZES    QUIZ_AVE

     6        7        8        9        7.71429
     8        8        .        8        8.00000
     .        .        .        3        8.00000
     9        .        .        7        7.85714
```

An interesting alternative to Program 7.10 is shown next. Here, a DO loop is used to add up the quiz scores, starting from the highest to the lowest. Look at the program and then study the explanation below:

Program 7.11: Alternate version of Program 7.10

```
***Primary function: ORDINAL
***Other functions: N and MIN;

DATA QUIZ_AVE2;
   INPUT ID $ QUIZ1-QUIZ9;
   N_OF_QUIZZES = N(OF QUIZ1-QUIZ9);
   SUM = 0;
   DO I = 1 TO MIN(N_OF_QUIZZES,7);
      SUM + ORDINAL(10 - I,OF QUIZ1-QUIZ9);
   END;
   QUIZ_AVE = SUM / MIN(N_OF_QUIZZES,7);
DATALINES;
001 6 7 8 9 8 7 6 7 8
002 6 8 8 8 8 8 8 8 .
003 7 8 9 . . . . . .
004 9 9 1 9 9 9 9 . .
;
PROC PRINT DATA=QUIZ_AVE2 NOOBS;
   TITLE "Listing of Data Set QUIZ_AVE2";
RUN;
```

Explanation

Although this program is shorter than the previous program, it's actually a bit more complicated. However, it is a good way to demonstrate the N, MIN, and ORDINAL functions.

The number of quizzes taken is computed using the N function and is assigned to the variable N_OF_QUIZZES. For each iteration of the DATA step, the SUM is initialized to 0. The DO loop starts from 1 and ends at the number of quizzes taken or the number 7, whichever is smaller. Next, each quiz score is added to the sum using a SUM statement, starting from the highest quiz score to the lowest, non-missing quiz score. Finally, the average is computed by dividing this sum by the number of quizzes taken or the number 7, whichever is smaller. The output from this program is identical to the output from Program 7.10 and will not be shown.

Using the ORDINAL Function to Sort Values within an Observation

As of Version 9, there are two experimental call routines (CALL SORTN and CALL SORTC), which sort values within an array. When these become available, you can throw out this macro (but it does provide a good demonstration of the ORDINAL function).

The program and macro in this section use the ORDINAL function to sort numerical values within an observation. For example, if you have variables X1–X10 and want to rearrange the values so that X1 holds the lowest value, X2, the next lowest value, and so forth, you can use this program to accomplish the task.

Program 7.12: Sorting values within an observation

```
***Primary function: ORDINAL
***Other functions: CALL SORTN;

DATA SORT;
   INPUT X1-X10;
   ARRAY X[10] X1-X10;
   ARRAY SORT_X[10] SORT_X1-SORT_X10;
   DO I = 1 TO 10;
      SORT_X[I] = ORDINAL(I,OF X1-X10);
   END;
   DROP I;
DATALINES;
5 2 9 1 3 6 . 22 7 0
PROC PRINT DATA=SORT NOOBS HEADING=H;
   TITLE "Listing of Data Set SORT";
RUN;

/***************************************************
Experimental:
CALL SORTN solution (with the result placed in the
                     original array)

DATA SORT;
   INPUT X1-X10;
   ARRAY X[10] X1-X10;
   CALL SORTN(OF X[*]);
DATALINES;
5 2 9 1 3 6 . 22 7 0
***************************************************/
```

Explanation

In one of my earlier books, I wrote a fairly long and complicated program to sort values within an observation, using a bubble sort algorithm. That was before I became familiar with the ORDINAL function. The use of this function greatly simplifies this task. Program 7.12 leaves the original values unchanged and creates a new set of variables to hold the sorted values. The key to the whole program is to use the DO loop index (I) as the first argument in the ORDINAL function, thus resulting in the new set of variables (SORT_Xn) in sorted order.

The output from the PRINT procedure is shown next:

```
                      Listing of Data Set SORT

   X1 X2 X3 X4 X5 X6 X7 X8 X9 X10  SORT_X1 SORT_X2 SORT_X3 SORT_X4

    5  2  9  1  3  6  . 22  7  0       .       0       1       2

   SORT_X5     SORT_X6     SORT_X7     SORT_X8     SORT_X9     SORT_X10

      3           5           6           7           9          22
```

If this is a task that you need to perform regularly, the sort macro presented below will sort the values for a set of variables and return the sorted values to the original variable names. For example, if your original variables were X1–X10, the same ten variables would have the values in sorted order after the macro was run. Here is the program:

Program 7.13: Macro to sort values within an observation

```
   ***Primary function: ORDINAL;

%MACRO SORT_ARRAY(DSN, BASE, N_OF_ELEMENTS);
   DATA &DSN;
      SET &DSN;
      ARRAY &BASE[&N_OF_ELEMENTS];
      ARRAY TEMP[&N_OF_ELEMENTS] _TEMPORARY_;
      ***Transfer values to temporary arry;
      DO I = 1 TO &N_OF_ELEMENTS;
         TEMP[I] = ORDINAL(I,OF &BASE.1 - &BASE&N_OF_ELEMENTS);
      END;
      ***Put them back in the original variable names in order;
```

```
      DO I = 1 TO &N_OF_ELEMENTS;
         &BASE[I]  = TEMP[I];
      END;
   RUN;
%MEND  SORT;
```

Explanation

This program uses a temporary array as a place to hold the sorted values so that they can be placed back into the original variable names. You could easily modify this program if you want to preserve the original variables and create a new series of variables to hold the sorted values. The code below shows the data set before the macro is called, the macro call, and a listing of the data set after the sorting has been done.

```
PROC PRINT DATA=SORT NOOBS;
   TITLE "Listing of Data Set SORT before macro";
   VAR X1-X10;
RUN;

%SORT_ARRAY(SORT,X,10);

PROC PRINT DATA=SORT NOOBS;
   TITLE "Listing of Data Set SORT after macro";
   VAR X1-X10;
RUN;
```

The two listings below show that the macro is working as desired.

```
                Listing of Data Set SORT before macro

    X1    X2    X3    X4    X5    X6    X7    X8    X9    X10

     5     2     9     1     3     6     .    22     7     0

                Listing of Data Set SORT after macro

    X1    X2    X3    X4    X5    X6    X7    X8    X9    X10

     .     0     1     2     3     5     6     7     9    22
```

Using the STD Function to Perform a *t* Test

This last section uses the STD function, along with several others, to perform a *t* test (a statistical test to compare the means of two groups) where all the values for one group are in one observation and all the values for the other group are in the next observation. In order to use PROC TTEST, a new data set would have to be created where each value was in a separate observation, along with the GROUP variable.

Program 7.14: Performing a *t* test where values for each group are in a single observation

```
***Primary function: STD
***Other functions: N, MEAN, SQRT, PROBT, ABS;

DATA _NULL_;
   FILE PRINT;
   INFILE DATALINES MISSOVER;
   INPUT GROUP $ X1-X50;
   RETAIN N1 MEAN1 SD1 GROUP1;
   IF _N_ = 1 THEN DO;
      GROUP1 = GROUP;
      N1 = N(OF X1-X50);
      MEAN1 = MEAN(OF X1-X50);
      SD1 = STD(OF X1-X50);
   END;
   IF _N_ = 2 THEN DO;
      GROUP2 = GROUP;
      N2 = N(OF X1-X50);
      MEAN2 = MEAN(OF X1-X50);
      SD2 = STD(OF X1-X50);
      DIFF = MEAN1 - MEAN2;
      SD_POOLED_2 = ((N1-1)*SD1**2 + (N2-1)*SD2**2)/(N1 + N2 - 2);
      T = ABS(DIFF) / SQRT(SD_POOLED_2/N1 + SD_POOLED_2/N2);
      PROB = 2*(1 - PROBT(T,N1+N2-2));

      ***Prepare the report;
      TITLE "T-Test Calculation";
      PUT @1  "Group " GROUP1 +(-1) ":"
          @10 "N = " N1 3.
          @20 "Mean = " MEAN1 7.3
          @35 "SD = " SD1 7.4 /
          @1  "Group " GROUP2 +(-1) ":"
          @10 "N = " N2  3.
          @20 "Mean = " MEAN2 7.3
          @35 "SD = " SD2 7.4 /
          @1 "Difference = " DIFF 7.3
```

```
        @25 "T = " T 7.4
        @40 "P(2-tail) = " PROB 7.4;
    END;
DATALINES;
A 4 5 8 7 6 5 7
B 9 7 8 8 6 7 9 9 11
;
```

Explanation

Since each group of values resides within a single observation, the SAS automatic variable _N_ allows you to determine if you are reading the first or second line of data. The three descriptive statistics functions N, MEAN, and STD compute the number of non-missing values, the mean, and the standard deviation, respectively. After these values have been computed for the second group, the steps to compute a *t*-value are performed. The SQRT function takes the square root of its argument. The ABS function takes the absolute value of the difference so that our *t*-value will always be positive. Finally, in order to print out the two-tailed *p*-value (the famous *p*-value that all researchers hope is less than .05), the PROBT function is used. This function computes the cumulative probability under the *t* distribution. Output from this program is shown below:

```
                    T-Test Calculation

    Group A: N =   7   Mean =   6.000 SD =   1.4142
    Group B: N =   9   Mean =   8.222 SD =   1.4814
    Difference =  -2.222    T =  3.0349    P(2-tail) =  0.0089
```

C h a p t e r 8

Mathematical Functions

Introduction

Most of the functions in this chapter perform basic mathematical tasks such as taking the log or exponent of a value. The MOD function is an exception. Although it is used in mathematical expressions, it has other, often overlooked, uses that will be covered here.

Commonly Used Mathematical Functions

Function: CONSTANT

Purpose: To compute numerical constants: (pi, E, and Euler's constant) and to determine various machine constants (the largest integer stored in *n* bytes, the largest double-precision number, the smallest double-precision number (its log and square root), the machine precision constant). Also, the log and square root of the last three constants.

Syntax: CONSTANT('*constant*' <,*parm*>)

constant, placed in quotation marks, is one of the following:

Mathematical Constants

E	is the base of natural logarithms.
EULER	is Euler's constant.
PI	is pi.

Machine Constants

EXACTINT	is the largest integer stored in *n* bytes (specified by *parm* = 2 to 8).
BIG	is the largest double-precision number stored in 8 bytes on your computer.
LOGBIG	is the logarithm of BIG. The default base is E, but you can specify a base with *parm*.
SQRTBIG	is the square root of BIG.
SMALL	is the smallest double-precision number stored in 8 bytes on your computer.
LOGSMALL	is the logarithm of SMALL (base specified with *parm*).
SQRTSMALL	is the square root of SMALL.

Machine Precision

MACEPS	is a machine-precision constant. This number is used to determine if one number is larger than another.
LOGMACEPS	is the log of MACEPS (base specified with *parm*).
SQRTMACEPS	is the square root of MACEPS.

Examples

These examples were run on a Windows platform.

Function	Returns
CONSTANT('PI')	3.1415926536
CONSTANT('EXACTINT',3)	8192
CONSTANT('EXACTINT',4)	2097152
CONSTANT('EXACTINT',8)	9.0071993E15
CONSTANT('BIG')	1.797693E308
CONSTANT('SMALL')	2.22507E-308
CONSTANT('MACEPS')	2.220446E-16

Program 8.1: Determining mathematical constants and machine constants using the CONSTANT function

```
***Primary function: CONSTANT;

DATA _NULL_;
   FILE PRINT;
   PI = CONSTANT('PI');
   E = CONSTANT('E');

   PUT "Mathematical Constants" /
       "Pi = " PI /
       "E = " E //
       "Largest Integers stored in 'n' bytes:";
   DO BYTES = 3 TO 8;
      INT = CONSTANT('EXACTINT',BYTES);
      PUT +5 "Largest Integer Stored in " BYTES "Bytes is: " INT;
   END;
   LARGE = CONSTANT('BIG');
   SMALL = CONSTANT('SMALL');
   PRECISION = CONSTANT('MACEPS');
   PUT / "Machine Constants" /
       "Largest 8 Byte Value is: " LARGE /
       "Smallest 8 Byte Value is: " SMALL /
       "Precision constant is: " PRECISION;
RUN;
```

Explanation

The CONSTANT function is used here to list some of the mathematical and machine constants. If you plan to change the default length of 8 for numerical values, it would be an excellent idea to use the CONSTANT function to determine the largest integer you could store exactly in the number of bytes you choose. The listing from this program (run on a Windows platform) is shown below:

```
Mathematical Constants
Pi = 3.1415926536
E = 2.7182818285

Largest Integers stored in 'n' bytes:
     Largest Integer Stored in 3 Bytes is: 8192
     Largest Integer Stored in 4 Bytes is: 2097152
     Largest Integer Stored in 5 Bytes is: 536870912
     Largest Integer Stored in 6 Bytes is: 137438953472
     Largest Integer Stored in 7 Bytes is: 3.5184372E13
     Largest Integer Stored in 8 Bytes is: 9.0071993E15

Machine Constants
Largest 8 Byte Value is: 1.797693E308
Smallest 8 Byte Value is: 2.22507E-308
Precision constant is: 2.220446E-16
```

Function: MOD

You probably have to think back to ninth grade to remember what modular arithmetic is. The MOD function returns the remainder of one number when it is divided by another. For example, 5 mod 3 is 2; 15 mod 3 is 0, 16 mod 3 is 1, and so forth. Two applications of the MOD function are presented here: one to select every *n*th observation from a SAS data set, and the other, a programming trick to use the MOD function as a toggle switch, allowing you to alternate two activities.

Purpose: To perform modular arithmetic. Also useful to select or process every *n*th observation

Syntax: MOD(*numeric-value*, *modulo*)

numeric-value is a numeric variable or expression.

modulo is a constant or a numeric variable. The function returns the remainder after *numeric-value* is divided by *modulo*.

Examples

Function	Returns
MOD(15,4)	3
MOD(4,15)	4
MOD(7,2)	1

Program 8.2: Using the MOD function to choose every *n*th observation from a SAS data set

```
***Primary function: MOD
***Other functions: INT, RANUNI;

***Create test input data set;
DATA BIG;
   DO SUBJ = 1 TO 20;
      X = INT(10*RANUNI(0)); /* Random integers from 0 to 9 */
      OUTPUT;
   END;
RUN;

%LET N = 4; /* Every 4th observation will be selected */

DATA EVERY_N;
   SET BIG;
   IF MOD(_N_ ,&N) = 1;
   /* Selects every nth observation, starting with the 1st */
RUN;

PROC PRINT DATA=EVERY_N NOOBS;
   TITLE "Listing of Data Set EVERY_N";
RUN;
```

Explanation

The first DATA step (the data set BIG) is included to produce a test data set with 20 subjects. The key to choosing every *n*th observation is the subsetting IF statement, using the MOD function to provide the condition. When the value of the automatic variable _N_ is 1, 5, 9, etc., the condition will be true and the observation is added to data set EVERY_N. The short listing below demonstrates that this program works as advertised.

```
                        Listing of Data Set EVERY_N

                        SUBJ     X

                        1        2
                        5        8
                        9        2
                        13       5
                        17       3
```

Program 8.3: Using the MOD function as a toggle switch, alternating group assignments

```
***Primary function: MOD;
***In this program, we want to assign every other subject into
   group A or group B;

DATA SWITCH;
   DO SUBJ = 1 TO 10;
      IF MOD(SUBJ,2) EQ 1 THEN GROUP = 'A';
      ELSE GROUP = 'B';
      OUTPUT;
   END;
RUN;
PROC PRINT DATA=SWITCH NOOBS;
   TITLE "Listing of Data Set SWITCH";
RUN;
```

Explanation

Since the second argument of the MOD function is a 2, the function will return either 1's or 0's alternately. This is a useful feature that can be used in any program where you need to perform two different activities in an alternating fashion. The listing from PROC PRINT is:

```
           Listing of Data Set SWITCH

           SUBJ    GROUP

             1       A
             2       B
             3       A
             4       B
             5       A
             6       B
             7       A
             8       B
             9       A
            10       B
```

Function: ABS

Purpose: To take the absolute value of its argument (i.e., throw away the minus sign if there is one).

Syntax: ABS(*numeric-value*)

numeric-value is a number, a numeric variable or expression.

Examples

Function	Returns
ABS(-15)	15
ABS(8)	8

Program 8.4: Computing Chi-square with Yates' correction, which requires an absolute value

```
***Primary function: ABS
***Other function: PROBCHI;

DATA YATES;
   INPUT A B C D;
   N = A + B + C + D;
   YATES = ( ABS(A*D - B*C) - N/2)**2 * N /
           ( (A+B)*(C+D)*(A+C)*(B+D) );
       PROB_YATES = 1 - PROBCHI(YATES,1);
DATALINES;
10 20 30 40
2 9 8 5
;
PROC PRINT DATA=YATES NOOBS;
   TITLE "Listing of Data Set YATES";
RUN;
```

Explanation

The formula for Chi-square with Yates' correction takes the absolute value of the numerator, thus requiring the use of the ABS function. The listing is:

```
                       Listing of Data Set YATES


                                                     PROB_
        A     B     C     D     N      YATES         YATES

        10    20    30    40    100    0.44643       0.50404
         2     9     8     5     24    2.99700       0.08342
```

Function: SQRT

Purpose: To take the square root of a value.

Syntax: SQRT(*numeric-value*)

numeric-value is a numeric variable or expression greater than or equal to zero.

Examples

Function	Returns
SQRT(16)	4
SQRT(-4)	missing value

Program 8.5: Program to compute and print out a table of integers and square roots

```
***Primary function: SQRT;

OPTIONS PS=15; /* So the panels will display in PROC REPORT */
DATA SQUARE_ROOT;
   DO N = 1 TO 40;
      SQUARE_ROOT = SQRT(N);
      OUTPUT;
   END;
RUN;

PROC REPORT DATA=SQUARE_ROOT NOWD PANELS=99;
   TITLE "Table of Integers and Square Roots";
   COLUMNS N SQUARE_ROOT;
   DEFINE N / DISPLAY WIDTH=3 FORMAT=3.0;
   DEFINE SQUARE_ROOT /'Square Root' WIDTH=7 FORMAT=7.6;
RUN;
```

Explanation

This very straightforward program uses a DO loop to generate the integers from 1 to 40. The SQRT function computes the square root of each integer, and the OUTPUT statement writes an observation to the SAS data set. In this example, PROC REPORT was used so that the PANELS option could be used. This option creates telephone-book style output. If the number of panels is more than will fit on the page, PROC REPORT attempts to fit as many panels as possible. Finally, in the listing below, the page size option was set to 15 so that the panels would appear in the space allowed.

```
                     Table of Integers and Square Roots

          Square              Square              Square              Square
    N      Root        N       Root        N       Root        N       Root
    1    1.00000      12     3.46410      23     4.79583      34     5.83095
    2    1.41421      13     3.60555      24     4.89898      35     5.91608
    3    1.73205      14     3.74166      25     5.00000      36     6.00000
    4    2.00000      15     3.87298      26     5.09902      37     6.08276
    5    2.23607      16     4.00000      27     5.19615      38     6.16441
    6    2.44949      17     4.12311      28     5.29150      39     6.24500
    7    2.64575      18     4.24264      29     5.38516      40     6.32456
    8    2.82843      19     4.35890      30     5.47723
    9    3.00000      20     4.47214      31     5.56776
   10    3.16228      21     4.58258      32     5.65685
   11    3.31662      22     4.69042      33     5.74456
```

Functions That Work with Exponentiation and Logarithms

These functions have been grouped together since they are all related and have similar syntax. I will describe the three functions and then follow with a single program that uses all three.

Function: **EXP**

Purpose: To return the value of the exponential function. EXP computes the value of E (the base of natural logarithms), raised to the power of the argument.

Syntax: EXP(*numeric-value*)

                numeric-value is a number, numeric variable, or expression.

Examples

Function	Returns
EXP(2.718)	15.150
EXP(100)	2.688
EXP(0)	1

Function: **LOG**

Purpose: To compute the natural logarithm (base E) of an argument.

Syntax: LOG(*numeric-value*)

numeric-value is a positive numeric variable or expression.

Examples

Function	Returns
LOG(2.718)	1.000
LOG(100)	4.605
LOG(1000)	6.908

Function: **LOG10**

Purpose: To compute the base-10 logarithm of an argument.

Syntax: LOG10(*numeric-value*)

numeric-value is a positive numeric variable or expression.

Examples

Function	Returns
LOG10(2.718)	.434
LOG10(100)	2
LOG10(1000)	3

Program 8.6: Creating tables of integers, their base-10 and base E logarithms and their value taken to the *n*th power

```
***Primary functions: EXP, LOG, LOG10;
***Program to print a pretty table of integers (from 1 to 100),
   results of the exponential function, base ten and base E logs;

DATA TABLE;
   DO N = 1 TO 40;
      E = .EXP(N);
      LN = LOG(N);
      LOG = LOG10(N);
      OUTPUT;
   END;
RUN;

PROC REPORT DATA=TABLE NOWD PANELS=99;
   TITLE "Table of Exponents, natural and base 10 logs";
   COLUMNS N E LN LOG;
   DEFINE N / DISPLAY RIGHT WIDTH=3 FORMAT=3.;
   DEFINE E / DISPLAY RIGHT WIDTH=8 FORMAT=BEST8. 'Exp';
   DEFINE LN / DISPLAY RIGHT WIDTH=7 FORMAT=7.4 'Natural Log';
   DEFINE LOG / DISPLAY RIGHT WIDTH=7 FORMAT=7.4 'Base 10 Log';
RUN;
```

```
         Table of Exponents, natural and base 10 logs

                 Natural    Base                      Natural    Base
    N      Exp      Log    10 Log     N      Exp        Log    10 Log
    1   2.718282  0.0000   0.0000    21   1.3188E9    3.0445   1.3222
    2   7.389056  0.6931   0.3010    22   3.5849E9    3.0910   1.3424
    3   20.08554  1.0986   0.4771    23   9.7448E9    3.1355   1.3617
    4   54.59815  1.3863   0.6021    24   2.649E10    3.1781   1.3802
    5   148.4132  1.6094   0.6990    25    7.2E10     3.2189   1.3979
    6   403.4288  1.7918   0.7782    26   1.957E11    3.2581   1.4150
    7   1096.633  1.9459   0.8451    27   5.32E11     3.2958   1.4314
    8   2980.958  2.0794   0.9031    28   1.446E12    3.3322   1.4472
    9   8103.084  2.1972   0.9542    29   3.931E12    3.3673   1.4624
   10   22026.47  2.3026   1.0000    30   1.069E13    3.4012   1.4771
   11   59874.14  2.3979   1.0414    31   2.905E13    3.4340   1.4914
   12   162754.8  2.4849   1.0792    32   7.896E13    3.4657   1.5051
   13   442413.4  2.5649   1.1139    33   2.146E14    3.4965   1.5185
   14   1202604   2.6391   1.1461    34   5.835E14    3.5264   1.5315
   15   3269017   2.7081   1.1761    35   1.586E15    3.5553   1.5441
   16   8886111   2.7726   1.2041    36   4.311E15    3.5835   1.5563
   17   24154953  2.8332   1.2304    37   1.172E16    3.6109   1.5682
   18   65659969  2.8904   1.2553    38   3.186E16    3.6376   1.5798
   19   1.7848E8  2.9444   1.2788    39   8.659E16    3.6636   1.5911
   20   4.8517E8  2.9957   1.3010    40   2.354E17    3.6889   1.6021
```

Factorial and Gamma Functions

Prior to Version 7, SAS did not include the FACT function. It was necessary to use the relationship that GAMMA(N + 1) was equal to N!.

Function: FACT

Purpose: To take the factorial of its argument. For example, 4! = FACT(4) = 4 x 3 x 2 x 1 = 24.

Syntax: FACT(*numeric-value*)

numeric-value is a numeric variable or expression that resolves to an integer that is greater than or equal to 0.

Examples

Function	Returns
FACT(4)	24
FACT(0)	1
FACT(20)	2.432902E18

Program 8.7: Creating a table of integers and factorials

```
***Primary function: FACT;

DATA FACTORIAL;
   DO N = 1 TO 12;
      FACTORIAL_N = FACT(N);
      OUTPUT;
   END;
   FORMAT FACTORIAL_N COMMA12.;
RUN;

PROC PRINT DATA=FACTORIAL NOOBS;
   TITLE "Listing of Data Set FACTORIAL";
RUN;
```

```
             Listing of Data Set FACTORIAL

              N      FACTORIAL_N

              1                1
              2                2
              3                6
              4               24
              5              120
              6              720
              7            5,040
              8           40,320
              9          362,880
             10        3,628,800
             11       39,916,800
             12      479,001,600
```

Function: **GAMMA**

Purpose: To compute the value of the Gamma function. For positive integers,
Gamma(X) = (X − 1)!.

Syntax: GAMMA(*numeric-value*)

numeric-value is a numeric variable or expression greater than or equal
to 0.

Examples

Function	Returns
GAMMA(4)	6
GAMMA(1)	1
GAMMA(4.5)	11.631728397

Program 8.8: Demonstrating the GAMMA function

```
***Primary function: GAMMA;

DATA TABLE;
   DO X = 1 TO 5 BY .05;
      GAMMA = GAMMA(X);
      OUTPUT;
   END;
RUN;

ODS RTF FILE='C:\BOOKS\FUNCTIONS\GAMMA.RTF';
GOPTIONS DEVICE=JPEG;
SYMBOL V=NONE I=SM;
PROC GPLOT DATA=TABLE;
   TITLE "Graph of Gamma Function from 1 to 5";
   PLOT GAMMA * X;
RUN;
ODS RTF CLOSE;
```

Explanation

Since the GAMMA function is not restricted to integers, this program computes the value of the GAMMA function from 1 to 5 with increments of .05. The GPLOT procedure is used to display this graph.

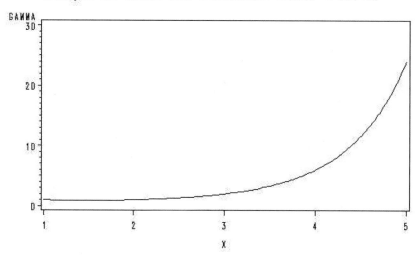

Graph of Gamma Function from 1 to 5

C h a p t e r   9

Random Number Functions

Introduction

This chapter focuses on the random number functions—functions that produce pseudo-random values according to a particular distribution. (Since computers can't create truly random numbers, the term pseudo-random numbers is the technically correct description of any computer-generated series of numbers. However, in this chapter, we will go ahead and call these **random numbers**.)

Only two of the numerous random number functions are described here. These are the two most widely used functions. See the SAS OnlineDoc for a list of the available random number distributions. Note: The wording of arguments in this book might differ from the wording of arguments in the *SAS OnlineDoc 9.1*.

Although most of the programs focus on statistical applications, you may find it useful to take a random subset of a SAS data set or to randomly generate test data sets whether you are a statistician or a non-statistician.

A Word about Random Number Seeds

It is important to understand how SAS generates a series of random numbers using the random number functions and the call routines. There are some important differences.

All of the random number functions share a common series of seeds. The random number functions can either use a seed that you supply (in which case you get the same series of random numbers every time you run the same DATA step) or a 0, in which case the first seed is generated using the computer clock. Regardless of what seed you designate for any subsequent uses of any random functions in your DATA step, it is only the **first** seed that matters in the random number functions.

If you choose to use one of the random number call routines, you can choose a new seed value any time you want. In addition, you can have a separate seed stream for each of several random number generators in your program.

To clarify how seed values affect a series of random numbers, look at the two programs below:

Program 9.1: Demonstrating differences between random functions and call routines (function example)

```
DATA RAN_FUNCTION;
   DO N = 1 TO 3;
      X = RANUNI(1234);
      Y = RANUNI(0);
      OUTPUT;
   END;
RUN;

PROC PRINT DATA=RAN_FUNCTION NOOBS;
   TITLE "Listing of Data Set RAN_FUNCTION - First Run";
RUN;

PROC PRINT DATA=RAN_FUNCTION NOOBS;
   TITLE "Listing of Data Set RAN_FUNCTION - Second Run";
RUN;
```

Explanation

This program demonstrates how seed values affect the results of random number functions. Notice in the listing below, that when this program is run twice, you get the same series of random numbers for both X and Y, even though you used a value of 0 for the seed of Y.

```
Listing of Data Set RAN_FUNCTION - First Run

N      X          Y

1    0.24381    0.089475
2    0.38319    0.097928
3    0.25758    0.088250

Listing of Data Set RAN_FUNCTION - Second Run

N      X          Y

1    0.24381    0.089475
2    0.38319    0.097928
3    0.25758    0.088250
```

Program 9.2: Demonstrating differences between random functions and call routines (call routine example)

```
DATA RAN_CALL;
   SEED1 = 1234;
   SEED2 = 0;
   DO N = 1 TO 3;
      CALL RANUNI(SEED1,X);
      CALL RANUNI(SEED2,Y);
      OUTPUT;
   END;
RUN;

PROC PRINT DATA=RAN_CALL NOOBS;
   TITLE "Listing of Data Set RAN_CALL - First Run";
RUN;

PROC PRINT DATA=RAN_CALL NOOBS;
   TITLE "Listing of Data Set RAN_CALL - Second Run";
RUN;
```

Explanation

Notice that the series of random numbers for Y in this example is different each time the program runs. This demonstrates one advantage of using random number call routines instead of random number functions—you can have complete control over the seed values. If you look closely at the values for X below, you will notice that the three values of X in the first three observations correspond to the first three random numbers produced in Program 9.1 (X in observation 1; Y in observation 1; X in observation 2).

```
Listing of Data Set RAN_CALL - First Run

    SEED1         SEED2        N      X         Y

  523580480     1181438451    1    0.24381    0.55015
  192146343     2112201917    2    0.08948    0.98357
  822902235     1184189980    3    0.38319    0.55143

Listing of Data Set RAN_CALL - Second Run

    SEED1         SEED2        N      X         Y

  523580480      199854308    1    0.24381    0.09306
  192146343      854037750    2    0.08948    0.39769
  822902235     2072455148    3    0.38319    0.96506
```

Functions That Generate Uniform Random Numbers

Function: **RANUNI**

Purpose: To generate a random number where each value is equally likely. The function generates uniform random numbers in the range from 0 to 1. By appropriate scaling, you can produce random numbers in any range you choose.

(Note: UNIFORM is another name for this function.)

Syntax: RANUNI(*seed*)

seed is a number less than 2,147,483,647 ($2^{31} - 1$). Every random number function needs to start with a seed, which is used to generate the first random number, and a new seed for the next time the function is executed. If the seed is less than or equal to 0, you will obtain a different series of random numbers each time you run your program (it uses the computer's clock to generate the seed). If you supply a positive seed, every time the program runs, it will produce the same series of random numbers.

Examples

Function	Returns
RANUNI(0)	Random number in the range 0 to 1 (clock-generated seed)
RANUNI(1357)	Random number in the range 0 to 1 (user-specified seed)

Program 9.3: Selecting an approximate *n*% random sample

```
***Primary function: RANUNI;

***This first DATA step generates a test data set;
DATA BIG;
   DO SUBJ = 1 TO 1000;
      OUTPUT;
   END;
RUN;

***This DATA step demonstrates how to select a random subset;
DATA RANDOM1;
   SET BIG (WHERE=(RANUNI(456) LE .10));
RUN;
```

Explanation

First, it is important to point out that the work of most of the programs in this chapter (programs that select random subsets or assign subjects to groups) can be accomplished with PROC SURVEYSELECT. However, the programs are useful in demonstrating how to use SAS random functions.

Each time the second DATA step iterates, the RANUNI function generates a random number between 0 and 1. Since a non-zero seed is supplied, this program will generate the same series of random numbers (and therefore, the same subset) each time it is run. Since all random numbers between 0 and 1 are equally likely, approximately 10% of the random numbers will be less than or equal to .10, thus selecting an approximate 10% sample.

Program 9.4: Selecting a random sample with exactly *n* observations

```
***Primary function: RANUNI;

DATA RANDOM2;
   SET BIG;
   SHUFFLE = RANUNI(0);
RUN;

PROC SORT DATA=RANDOM2;
   BY SHUFFLE;
RUN;

DATA EXACT_N;
   SET RANDOM2(DROP=SHUFFLE);
   IF _N_ GT 100 THEN STOP;
RUN;
```

Explanation

The first DATA step makes a copy of the original data set (BIG) and adds a uniform random number to each observation. Sorting the data set by the random number, in effect, shuffles the order of the observations. Finally, by using the _N_ automatic variable, you can pick off the first 100 observations (or any number you choose) to create a subset with exactly *n* observations. You would probably want to avoid using this technique on very large data sets because of the extensive time needed to perform the sort. You might use Program 9.3 to obtain a random sample that is a bit larger than you need, and then use this technique to select exactly *n* observations.

Program 9.5: Simulating random throws of two dice

```
***Primary function: RANUNI
***Other function: INT;

DATA DICE;
   DO I = 1 TO 1000; /* Generate 1000 throws */
      DIE_1 = INT(RANUNI(0)*6 + 1);
      DIE_2 = INT(RANUNI(0)*6 + 1);
      THROW = DIE_1 + DIE_2;
      OUTPUT;
   END;
RUN;
```

```
PROC FREQ DATA=DICE;
   TITLE "Frequencies of Dice Throws";
   TABLES DIE_1 DIE_2 THROW / NOCUM NOPERCENT;
RUN;
```

Explanation

The main point of this program is to demonstrate how to generate uniform random integers in a given range—in this case from 1 to 6. At first glance, you may be tempted to multiply the result of the RANUNI function by 5 and add 1. You have to remember that the maximum value that is returned by this function is 1. However, it's best to think of the returned values as ranging from 0 to just a tiny bit less than 1 (the chances that the result would be exactly 1.0 are almost 0). So, when you multiply the RANUNI function by 6, the resulting values range from 0 to just less than 6. Adding 1 moves the values from 1 to just less than 7, and taking the integer of this results in integers from 1 to 6. If you want to use the ROUND function instead of the INT function to produce integers, you need to first generate values .5 below and .5 above the range that you want.

To see that you are producing integers in the proper range, the listing from the FREQ procedure is shown below:

```
              Frequencies of Dice Throws

              The FREQ Procedure

              DIE_1     Frequency
              ─────────────────────
                 1          180
                 2          170
                 3          160
                 4          143
                 5          160
                 6          187


              DIE_2     Frequency
              ─────────────────────
                 1          160
                 2          146
                 3          187
                 4          173
```

Output (*continued*)

THROW	Frequency
5	161
6	173

THROW	Frequency
2	25
3	43
4	88
5	112
6	142
7	175
8	138
9	117
10	75
11	53
12	32

Program 9.6: Randomly assigning *n* subjects into two groups: Method 1 — Approximate number of subjects in each group

```
***Primary function: RANUNI;

DATA ASSIGN1;
   DO SUBJ = 1 TO 12;
      IF RANUNI(123) LT .5 THEN GROUP = 'A';
     ELSE GROUP = 'B';
      OUTPUT;
   END;
RUN;

PROC PRINT DATA=ASSIGN1 NOOBS;
   TITLE "List of Random Assignments";
RUN;
```

Explanation

The DO loop generates 12 subject numbers (SUBJ). Since the RANUNI function generates uniform random numbers in the range 0 to 1, the function should return a value less than .5 about half the time. When this happens, GROUP is set to 'A'. If the number is greater than or equal to .5, GROUP gets set to 'B'. By the way, there is no need to worry that the program uses a less than operator (LT) to assign subject into group A and all others into B. The probability of returning a value exactly equal to .5 is so small that it can be ignored. When you use this method of random assignment, you are not guaranteed to assign equal numbers of subjects to groups A and B. If that is important to you, use the logic in the next program.

```
                    List of Random Assignments

                      SUBJ      GROUP

                        1         B
                        2         A
                        3         A
                        4         B
                        5         A
                        6         A
                        7         B
                        8         A
                        9         A
                       10         A
                       11         B
                       12         A
```

**Program 9.7: Randomly assigning *n* subjects into two groups: Method 2 —
Equal number of subjects in each group**

```
***Primary function: RANUNI;

PROC FORMAT;
   VALUE GRPFMT 0 = 'A'  1 = 'B';
RUN;

DATA ASSIGN2;
   DO SUBJ = 1 TO 12;
      GROUP = RANUNI(123);
      OUTPUT;
   END;
RUN;

PROC RANK DATA=ASSIGN2 OUT=RANDOM GROUPS=2;
   VAR GROUP;
RUN;

PROC PRINT DATA=RANDOM NOOBS;
```

```
    TITLE "Random assignment of subjects, equal number in each group";
    ID SUBJ;
    VAR GROUP;
    FORMAT GROUP GRPFMT.;
RUN;
```

Explanation

The DATA step creates a data set consisting of 12 observations. Each observation has a subject number and a variable called GROUP, which is a random number between 0 and 1. The heart of this program is PROC RANK. This procedure is commonly used to replace data values with their ranks. The smallest value is rank 1, the next smallest value rank 2, etc. When you add the GROUPS= option to PROC RANK, the procedure places all the observations into the number of groups you specify. In this program where we have coded GROUPS=2, all values of GROUP below the median will be given the value of 0, and all values above the median will be given the value of 1. (Without the GROUPS= option, PROC RANK starts counting from 1; with the GROUPS= option, the groups begin at 0.)

So, the output data set created by PROC RANK now has a variable called GROUP with values of 0 and 1. The PRINT procedure applies the user-defined format GRPFMT to the GROUP variable so the listing consists of A's and B's. As long as there is an even number of subjects, this program can be used to randomly assign subjects to two groups with the same number of subjects in each group.

```
          Random assignment of subjects, equal number in each group

                        SUBJ      GROUP

                          1         B
                          2         A
                          3         A
                          4         B
                          5         A
                          6         A
                          7         B
                          8         B
                          9         A
                         10         A
                         11         B
                         12         B
```

**Program 9.8: Randomly assigning *n* subjects into two groups: Method 3 —
Equal number of subjects in each group within blocks of four
subjects**

```
*** Primary function: RANUNI;

DATA ASSIGN3;
   DO BLOCK = 1 TO 3;
      DO I = 1 TO 4;
         SUBJ + 1;
         GROUP = RANUNI(123);
         OUTPUT;
      END;
   END;
   DROP I;
RUN;

PROC RANK DATA=ASSIGN3 OUT=RANDOM GROUPS=2;
   BY BLOCK;
   VAR GROUP;
RUN;

PROC PRINT DATA=RANDOM NOOBS;
   TITLE "Random assignment of subjects, blocks of four";
   ID SUBJ;
   VAR GROUP;
   FORMAT GROUP GRPFMT.;
RUN;
```

Explanation

When you are assigning subjects to random groups, chance can deal you some strange
results. You may wind up with quite a few subjects in a row all in the same group. There
are times when you want to avoid this. This program assigns a random group to blocks of
four subjects. Thus, to randomly assign 12 subjects to two groups, you need to generate
three blocks of 4. With this method, you can be sure that you will not have too many
subjects in a row assigned to one group.

```
                Random assignment of subjects, blocks of four

                          SUBJ      GROUP

                            1         B
                            2         A
                            3         A
                            4         B
                            5         A
                            6         A
                            7         B
                            8         B
                            9         A
                           10         A
                           11         B
                           12         B
```

Two Macros to Assign *n* Subjects into *k* Groups

For those who need to provide random assignments of subjects for experimental purposes, the following two macros are presented. The first macro performs a simple random assignment with an equal number of subjects in each group (providing that the total number of subjects is a multiple of the number of groups). The second macro performs the same function but goes one step further by randomizing subjects within blocks to attempt to avoid long runs of subjects assigned to the same group. Since these macros are included only as a convenience to those needing to perform this function, an explanation is not included.

Program 9.9: Macro to assign *n* subjects into *k* groups

```
***Primary function: RANUNI;

***Macro to assign n subjects into k groups;
*----------------------------------------------------------------*
| Macro Name: ASSIGN                                             |
| Purpose: Random assignment of k treatments for n subjects     |
| Arguments: DSN     : Data set to hold output                  |
|            N       : Number of subjects                       |
|            K       : Number of groups                         |
|            SEED=   : Number for seed, seed is 0 if omitted    |
|            REPORT= : NO if no report is desired               |
| Example: %ASSIGN (MYDATA, 100, 4) will assign 100 subjects    |
|          into four (equal) groups                             |
| Example: %ASSIGN (MYDATA, 100, 2, SEED=123, REPORT=NO)        |
|          100 subjects assigned to two groups, the random      |
|          seed is 123 and no report is desired                 |
*----------------------------------------------------------------*;
%MACRO ASSIGN(DSN,N,K,SEED=0,REPORT=YES);
   DATA _TEMP_;
      DO SUBJ = 1 TO &N;
         GROUP = RANUNI(&SEED);
         OUTPUT;
      END;
      RUN;
   PROC RANK DATA=_TEMP_ OUT=&DSN GROUPS=&K;
      VAR GROUP;
   RUN;
   ***Increment GROUP so group numbers start with 1;
   DATA &DSN;
      SET &DSN;
      GROUP = GROUP + 1;
   RUN;
   %IF &REPORT EQ YES %THEN %DO;
      PROC REPORT DATA=&DSN NOWD PANELS=99;
         TITLE "&N of Subjects Randomly Assigned to &K Groups";
         COLUMNS SUBJ GROUP;
         DEFINE SUBJ / DISPLAY WIDTH=4 RIGHT FORMAT=4.0 'Subj';
         DEFINE GROUP / DISPLAY WIDTH=5 CENTER FORMAT=2. 'Group';
      RUN;
   %END;
   PROC DATASETS LIBRARY=WORK;
      DELETE _TEMP_;
   RUN;
   QUIT;
%MEND ASSIGN;
```

To demonstrate this macro, I provide the following calling sequence to create a SAS data set called RANDOM, with 100 subjects assigned to four groups. In addition, the sequence uses a user-selected seed of 123 and produces a report, listing the subject numbers and group assignments.

```
%ASSIGN(RANDOM,100,4,SEED=123,REPORT=YES);
```

A truncated listing from this program is shown below:

```
            100 of Subjects Randomly Assigned to 4 Groups

                Subj  Group      Subj  Group
                 1      3         52      4
                 2      2         53      4
                 3      1         54      2
                 4      4         55      4
                 5      2         56      2
                 6      1         57      3
                 7      4         58      4
                 8      2         59      1
                 9      1         60      1
                10      1         61      1
                11      4         62      1
                12      2         63      4
                13      4         64      3
                              etc.
```

Program 9.10: Macro to assign *n* subjects into *k* groups, with *b* subjects per block

```
***Primary function: RANUNI;

***Macro to assign n subjects into k groups with b subjects
   per block;
*------------------------------------------------------------*
| Macro Name: ASSIGN_BALANCE                                 |
| Purpose: Random assignment of k treatments for n subjects  |
| Arguments: DSN      : Data set to hold output              |
|            N        : Number of subjects                   |
|            K        : Number of groups                     |
|            B        : Number of subjects per block         |
|                       B must be evenly divisible by k      |
```

```
|               SEED=    : Number for seed, seed is 0 if omitted |
|               REPORT= : NO if no report is desired             |
|  Example: %ASSIGN (MYDATA, 100, 4, 20) will assign 100         |
|           subjects into four (equal) groups, with the same     |
|           number of subjects in each of the k groups in        |
|           every block of 20 subjects.                          |
|  Example: %ASSIGN (MYDATA, 100, 2, 100,SEED=123, REPORT=NO)    |
|           100 subjects assigned to two groups, the random      |
|           seed is 123 and no report is desired                 |
*----------------------------------------------------------------*;
%MACRO ASSIGN_BALANCE(DSN, N, K, B, SEED=0,REPORT=YES);
   DATA _TEMP_;
   %IF %EVAL(%SYSEVALF(&B/&K, FLOOR) - %SYSEVALF(&B/&K, CEIL))
      NE 0 %THEN %DO;
      FILE PRINT;
      PUT "The number of subjects per group (&B) is not"/
         "evenly divisible by the number of groups (&K)";
      STOP;
   %END;
      %LET N_BLOCKS = %SYSEVALF(&N/&B,FLOOR);
      DO BLOCK = 1 TO &N_BLOCKS;
         DO J = 1 TO &B;
            SUBJ + 1;
            GROUP = RANUNI(&SEED);
            OUTPUT;
         END;
      END;
   RUN;
   PROC RANK DATA=_TEMP_ OUT=&DSN GROUPS=&K;
      BY BLOCK;
      VAR GROUP;
   RUN;
   ***Increment GROUP so group numbers start with 1;
   DATA &DSN;
      SET &DSN(DROP = BLOCK);
      GROUP = GROUP + 1;
   RUN;
   %IF &REPORT EQ YES %THEN %DO;
   PROC REPORT DATA=&DSN NOWD PANELS=99;
      TITLE1 "&N of Subjects Randomly Assigned to &K Groups";
      TITLE2 "Equal number of subjects in each group of &B subjects";
      COLUMNS SUBJ GROUP;
      DEFINE SUBJ / DISPLAY WIDTH=4 RIGHT FORMAT=4.0 'Subj';
      DEFINE GROUP / DISPLAY WIDTH=5 CENTER FORMAT=2. 'Group';
   RUN;
   %END;
```

```
    PROC DATASETS LIBRARY=WORK;
       DELETE _TEMP_;
    RUN;
    QUIT;
 %MEND ASSIGN_BALANCE;
```

Function: CALL RANUNI

As discussed in the introduction to this chapter, all of the random number functions have a corresponding call routine. The syntax for all of the call routines is identical.

Purpose: To generate one or more random numbers where each value is equally likely. The function generates uniform random numbers in the range from 0 to 1. By appropriate scaling, you can produce random numbers in any range you choose.

Syntax: CALL RANUNI(*seed, value*)

seed is an integer less than 2,147,483,647 ($2^{31} - 1$). If the seed is less than or equal to 0, you obtain a different series of random numbers each time you run your program (it uses the computer's clock to generate the seed). If you supply a positive seed, every time the program runs, it will produce the same series of random numbers. You need to initialize the seed before you call RANUNI for the first time.

value is the name of a variable that will hold the uniform random number.

Examples
For these examples SEED1 = 0 and SEED2 = 1234567

Function	Returns
CALL RANUNI(SEED1, X)	A value for X in the range 0 to 1 (clock generated seed)
CALL RANUNI(SEED2, Y)	A value for Y in the range 0 to 1 (user specified seed)

See Program 9.2 for an example of the RANUNI call routine.

Functions That Generate Normally Distributed Numbers

Function: **RANNOR**

Purpose: To generate random numbers that are normally distributed. This function generates random numbers that come from a distribution with a mean of 0 and a standard deviation of 1. You can easily scale this to generate any normally distributed values. For example, to generate normally distributed numbers with a mean of 100 and a standard deviation of 10, you multiply the result of the RANNOR function by 10 and add 100.

Syntax: RANNOR(*seed*)

seed is either a 0 in which case you will obtain a different series of normally distributed random numbers each time you run your program (it uses the computer's clock to generate the seed) or a number of your choosing, in which case, every time the program runs, it produces the same series of random numbers.

Examples

Function	Returns
RANNOR(0)	A random number from a normal distribution (mean = 0, standard deviation = 1) with a machine-generated seed
RANNOR(1234)	A random number from a normal distribution (mean = 0, standard deviation = 1) with user-defined seed
10*RANNOR(0) + 100	A random number from a normal distribution (mean = 100, standard deviation = 10) with a machine-generated seed

The program that follows uses the RANNOR function to demonstrate how to run a Monte-Carlo simulation using SAS. Two groups are defined with their own mean, standard deviation, and sample size. The program then generates 1,000 sets of two samples, runs 1,000 *t* tests on the 1,000 samples, and uses the Output Delivery System (ODS) to capture the *p*-values from each of these 1,000 samples. From this, the power of the *t* tests can be determined. This same technique can be used with other distributions or other statistical tests.

Program 9.11: Demonstrating a Monte-Carlo simulation to determine the power of a *t* test

```
***Primary function: RANNOR;

/*****************************************************************
   Group 1:mean = 100 n = 8 standard deviation = 10
   Group 2:mean = 115 n = 6 standard deviation = 12
   Scores are normally distributed in each group.
   This program generates 1000 samples;
 *****************************************************************/
DATA GENERATE;
   DO BLOCK = 1 TO 1000;
      DO GROUP = 'A', 'B';
         IF GROUP = 'A' THEN DO SUBJ = 1 TO 6;
            X = RANNOR(123)*10 + 100;
            OUTPUT;
         END;
         ELSE IF GROUP = 'B' THEN DO SUBJ = 1 TO 8;
            X = RANNOR(123)*12 + 115;
            OUTPUT;
         END;
      END;
   END;
RUN;

***Test the distributions;
PROC MEANS DATA=GENERATE N MEAN STD;
   TITLE "Mean and Standard Deviation of the 1000 Samples";
   CLASS GROUP;
   VAR X;
RUN;
```

```
***Run 1000 t-tests and capture the p-values;
ODS LISTING CLOSE;
ODS OUTPUT TTESTS=WORK.P_VALUES;
PROC TTEST DATA=GENERATE;
   BY BLOCK;
   CLASS GROUP;
   VAR X;
RUN;
ODS OUTPUT CLOSE;
ODS LISTING;

***Examine the results;
DATA POWER_T;
   SET P_VALUES;
   IF PROBT LE .05 THEN RESULT = 'Power';
   ELSE RESULT = 'Beta';
RUN;
PROC TABULATE DATA=POWER_T;
   TITLE "Power of a t-test for assumptions of equal or unequal
variance";
   CLASS VARIANCES RESULT;
   TABLES VARIANCES , (RESULT ALL)*PCTN<RESULT ALL>=' ';
RUN;
PROC CHART DATA=P_VALUES;
   TITLE "Power of a T-Test with Equal Variances";
   WHERE VARIANCES = 'Equal';
   VBAR PROBT / MIDPOINTS = 0 TO .7 BY .05;
RUN;
QUIT;
```

Explanation

The first DATA step generates the 1,000 samples (the data set BLOCKS). Remember that a DO loop can use character values as well as numerical ones. Here, GROUP is first set to 'A'. Then six values of X are generated where X has a mean of 100 and a standard deviation of 10. The next time through this inner loop, GROUP gets set to 'B,' and eight values of X are generated where X has a mean of 115 and a standard deviation of 12.

Just to be sure that this DATA step is working properly, PROC MEANS is run to determine the mean and standard deviation of the 1,000 samples of GROUP 'A' and GROUP 'B'. This output is shown next:

```
            Mean and Standard Deviation of the 1000 Samples

        The MEANS Procedure

                        Analysis Variable : X

        GROUP    N Obs      N          Mean          Std Dev

        A         6000     6000     99.6789555      10.0285852

        B         8000     8000    115.0191877      11.9847446
```

Notice that these values are close to the specified values.

Next, two ODS statements are submitted. The first closes the listing file so that the output window doesn't fill up. The next ODS statement creates a SAS data set called P_VALUES, containing part of the *t* test output containing the *p*-values. To determine what goes into this data set, you need to know the names of the various output objects from each procedure. To do that, you can run the desired procedure once, preceded by the ODS TRACE statement with the ON argument to obtain a list of the output objects from that procedure. With PROC TTEST, the output object you want is called TTESTS. You will need to run a PROC PRINT on this data set to see exactly what it looks like. Having done that, you will find that the *p*-values from each of the 1,000 *t* tests were stored in a variable called PROBT. Therefore, for each sample where the p-value was less than or equal to .05, the variable RESULT was assigned a value of Power. Otherwise it was set to Beta. Running a simple PROC FREQ step would have sufficed to determine the percentage of samples where RESULT was equal to Power (the power of the test) or Beta (the beta error). In this case, the fancier listing from PROC TABULATE was used to make a prettier listing. It is shown below:

```
Power of a t-test for assumptions of equal or unequal variance
```

	RESULT		
	Beta	Power	All
Variances			
Equal	35.40	64.60	100.00
Unequal	34.60	65.40	100.00

Finally, a power curve is displayed by running PROC CHART.

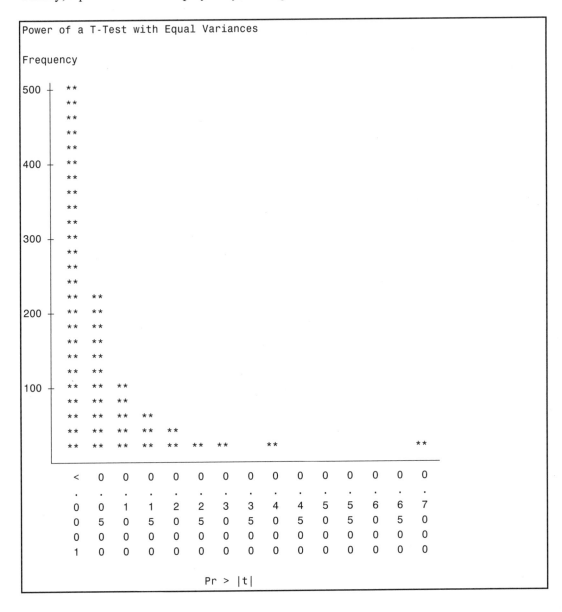

Function: CALL RANNOR

Purpose: To generate random numbers that are normally distributed. This call routine generates random numbers that come from a distribution with a mean of 0 and a standard deviation of 1. You can easily scale this to generate any normally distributed values. For example, to generate normally distributed numbers with a mean of 100 and a standard deviation of 10, you would multiply the result of the RANNOR function by 10 and add 100.

Syntax: CALL RANNOR(*seed, value*)

seed is either a 0, in which case you obtain a different series of normally distributed random numbers each time you run your program (it uses the computer's clock to generate the **seed**) or a number of your choosing, in which case *seed* produces the same series of random numbers every time the program runs.

value is the name of a variable that holds the normally distributed random number.

Examples

For these examples SEED1 = 0 and SEED2 = 1234567

Function	Returns
CALL RANNOR(SEED1, X)	A value for X from a normal distribution with a mean of 0 and a standard deviation of 1 (clock-generated seed)
CALL RANNOR(SEED2, Y)	A value for Y from a normally distributed distribution with a mean of 0 and a standard deviation of 1 (user-specified seed)

Program 9.12: Program to generate random values of heart rates that are normally distributed

```
***Primary function: RANNOR;
***Other function: ROUND;

DATA GENERATE;
   SEED = 0;
   DO SUBJ = 1 TO 100;
      CALL RANNOR(SEED, HR);
      HR = ROUND(15*HR + 70);
      OUTPUT;
   END;
RUN;

OPTIONS PS=16;
PROC REPORT DATA=GENERATE PANELS=99 NOWD;
   TITLE "Listing of Data Set GENERATE";
   COLUMNS SUBJ HR;
   DEFINE SUBJ / DISPLAY WIDTH=4;
   DEFINE HR / DISPLAY WIDTH=4 FORMAT=4.0;
RUN;
```

Explanation

The values for heart rate (HR) are generated from a normal distribution with a mean of 70 and a standard deviation of 15. Since *seed* is set to 0, you will obtain a different series of heart rates every time you run the program. PROC REPORT was used with the PANELS option so that the output could be shown in multi-column format. The listing is shown below:

```
                    Listing of Data Set GENERATE

   SUBJ    HR     SUBJ    HR     SUBJ    HR     SUBJ    HR
     53    82       66    67       79    66       92    70
     54    78       67    69       80    59       93    85
     55    61       68    79       81    72       94    86
     56    56       69    79       82    58       95   112
     57    79       70    73       83    80       96    75
     58    60       71    56       84    66       97    69
     59    99       72    85       85    65       98    88
     60    47       73    88       86    83       99    79
     61   101       74    75       87    87      100    66
     62    95       75    77       88    64
     63    56       76    45       89    92
     64    88       77    79       90    42
     65    60       78    66       91    44
```

C h a p t e r   1 0

Special Functions

Introduction

The title of this chapter may cause you to think that these functions are somehow esoteric or unimportant. In fact, these four functions are some of the most commonly used functions in the SAS arsenal—they just don't fit easily into any of the other categories of SAS functions.

Functions That Obtain Values from Previous Observations

These two functions are grouped together because of their similar applications. The LAG function returns the value of its argument the last time the function executed. If you execute the LAG function in every iteration of the DATA step, you can interpret the result of the LAG function as the value of its argument in the previous observation. There is actually a whole class of LAG and DIF functions: LAG1, LAG2, etc., which return the value from the previous iteration of the DATA step, the iteration before that, etc. Each of the family of DIF functions operates in a similar manner to the family of LAG functions except that the difference between the current value and a previous value is returned. For example, DIF(X) returns the current value of X minus the value of X the last time the DIF function executed. Thus, DIF is very useful in determining the difference between a value in the current observation and a value in a previous observation.

Functions: LAG and LAG*n*

Purpose: To obtain the value of a variable from a previous observation or *n* observations previous to the current observation.

Caution: This application of the LAG and LAG*n* functions requires that you execute the function in **every** iteration of the DATA step. If you conditionally execute a LAG*n* function, the results you get may be unexpected and unwanted.

Syntax: LAG(*value*)
LAG*n*(*value*)

value is any numeric variable.

n is the number of lagged values. LAG and LAG1 are equivalent.

Examples

For these examples, the value of X in the current observation is 9, the value of X in the previous observation is 7, and the value of X in the observation previous to that is 5.

Function	Returns
LAG(X)	7
LAG2(X)	5
LAG3(X)	missing

Program 10.1: Using the LAGn functions to compute a moving average

```
***Primary functions: LAG and LAG2
***Other function: MEAN;

***Program to compute a moving average, based on three observations;
DATA MOVING;
    INPUT X @@;
    X1 = LAG(X);
    X2 = LAG2(X);
    MOVING = MEAN(X, X1, X2);
    IF _N_ GE 3 THEN OUTPUT;
DATALINES;
1 3 9 5 7 10
;
PROC PRINT DATA=MOVING NOOBS;
    TITLE "Listing of Data Set MOVING";
RUN;
```

Explanation

In the first iteration of the DATA step, X has a value of 1; X1 and X2 are both missing. During the second iteration of the DATA step, X has a value of 3, X1 is equal to 1, and X2 is missing. Finally, in the third iteration of the DATA step, X is equal to 9, X1 is equal to 3, and X2 is equal to 1. Since _N_ is now equal to 3, the OUTPUT statement is executed, and the first observation in the data set MOVING is written out. See the listing below:

```
            Listing of Data Set MOVING

            X    X1    X2    MOVING

            9     3     1    4.33333
            5     9     3    5.66667
            7     5     9    7.00000
           10     7     5    7.33333
```

Functions: DIF and DIF*n*

Purpose: To compute the difference between a value in the current observation and a value from one or more previous observations. Note that DIF(X) is equivalent to X - LAG(X).

Syntax: DIF(*value*)
DIF*n*(*value*)

value is any numeric variable.

n is the number of lagged values. LAG and LAG1 are equivalent.

Examples

For these examples, the value of X in the current observation is 9, the value of X in the previous observation is 7, and the value of X in the observation previous to that is 5.

Function	Returns
DIF(X)	2
DIF2(X)	4
DIF3(X)	.(missing)

Program 10.2: Computing changes in blood pressure from one visit to another

```
***Primary function: DIF;
***Create a test data set of patient visits;

DATA VISITS;
   INPUT ID VISIT_DATE : MMDDYY10. SBP DBP @@;
   FORMAT VISIT_DATE DATE9.;
   LABEL SBP = 'Systolic Blood Pressure'
         DBP = 'Diastolic Blood Pressure';
DATALINES;
1 02/01/2003 180 110    1 03/02/2003 178 100   1 04/01/2003 170 90
2 03/03/2003 170 100    2 04/01/2003 172 100
3 04/01/2003 130 80     3 06/01/2003 128 82    3 08/01/2003 128 78
;
```

```
PROC SORT DATA=VISITS;
   BY ID VISIT_DATE;
RUN;

***Program to compute changes between visits;
DATA CHANGE;
   SET VISITS;
   BY ID;

   ***Delete any subject with only one visit;
   IF FIRST.ID AND LAST.ID THEN DELETE;

   DIFF_SBP = DIF(SBP);
   DIFF_DBP = DIF(DBP);
   IF NOT FIRST.ID THEN OUTPUT;
RUN;

PROC PRINT DATA=CHANGE NOOBS;
   TITLE "Listing of Data Set CHANGE";
RUN;
```

Explanation

Notice that the DIF function is executed during every iteration of the DATA step. For the first visit for subject one (the first observation in VISITS), the value of the DIF function will be missing (the current value minus a missing value). For the second visit, the DIF function will take the current value of SBP (178) minus the value from the previous visit (180) and return a value of –2. Now, what happens when the DATA stop reaches the first visit for the second subject? It is actually computing the difference between the current value of SBP (170) and the value of SBP from the previous subject! This is OK. You need to execute the DIF function for every iteration of the DATA step, but, because of the IF NOT FIRST.ID statement (a subsetting IF statement), the DATA step does not output an observation when it is processing the first visit for every patient. You need to delete any subject with only one visit or you will be computing the difference between his or her values and the last value from the previous subject. Notice that the values for the first visit for each patient are missing from the listing below:

```
                      Listing of Data Set CHANGE


                   VISIT_
            ID      DATE     SBP    DBP    DIFF_SBP   DIFF_DBP


             1    02MAR2003   178   100      -2         -10
             1    01APR2003   170    90      -8         -10
             2    01APR2003   172   100       2           0
             3    01JUN2003   128    82      -2           2
             3    01AUG2003   128    78       0          -4
```

**Program 10.3: Computing the difference in blood pressure between the
first and last visit for each patient**

```
***Primary function: DIF;
***This example uses the data set VISITS from the example above;

DATA FIRST_LAST;
   SET VISITS;
   BY ID;
   ***Note: The DIF function is being executed conditionally.
      Be VERY careful if you do this;
   ***Delete any subject with only one visit;
   IF FIRST.ID AND LAST.ID THEN DELETE;

   IF FIRST.ID OR LAST.ID THEN DO;
      DIFF_SBP = DIF(SBP);
      DIFF_DBP = DIF(DBP);
   END;
   IF LAST.ID THEN OUTPUT;
RUN;

PROC PRINT DATA=FIRST_LAST NOOBS;
   TITLE "Listing of Data Set FIRST_LAST";
RUN;
```

Explanation

This example clearly demonstrates what happens when you conditionally execute the DIF
(or LAG) function. Notice that the DIF function is executed only for the first or last visit for
each subject. As before, the value obtained during the first visit is either the current value
minus a missing value (first subject) or the current value minus the last value for the

previous subject. This is necessary to "prime the pump" and ensure that the next time the DIF function is executed, it will be computing the difference between the first and last visit. Notice also that an observation is output only when the DATA step is processing the last visit for each subject. This is a very unusual application of the DIF function and you should always use extreme care if the DIF or LAG functions are executed conditionally. As before, you need to omit the values from any subject who has only one visit. The listing below shows one observation for each subject, with the current value of SBP and DBP and the difference between the first and last visit.

```
              Listing of Data Set FIRST_LAST


              VISIT_
    ID         DATE    SBP    DBP    DIFF_SBP    DIFF_DBP


     1      01APR2003   170    90       -10         -20
     2      01APR2003   172   100        2           0
     3      01AUG2003   128    78       -2          -2
```

Functions That Perform Character-to-Numeric or Numeric-to-Character Conversion

Function: INPUT

The first two functions in this group (INPUT and PUT) are being grouped together since they have something in common: They are commonly used to perform character-to-numeric (INPUT) or numeric-to-character (PUT) conversion. These two functions may be confusing at first, but they are extremely useful once you get the hang of them.

Purpose: To perform character-to-numeric conversion. Also useful in converting character values such as dates into true SAS numeric date values.

Syntax: INPUT(*value, informat*)

value is a character variable or character expression.

informat is a SAS or user-defined informat.

Examples

For these examples N_CHAR = '123' and CHAR_DATE = '10/21/1980'

Function	Returns
INPUT(N_CHAR,3.)	123 (numeric)
INPUT(N_CHAR,9.)	123 (numeric)
INPUT(CHAR_DATE,MMDDYY10.)	7599 (equals 10/21/1980)

Program 10.4: Using the INPUT function to perform character-to-numeric conversion

```
***Primary function: INPUT;
***Create test data set;

DATA CHAR;
   INPUT NUM $ DATE1 : $10. DATE2 : $9. MONEY : $12.;
DATALINES;
123 10/21/1980 21OCT1980 $123,000.45
XYZ 11/11/2003 01JAN1960 $123
;
DATA CONVERT;
   SET CHAR(RENAME=(NUM=C_NUM));
   NUM = INPUT(C_NUM,9.);
   SASDATE1 = INPUT(DATE1,MMDDYY10.);
   SASDATE2 = INPUT(DATE2,DATE9.);
   DOLLAR = INPUT(MONEY,COMMA12.);
   FORMAT SASDATE1 SASDATE2 MMDDYY10.;
RUN;

PROC PRINT DATA=CONVERT NOOBS;
   TITLE "Listing of Data Set CONVERT";
RUN;
```

Explanation

All the variables in the CHAR data set are character. Although you can force SAS to do a character-to-numeric conversion by multiplying the character variable by 1 or adding 0, that causes SAS to write messages to the log, and is considered by most SAS programmers to be sloppy programming. In this example, the user wanted to use the same variable name (NUM) for the numeric variable that was in the CHAR data set as a character variable. The usual trick is to use the RENAME= data set option to rename the character variable, which allows you to keep the same name for the numeric equivalent. A SAS variable cannot be both a character and a numeric value at the same time.

The two dates were read as character values (this happens frequently when you are importing dates from various data bases or spread sheets). The INPUT function allows you to "reread" these values using the correct SAS date informats. Finally, the value with dollar signs and commas is converted to a numeric value by using the comma informat. Although not readily apparent, the dates in the listing below are true SAS dates which have been formatted using the MMDDYY10. format.

```
                    Listing of Data Set CONVERT

          C_NUM      DATE1          DATE2         MONEY

           123     10/21/1980     21OCT1980     $123,000.45
           XYZ     11/11/2003     01JAN1960     $123


           NUM     SASDATE1       SASDATE2       DOLLAR

           123     10/21/1980     10/21/1980    123000.45
            .      11/11/2003     01/01/1960       123.00
```

If you examine the SAS log (shown below), you will see a note there that the character value of XYZ could not be read with a numeric informat.

```
NOTE: Invalid argument to function INPUT at line 203 column 10.
C_NUM=XYZ DATE1=11/11/2003 DATE2=01JAN1960 MONEY=$123 NUM=.
SASDATE1=11/11/2003 SASDATE2=01/01/1960 DOLLAR=123 _ERROR_=1 _N_=2
NOTE: Mathematical operations could not be performed at the following
      places. The results of the operations have been set to missing
      values.
      Each place is given by: (Number of times) at (Line):(Column).
      1 at 203:10
```

To avoid error messages in the SAS log, you can use a ?? modifier with the INPUT function, much in the same way as you can with the INPUT statement. So, if you rewrote the line in question like this, there would be no errors listed in the SAS log.

```
INPUT (C_NUM,?? 9.);
```

Function: INPUTC

The next two functions in this group (INPUTC and INPUTN) are similar to the INPUT function with one important difference: They can assign the informat at run time. The INPUTC function is used for character informats and the INPUTN function is used with numeric formats. These functions are useful when you want to select an informat from information obtained from the data itself.

Purpose: Similar to the INPUT function except that the character informat can be assigned at run time.

Syntax: INPUTC(*value, char-informat*)

value is a character variable or character expression.

char-informat is a SAS or user-defined informat.

Examples

For these examples INFOR1 = "$GENDER.", INFOR2 = "$YESNO.", VALUE1 = "1", and VALUE2 = "2" ($GENDER AND $YESNO are user written informats)

Function	Returns
INPUTC(VALUE1, INFOR1)	"Male"
INPUTC(VALUE2, INFOR2)	"Yes"

Program 10.5: Using the INPUTC function to specify an informat at run time

```
***Primary function: INPUTC
***Other functions: PUT;

PROC FORMAT;
   INVALUE $CODEA 'A' = 'Chair'
                  'B' = 'Desk'
                  'C' = 'Table';
   INVALUE $CODEB 'A' = 'Office Chair'
                  'B' = 'Big Desk'
                  'C' = 'Coffee Table';
```

```
      VALUE CODE 1 = '$CODEA.'
                 2 = '$CODEB.';
   RUN;

   DATA ITEMS;
      INPUT YEAR LETTER : $1. @@;
      LENGTH ITEM $ 12;
      ITEM = INPUTC(LETTER, PUT(YEAR, CODE.));
   DATALINES;
   1 A  1 B  2 A  1 C  2 C  2 B
   ;
   PROC PRINT DATA=ITEMS NOOBS;
      TITLE "Listing of Data Set ITEMS";
   RUN;
```

Explanation

In this example, there are two sets of codes for office furniture, described by the two informats $CODEA and $CODEB. The variable YEAR, read in as a data value, tells the program which informat to use. If YEAR is equal to 1, the result of PUT(YEAR, CODE.) is the character value "$CODEA." If YEAR is 2, the PUT function returns "$CODEB." This value is then used in the INPUTC function in the next line. Reading an "A" using the $CODEA informat results in the value "Chair." Reading an "A" using the $CODEB informat results in the value "Office Chair," etc. A listing of data set ITEMS is shown below:

```
                  Listing of Data Set ITEMS

            YEAR     LETTER     ITEM

             1         A        Chair
             1         B        Desk
             2         A        Office Chair
             1         C        Table
             2         C        Coffee Table
             2         B        Big Desk
```

Function: INPUTN

Purpose: Similar to the INPUT function except that the numeric informat can be assigned at run time.

Syntax: INPUTN(*value, num-informat*)

value is a character variable or character expression.

num-informat is a SAS or user-defined informat.

Examples

For these examples DATE1 = "10/21/1980", DATE2 = "21OCT1980", INFOR1 = "MMDDYY!).", and INFOR2 = "DATE9."

Function	Returns
INPUTN(DATE1, INFOR1)	7599
INPUTN(DATE2, INFOR2)	7599

Program 10.6: Using the INPUTN function to read dates in mixed formats

```
***Primary function: INPUTN
***Other function: PUT;

PROC FORMAT;
   VALUE WHICH 1 = 'MMDDYY10.'
               2 = 'DATE9.';
RUN;

DATA MIXED_DATES;
   INPUT WHICH_ONE DUMMY : $10.;
   DATE = INPUTN(DUMMY, PUT(WHICH_ONE, WHICH.));
   FORMAT DATE WEEKDATE.;
DATALINES;
1 10/21/1980
2 21OCT1980
1 01/01/1960
2 03NOV2003
;
```

```
PROC PRINT DATA=MIXED_DATES NOOBS;
   TITLE "Listing of Data Set MIXED_DATES";
RUN;
```

Explanation

Although there are simpler ways to solve this problem of mixed-date formats, this solution helps demonstrate the INPUTN function. The informat to use as the second argument of the INPUTN function is obtained by the result of the PUT function and the WHICH format. When the variable WHICH_ONE is equal to 1, the statement PUT(WHICH_ONE, WHICH.) returns the character value "MMDDYY10." When WHICH_ONE is equal to 2, the PUT function returns the value "DATE9." The INPUTN function uses these values at run time to determine which informat to use to read the date properly. The data set MIXED_DATES is shown below:

```
                    Listing of Data Set MIXED_DATES

      WHICH_
       ONE       DUMMY                    DATE

        1       10/21/1980     Tuesday, October 21, 1980
        2       21OCT1980      Tuesday, October 21, 1980
        1       01/01/1960       Friday, January 1, 1960
        2       03NOV2003      Monday, November 3, 2003
```

Function: **PUT**

Purpose: To perform numeric-to-character conversion or to create a character variable from a user-defined format. The result of a PUT function is always a character value.

Syntax: **PUT(*value, format*)**

value is a character or numeric SAS variable or expression.

format is a SAS or user-defined format.

Examples

For these examples, let X = 3 (numeric), DATE = "21OCT1980"

Function	Returns
PUT(X,3.)	"3" (character)
PUT(7599,MMDDYY10.)	"10/21/1980"
PUT(INPUT(DATE, DATE9.), MMDDYY10.)	"21OCT1980"
PUT(X, WEEKDATE3.)	"Mon"

Program 10.7: Performing a table look-up using a format and the PUT function

```
***Primary functions: PUT, INPUT;

PROC FORMAT;
   VALUE ITEM 1 = 'APPLE'
              2 = 'PEAR'
              3 = 'GRAPE'
              OTHER = 'UNKNOWN';
   VALUE $COST 'A' - 'C' = '44.45'
               'D'       = '125.'
               OTHER     = ' ';
RUN;

DATA TABLE;
   INPUT ITEM_NO CODE $ @@;
   ITEM_NAME = PUT(ITEM_NO, ITEM.);
   AMOUNT = INPUT(PUT(CODE, $COST.),9.);
DATALINES;
1 B   2 D   3 X   4 C
;
PROC PRINT DATA=TABLE NOOBS;
   TITLE "Listing of Data Set TABLE";
RUN;
```

Explanation

In order to associate an item name with the item number, the PUT function takes the formatted value of the item number and assigns this value to the character variable ITEM_NAME. The result of using the PUT function with the variable COST are the character values defined by the $COST format. Since the result of a PUT function is always a character value, in order to obtain the amount as a numeric value, the INPUT function

performs a character-to-numeric conversion. In the listing below, the variable AMOUNT is
a numeric value.

```
                 Listing of Data Set TABLE


                            ITEM_
        ITEM_NO    CODE     NAME       AMOUNT


           1        B       APPLE       44.45
           2        D       PEAR       125.00
           3        X       GRAPE          .
           4        C       UNKNOWN     44.45
```

Function: PUTC

Just as with the INPUTC and INPUTN functions, the last two functions in this group (PUTC
and PUTN) allow you to specify a character or numeric format at run time, respectively.

Purpose: Similar to the PUT function except that the character format can be assigned
at run time.

Syntax: PUTC(*value, char-format*)

value is a character variable or character expression.

char-format is a SAS or user-defined character format.

Examples

For these examples FOR1 = "$GENDER.", FOR2 = "$YESNO.", VALUE1 = 1,
and VALUE2 = 2 ($GENDER and $YESNO are user-written character formats)

Function	Returns
PUTC(VALUE1, FOR1)	"Male"
PUTC(VALUE2, FOR2)	"Yes"

Program 10.8: Using the PUTC function to assign a value to a character variable at run time

```
***Primary function: PUTC
***Other function: PUT;

PROC FORMAT;
   VALUE $TOOL '1' = 'Hammer'
               '2' = 'Pliers'
               '3' = 'Saw';
   VALUE $SUPPLY '1' = 'Paper'
                 '2' = 'Pens'
                 '3' = 'Paperclips';
   VALUE TYPE 1 = '$TOOL.'
              2 = '$SUPPLY.';
RUN;

DATA TOOLS_SUPPLIES;
   INPUT TYPE VALUE $;
   LENGTH NAME $ 10;
   FORMAT = PUT(TYPE, TYPE.);
   NAME = PUTC(VALUE, FORMAT);
DATALINES;
1 1
2 1
1 2
2 3
;
PROC PRINT DATA=TOOLS_SUPPLIES NOOBS;
   TITLE "Listing of Data Set TOOLS_SUPPLIES";
RUN;
```

Explanation

In this program, the PUT function, along with a format, assigns the proper value to the variable FORMAT. This, in turn, is used in the PUTC function to supply the proper character format (either $TOOLS or $SUPPLY) to use in the PUTC function. A listing of data set TOOLS_SUPPLIES is shown below:

```
        Listing of Data Set TOOLS_SUPPLIES

     TYPE    VALUE    NAME          FORMAT

       1       1      Hammer        $TOOL.
       2       1      Paper         $SUPPLY.
       1       2      Pliers        $TOOL.
       2       3      Paperclips    $SUPPLY.
```

Function: **PUTN**

Purpose: Similar to the PUT function except that the numeric format can be assigned at run time.

Syntax: PUTN(*value, numeric-format*)

value is a character variable or character expression.

numeric-format is a SAS or user-defined numeric format.

Examples

For these examples FOR1 = "GENDER.", FOR2 = "YESNO.", VALUE1 = 1, and VALUE2 = 2 (GENDER and YESNO are user-written numeric formats)

Function	Returns
PUTC(VALUE1, FOR1)	"Male"
PUTC(VALUE2, FOR2)	"Yes"

Program 10.9: Using the PUTN function to assign a value to a character variable at run time

```
***Primary function: PUTN;

PROC FORMAT;
    VALUE TOOL 1 = 'Hammer'
               2 = 'Pliers'
               3 = 'Saw';
    VALUE SUPPLY 1 = 'Paper'
                 2 = 'Pens'
                 3 = 'Paperclips';
RUN;
DATA TOOLS_SUPPLIES;
    INPUT TYPE $ VALUE;
    NAME = PUTN(VALUE, TYPE);
DATALINES;
TOOL. 1
SUPPLY. 1
TOOL. 2
SUPPLY. 2
;
PROC PRINT DATA=TOOLS_SUPPLIES NOOBS;
    TITLE "Listing of Data Set TOOLS_SUPPLIES";
RUN;
```

Explanation

To keep this program very simple, the actual format (TOOL or SUPPLY) was read into the variable TYPE. This value was then used in the PUTN function to translate the numeric values into either a list of tools or a list of supplies. A listing of TOOLS_SUPPLIES is shown next:

```
              Listing of Data Set TOOLS_SUPPLIES

              TYPE        VALUE      NAME

              TOOL.         1        Hammer
              SUPPLY.       1        Paper
              TOOL.         2        Pliers
              SUPPLY.       2        Pens
```

Chapter 11

State and Zip Code Functions

Introduction

This group of functions allows you to convert between FIPS (Federal Information Processing Standards) codes, zip codes, two-digit state postal codes, and state names and abbreviations. For example, these functions let you store a zip code and print out a state name or abbreviation, computed from the code.

Functions That Convert FIPS Codes

This group of functions takes a FIPS code as an argument and produces either an uppercase state name, a mixed-case state name, or a two-character standard state abbreviation.

Function: **FIPNAME**

Purpose: To convert a FIPS code to an uppercase state name.

Syntax: `FIPNAME(FIPS-code)`

`FIPS-code` is a numeric variable or an expression that represents a standard FIPS code.

Examples

For these examples, `FIPS1 = 27, FIPS2 = 2`

Function	Returns
FIPNAME(FIPS1)	MINNESOTA
FIPNAME(FIPS2)	ALASKA
FIPNAME(34)	NEW JERSEY
FIPNAME(999)	Error written to the SAS log

See Program 11.1 for a sample program.

Function: **FIPNAMEL**

Purpose: To convert a FIPS code to a mixed-case state name.

Syntax: `FIPNAMEL(FIPS-code)`

`FIPS-code` is a numeric variable or an expression that represents a standard FIPS code.

Examples

For these examples, FIPS1 = 27, FIPS2 = 2

Function	Returns
FIPNAMEL(FIPS1)	Minnesota
FIPNAMEL(FIPS2)	Alaska
FIPNAMEL(34)	New Jersey
FIPNAMEL(999)	Error written to the SAS log

See Program 11.1 for a sample program.

Function: FIPSTATE

Purpose: To convert a FIPS code to a two-character state code.

Syntax: FIPSTATE(*FIPS-code*)

FIPS-code is a numeric variable or an expression that represents a standard FIPS code.

Examples

For these examples, FIPS1 = 27, FIPS2 = 2

Function	Returns
FIPSTATE(FIPS1)	MN
FIPSTATE(FIPS2)	AL
FIPSTATE(34)	NJ
FIPSTATE(999)	Error written to the SAS log

Program 11.1: Converting FIPS codes to state names and abbreviations

```
***Primary functions: FIPNAME, FIPNAMEL, and FIPSTATE;

DATA FIPS;
   INPUT FIPS @@;
   UPPER_STATE = FIPNAME(FIPS);
   MIXED_STATE = FIPNAMEL(FIPS);
   ABBREV      = FIPSTATE(FIPS);
DATALINES;
1 2 3 4 5 34 . 50 95 99
;
PROC PRINT DATA=FIPS NOOBS;
   TITLE "Listing of Data Set FIPS";
RUN;
```

Explanation

This straightforward program converts each of the FIPS codes to an uppercase and a mixed-case state name as well as a two-character state abbreviation. When the argument for these functions is not a valid FIPS code (which range from 1 to 95, as of this writing), the state name is "INVALID CODE" (in either upper- or mixed-case) or two dashes for the state abbreviation (for example, the FIPS code 3). FIPS codes resulting in locations outside the U.S. result in territory names as values and values of – – for the state abbreviations (for example, FIPS code 95). A missing value produces blanks for all three values. Values greater than the number of valid FIPS codes cause an error message to be printed to the log, and missing values result from all three functions. You can verify this by inspecting the listing below:

```
                    Listing of Data Set FIPS

      FIPS    UPPER_STATE      MIXED_STATE      ABBREV

        1     ALABAMA          Alabama          AL
        2     ALASKA           Alaska           AK
        3     INVALID CODE     Invalid Code     --
        4     ARIZONA          Arizona          AZ
        5     ARKANSAS         Arkansas         AR
       34     NEW JERSEY       New Jersey       NJ
        .
       50     VERMONT          Vermont          VT
       95     PALMYRA ATOLL    Palmyra Atoll    --
       99
```

Functions That Convert State Codes

This set of functions all take two-character state codes and return FIPS codes or state names.

Function: **STFIPS**

Purpose: To convert a two-character state code (e.g., 'NJ') to a FIPS code.

Syntax: STFIPS(*state-code*)

state-code is a two-character standard state abbreviation. This can be a SAS character variable, an expression, or a character constant and can be in upper- or lowercase.

Examples

For these examples, STATE1 = 'NJ' and STATE2 = 'nc'

Function	Returns
STFIPS(STATE1)	34
STFIPS(STATE2)	37
STFIPS('TX')	48
STFIPS('XX')	missing value

See Program 11.2 for a sample program.

Function: **STNAME**

Purpose: Takes a two-character state code (e.g., 'NJ') and returns a state name in uppercase letters.

Syntax: STNAME(*state-code*)

state-code is a two-character standard state abbreviation. This can be a SAS character variable, an expression, or a character constant and can be in upper- or lowercase.

Examples

For these examples, STATE1 = 'NJ' and STATE2 = 'nc'

Function	Returns
STNAME(STATE1)	NEW JERSEY
STNAME(STATE2)	NORTH CAROLINA
STNAME('TX')	TEXAS

See Program 11.2 for a sample program.

Function: **STNAMEL**

Purpose: To convert a two-character state code (e.g., 'NJ') to a state name in mixed case.

Syntax: STNAME(*state-code*)

state-code is a two-character standard state abbreviation. This can be a SAS character variable, an expression, or a character constant and can be in upper- or lowercase.

Examples

For these examples, STATE1 = 'NJ' and STATE2 = 'nc'

Function	Returns
STNAME(STATE1)	New Jersey
STNAME(STATE2)	North Carolina
STNAME('TX')	Texas

Program 11.2: Converting state abbreviations to zip codes, FIPS codes, and state names

```
***Primary functions: STFIPS, STNAME, and STNAMEL;

DATA STATE_TO_OTHER;
   INPUT STATE : $2. @@;
   FIPS = STFIPS(STATE);
   UPPER_NAME = STNAME(STATE);
   MIXED_NAME = STNAMEL(STATE);
DATALINES;
NY NJ nj NC AL
;
PROC PRINT DATA=STATE_TO_OTHER NOOBS;
   TITLE "Listing of Data Set STATE_TO_OTHER";
RUN;
```

Explanation

This program uses the three ST functions to take a two-letter state abbreviation (in upper- or lowercase) and output a FIPS code or a state name. See the listing below:

```
            Listing of Data Set STATE_TO_OTHER

         STATE    FIPS    UPPER_NAME        MIXED_NAME

          NY       36     NEW YORK          New York
          NJ       34     NEW JERSEY        New Jersey
          nj       34     NEW JERSEY        New Jersey
          NC       37     NORTH CAROLINA    North Carolina
          AL        1     ALABAMA           Alabama
```

Functions That Convert Zip Codes

These four functions take a character or numeric zip code and return FIPS codes, state names (uppercase or mixed case), and state abbreviations.

Function: **ZIPFIPS**

Purpose: To convert a zip code (character or numeric) to a two-digit FIPS code (numeric).

Syntax: ZIPFIPS(*zip-code*)

zip-code is a numeric variable, expression, or constant (for a zip code starting with 0, the leading 0 is not necessary) or a character variable, expression, or constant.

Examples

For these examples, ZIPN = 12345, ZIPC = '08822'

Function	Returns
ZIPFIPS(ZIPN)	36
ZIPFIPS(ZIPC)	34
ZIPFIPS(2*12222)	51

See Program 11.3 for a sample program.

Function: **ZIPNAME**

Purpose: To convert a zip code (character or numeric) to a state name (in uppercase).

Syntax: ZIPNAME(*zip-code*)

zip-code is a numeric variable, expression, or constant (for a zip code starting with 0, the leading 0 is not necessary) or a character variable, expression, or constant.

Examples

For these examples, ZIPN = 12345, ZIPC = '08822'

Function	Returns
ZIPNAME(ZIPN)	"NEW YORK"
ZIPNAME(ZIPC)	"NEW JERSEY"
ZIPNAME(2*12222)	"VIRGINIA"

See Program 11.3 for a sample program.

Function: ZIPNAMEL

Purpose: To convert a zip code (character or numeric) to a state name (in mixed case).

Syntax: ZIPNAMEL(*zip-code*)

zip-code is a numeric variable, expression, or constant (for a zip code starting with 0, the leading 0 is not necessary) or a character variable, expression, or constant.

Examples

For these examples, ZIPN = 12345, ZIPC = '08822'

Function	Returns
ZIPNAMEL(ZIPN)	"New York"
ZIPNAMEL(ZIPC)	"New Jersey"
ZIPNAMEL(2*12222)	"Virginia"

See Program 11.3 for a sample program.

Function: ZIPSTATE

Purpose: To convert a zip code (character or numeric) to a standard two-character state abbreviation.

Syntax: ZIPSTATE(*zip-code*)

zip-code is a numeric variable, expression, or constant (for a zip code starting with 0, the leading 0 is not necessary) or a character variable, expression, or constant.

Examples

For these examples, ZIPN = 12345, ZIPC = '08822'

Function	Returns
ZIPSTATE(ZIPN)	"NY"
ZIPSTATE(ZIPC)	"NJ"
ZIPSTATE(2*12222)	"VA"

Program 11.3: Converting zip codes to FIPS codes, state names, and state abbreviations

```
***Primary functions: ZIPFIPS, ZIPNAME, ZIPNAMEL, and ZIPSTATE;

DATA ZIP_TO_OTHER;
   INPUT ZIP @@;
   FIPS = ZIPFIPS(ZIP);
   STATE_CAPS = ZIPNAME(ZIP);
   STATE_MIXED = ZIPNAMEL(ZIP);
   STATE_ABBRE = ZIPSTATE(ZIP);
   FORMAT ZIP Z5.;
DATALINES;
1234 12345 08822 98765
;
PROC PRINT DATA=ZIP_TO_OTHER NOOBS;
   TITLE "Listing of Data Set ZIP_TO_OTHER";
RUN;
```

Explanation

This program uses a numeric value for the zip code (remember, these functions can also take character arguments) and returns the FIPS code, the state name (uppercase and mixed case), and standard state abbreviations. See the listing below:

```
                    Listing of Data Set ZIP_TO_OTHER


                                                      STATE_
       ZIP    FIPS    STATE_CAPS      STATE_MIXED      ABBRE

      01234    25     MASSACHUSETTS   Massachusetts     MA
      12345    36     NEW YORK        New York          NY
      08822    34     NEW JERSEY      New Jersey        NJ
      98765    53     WASHINGTON      Washington        WA
```

Program 11.4: Adding a state abbreviation to an address containing only city and zip code

```
***Primary function: ZIPSTATE;

DATA ADDRESS;
   INPUT #1 NAME $30.
         #2 STREET $40.
         #3 CITY & $20. ZIP;
   STATE = ZIPSTATE(ZIP);

   FILE PRINT;
   ***Create Mailing list;
   PUT NAME /
       STREET /
       CITY +(-1) ", " STATE ZIP Z5.//;
DATALINES;
Mr. James Joyce
123 Sesame Street
East Rockaway  11518
Mrs. Deborah Goldstein
87 Hampton Corner Road
Flemington  08822
;
```

Explanation

This program reads in three lines of an address. Note that in the third line, only a city and zip code are entered. The program uses the ZIPSTATE function to obtain the two-character state abbreviation and insert it into the address. Note the use of the ampersand informat modifier on the third line of the INPUT statement. This causes the delimiter to be two or more blanks, so that city names containing blanks can be read correctly. Notice that there are at least two blanks between the city name and the zip code. The addresses are then sent to the output device, using PUT statements (see below).

```
                    Mr. James Joyce
                    123 Sesame Street
                    East Rockaway, NY 11518


                    Mrs. Deborah Goldstein
                    87 Hampton Corner Road
                    Flemington, NJ 08822
```

C h a p t e r   1 2

Trigonometric Functions

Introduction

Rather than cover all the trigonometric functions, I've decided to demonstrate just the three basic ones and their inverses. The remaining trigonometric functions work essentially the same way and their use is left as an "exercise for the reader."   The salient point to remember when dealing with the trigonometric functions is that the angles are always expressed in radians.

Three Basic Trigonometric Functions

All three functions are demonstrated in the single program that follows the syntax and examples.

Function: COS

Purpose: To compute the cosine of an angle (expressed in radians).

Syntax: COS(*angle*)

angle is the angle in radians. Note: multiply the angle in degrees by $\pi/180$ to convert to radians. For example, the cosine of 60 degrees (1.0472 radians) is equal to .5.

Examples

Function	Returns
COS(0)	1
COS(.5236)	.8660

Note: .5236 radians = 30 degrees.

Function: SIN

Purpose: To compute the sine of an angle (expressed in radians).

Syntax: SIN(*angle*)

angle is the angle in radians. Note: multiply the angle in degrees by $\pi/180$ to convert to radians. For example, the sine of 30 degrees (.5236 radians) is equal to .5.

Examples

Function	Returns
SIN(0)	0
SIN(.5236)	.5

Note: .5236 radians = 30 degrees.

Function: **TAN**

Purpose: To compute the tangent of an angle (expressed in radians).

Syntax: TAN(*angle*)

angle is the angle in radians. Note: multiply the angle in degrees by $\pi/180$ to convert to radians. For example, the tangent of 45 degrees (.7854 radians) is equal to 1.

Examples

Function	Returns
TAN(0)	0
TAN(.5236)	.5774

Note: .5236 radians = 30 degrees.

Program 12.1: Creating a table of trigonometric functions

```
***Primary functions: COS, SIN, TAN
***Other function: CONSTANT;

DATA TRIG_TABLE;
   IF _N_ = 1 THEN PI = CONSTANT('PI');
   RETAIN PI;

   DO ANGLE = 0 TO 360 BY 10;
      RADIAN = PI*ANGLE/180;
      SIN = SIN(RADIAN);
      COS = COS(RADIAN);
      TAN = TAN(RADIAN);
      OUTPUT;
   END;

   DROP PI RADIAN;
RUN;

OPTIONS LS=22 MISSING='-';
PROC REPORT DATA=TRIG_TABLE NOWD PANELS=99;
   TITLE "Table of Basic Trig Functions";
```

```
   COLUMNS ANGLE SIN COS TAN;
   DEFINE ANGLE / DISPLAY 'Angle' WIDTH=5 FORMAT=4.;
   DEFINE SIN / DISPLAY 'Sin' WIDTH=6 FORMAT=6.4;
   DEFINE COS / DISPLAY 'Cos' WIDTH=6 FORMAT=6.4;
   DEFINE TAN / DISPLAY 'Tan' WIDTH=6 FORMAT=6.2;
RUN;
```

Explanation

The CONSTANT function is a convenient way to obtain an accurate value for π. With efficiency in the back (or front) of your mind, you realize you don't want to compute this value for each iteration of the DATA step. The IF-THEN statement (IF _N_ = 1) ensures that the calculation is performed only once and the RETAIN statement ensures that the value does not get replaced by a missing value as the DATA step iterates.

In this program, to make the output smaller, I set up the trigonometric table to show the values for every 10 degrees. To make the output look nicer than the standard PROC PRINT output and to print multiple columns on a single page, I used PROC REPORT. One of my main reasons for using PROC REPORT (since I do very little fancy reporting) is to use the PANELS option. If you set the value to a large number (such as 99), PROC REPORT will fit as many panels as it can on the page, provided that the number of lines of output is greater than the pagesize value (PAGESIZE was set to 22 for this program.). The nice-looking table produced by this report is shown below:

```
                Table of Basic Trig Functions

   Angle    Sin     Cos     Tan      Angle    Sin     Cos     Tan
       0  0.0000  1.0000   0.00        190  -.1736  -.9848   0.18
      10  0.1736  0.9848   0.18        200  -.3420  -.9397   0.36
      20  0.3420  0.9397   0.36        210  -.5000  -.8660   0.58
      30  0.5000  0.8660   0.58        220  -.6428  -.7660   0.84
      40  0.6428  0.7660   0.84        230  -.7660  -.6428   1.19
      50  0.7660  0.6428   1.19        240  -.8660  -.5000   1.73
      60  0.8660  0.5000   1.73        250  -.9397  -.3420   2.75
      70  0.9397  0.3420   2.75        260  -.9848  -.1736   5.67
      80  0.9848  0.1736   5.67        270  -1.000  -.0000     -
      90  1.0000  0.0000     -         280  -.9848  0.1736  -5.67
     100  0.9848  -.1736  -5.67        290  -.9397  0.3420  -2.75
     110  0.9397  -.3420  -2.75        300  -.8660  0.5000  -1.73
     120  0.8660  -.5000  -1.73        310  -.7660  0.6428  -1.19
     130  0.7660  -.6428  -1.19        320  -.6428  0.7660  -0.84
```

Output (*continued*)

```
140  0.6428  -.7660   -0.84      330  -.5000  0.8660   -0.58
150  0.5000  -.8660   -0.58      340  -.3420  0.9397   -0.36
160  0.3420  -.9397   -0.36      350  -.1736  0.9848   -0.18
170  0.1736  -.9848   -0.18      360  -.0000  1.0000   -0.00
180  0.0000  -1.000   -0.00
```

Three Inverse Trigonometric Functions

These functions compute the inverse of the three basic trigonometric functions. Given a value, these functions compute an angle (expressed in radians).

Function: ARCOS

Purpose: To compute the inverse cosine or arccosine. The resulting angle is in radians. To convert from radians to degrees, multiply by the fraction $(180/\pi)$. For example, the arccosine of .5 is 1.0472, which is equal to 60 degrees.

Syntax: ARCOS(*value*)

value is a numeric value between -1 and $+1$.

Examples

Function	Returns
ARCOS(.5)	1.0472 (60 degrees)
ARCOS(1)	0

See Program 12.2 for a sample program.

Function: ARSIN

Purpose: To compute the inverse sine or arcsine. The resulting angle is in radians. To convert from radians to degrees, multiply by the fraction $(180/\pi)$. For example, the arcsine of .5 is 0.5236 which is equal to 30 degrees.

Syntax: ARSIN(*value*)

value is a numeric value between –1 and +1.

Examples

Function	Returns
ARSIN(.5)	.5326 (30 degrees)
ARSIN(1)	1.5708 (90 degrees)

Program 12.2: Computing arccosines and arcsines

```
***Primary functions: ARCOS and ARSIN
***Other function: CONSTANT;

DATA ARC_D_TRIUMPH;
   IF _N_ = 1 THEN PI = CONSTANT('PI');
   RETAIN PI;
   DROP PI;

   DO VALUE = 0 TO 1 BY .1;
      COS_RADIAN = ARCOS(VALUE);
      COS_ANGLE = COS_RADIAN * 180/PI;
      SIN_RADIAN = ARSIN(VALUE);
      SIN_ANGLE = SIN_RADIAN * 180/PI;
      OUTPUT;
   END;
RUN;

PROC PRINT DATA=ARC_D_TRIUMPH NOOBS;
   TITLE "Listing of Data Set ARC_D_TRIUMPH";
RUN;
```

Explanation

For each of the values between 0 and 1, this program computes the angle in radians and degrees, corresponding to the arccosine and arcsine values. The listing is shown below:

```
              Listing of Data Set ARC_D_TRIUMPH

                  COS_        COS_        SIN_        SIN_
       VALUE     RADIAN      ANGLE      RADIAN      ANGLE

        0.0      1.57080    90.0000    0.00000     0.0000
        0.1      1.47063    84.2608    0.10017     5.7392
        0.2      1.36944    78.4630    0.20136    11.5370
        0.3      1.26610    72.5424    0.30469    17.4576
        0.4      1.15928    66.4218    0.41152    23.5782
        0.5      1.04720    60.0000    0.52360    30.0000
        0.6      0.92730    53.1301    0.64350    36.8699
        0.7      0.79540    45.5730    0.77540    44.4270
        0.8      0.64350    36.8699    0.92730    53.1301
        0.9      0.45103    25.8419    1.11977    64.1581
        1.0      0.00000     0.0000    1.57080    90.0000
```

Function: **ATAN**

Purpose: To compute the inverse tangent or arctangent. The resulting angle is in radians. To convert from radians to degrees, multiply by the fraction $(180/\pi)$. For example, the arctangent of .5 is .4646.

Syntax: `ATAN(value)`

`value` is a numeric value.

Examples

Function	Returns
ATAN(99999)	1.5708 (89.9999 degrees)
ATAN(1)	.7854 (45 degrees)
ATAN(10)	1.47113 (84.2842 degrees)

Program 12.3: Computing arctangents

```
***Primary function: ATAN;
***Other function: CONSTANT;

DATA ON_A_TANGENT;
   IF _N_ = 1 THEN PI = CONSTANT('PI');
   RETAIN PI;
   DROP PI;

   DO VALUE = 0 TO 10;
      TAN_RADIAN = ATAN(VALUE);
      TAN_ANGLE = TAN_RADIAN * 180/PI;
      OUTPUT;
   END;
RUN;

PROC PRINT DATA=ON_A_TANGENT NOOBS;
   TITLE "Listing of Data Set ON_A_TANGENT";
RUN;
```

Explanation

This program is similar to Program 12.2 except that the values go from 0 to 10. The output is below:

```
              Listing of Data Set ON_A_TANGENT


                        TAN_         TAN_
             VALUE      RADIAN       ANGLE

               0       0.00000      0.0000
               1       0.78540     45.0000
               2       1.10715     63.4349
               3       1.24905     71.5651
               4       1.32582     75.9638
               5       1.37340     78.6901
               6       1.40565     80.5377
               7       1.42890     81.8699
               8       1.44644     82.8750
               9       1.46014     83.6598
              10       1.47113     84.2894
```

C h a p t e r   1 3

Macro Functions

Introduction

This chapter covers only those macro functions that you can use during DATA step execution. Even these functions are discussed only briefly. If you want to learn more about these functions and the extensive set of functions used in the macro language, see the many fine books and reference materials currently available. In particular, *SAS Macro Programming Made Easy*, by Michele Burlew, and *SAS 9.1 Macro Language: Reference* are highly recommended.

Two of these macro functions, CALL SYMPUT and CALL SYMPUTX, are used to assign the values of DATA step variables to existing macro variables. They can also create a new macro variable and assign it a value during the execution of the DATA step. The only difference between these two call routines is that SYMPUTX removes leading and trailing blanks before assigning the value to the macro variable.

Function: CALL SYMPUT

Purpose: To assign a value to a macro variable during the execution of a DATA step.

Syntax: `CALL SYMPUT (macro-var, character-value)`

macro-var is the name of a new or existing macro variable. It is either a character literal in quotation marks, a character variable, or a character expression.

character-value is a character literal, a character variable, or a character expression.

Examples

For these examples, `CHAR = "BIGMAC"` and `STRING = "Hello"`

Function	Returns
`CALL SYMPUT(CHAR, STRING)`	Macro variable `BIGMAC` has a value of `"Hello"`
`CALL SYMPUT("MAC", STRING)`	Macro variable `MAC` has a value of `"Hello"`
`CALL SYMPUT("MAC", "Goodbye")`	Macro variable `MAC` has a value of `"Goodbye"`

SAS9.1 Function: CALL SYMPUTX

Purpose: To assign a value to a macro variable during the execution of a DATA step. Leading and trailing blanks are removed from the value before it is assigned to the macro variable.

Syntax: `CALL SYMPUTX (macro-var, character-value)`

macro-var is the name of a new or existing macro variable. It is either a character literal in quotation marks, a character variable, or a character expression.

character-value is a character literal, a character variable, or a character expression. This value is stripped of leading and trailing blanks.

Examples

For these examples, CHAR = "BIGMAC" and STRING = " Hello"

Function	Returns
CALL SYMPUTX(CHAR, STRING)	Macro variable BIGMAC has a value of "Hello"
CALL SYMPUTX("MAC", STRING)	Macro variable MAC has a value of "Hello"
CALL SYMPUTX("MAC"," Goodbye ")	Macro variable MAC has a value of "Goodbye"

Program 13.1: Using the SYMPUT and SYMPUTX call routines to assign a value to a macro variable during the execution of a DATA step

```
***Primary functions: SYMPUT and SYMPUTX;

DATA TEST;
   INPUT STRING $CHAR10.;
   CALL SYMPUT("NOTX",STRING);
   CALL SYMPUTX("YESX",STRING);
DATALINES;
   abc
;
DATA _NULL_;
   NOSTRIP = ":" || "&NOTX" || ":";
   STRIP   = ":" || "&YESX" || ":";
   PUT "Value of NOSTRIP is  " NOSTRIP;
   PUT "Value of STRIP is  " STRIP;
RUN;
```

Explanation

The value of STRING is three blanks, followed by the letters abc, followed by four blanks. When CALL SYMPUT is used to assign this value to the macro variable NOTX, the leading and trailing blanks are included in the value; when CALL SYMPUTX is used, the leading and trailing blanks are stripped. To see that this is the case, examine the results of the

DATA _NULL_ step. It concatenates colons to the beginning and end of the macro variable so that the blanks can be visualized. The two lines sent to the SAS log are:

```
Value of NOSTRIP is :    abc    :
Value of STRIP is  :abc:
```

Program 13.2: Passing DATA step values from one step to another, using macro variables created by CALL SYMPUT and CALL SYMPUTX

```
***Primary functions: SYMPUT and SYMPUTX
***Other functions: STRIP and PUT;

DATA SUM;
   INFILE "C:\BOOKS\FUNCTIONS\DATA.DTA" END=LAST;
   INPUT N @@;
   SUM + N;
   COUNT + 1;
   IF LAST THEN DO;
      CALL SYMPUT("SUM_OF_N",STRIP(PUT(SUM,3.)));
      CALL SYMPUTX("NUMBER",PUT(COUNT,3.));
   END;
RUN;

PROC PRINT DATA=SUM NOOBS;
   TITLE "Listing of Data Set NEXT";
   TITLE2 "Summary data: There were &NUMBER values";
   TITLE3 "The sum was &SUM_OF_N";
   VAR N;
RUN;
```

Explanation

In this example, you want to put summary information computed in a DATA step in the titles of the PROC PRINT step that follows. Both SYMPUT and SYMPUTX are used in order to demonstrate the difference between them. In the first call to SYMPUT, the STRIP function was needed to strip leading and trailing blanks from the value SUM, before assigning it to the macro variable SUM_OF_N. The next call to SYMPUTX shows the advantage of using this function: The macro variable NUMBER does not contain any leading or trailing blanks. The output from PROC PRINT is shown next:

```
                    Listing of Data Set NEXT
                    Summary data: There were 6 values
                    The sum was 29

                    N

                    1
                    6
                    3
                    4
                    8
                    7
```

Function: **RESOLVE**

This function is similar to SYMGET. However, it is more flexible. Since it operates during the execution stage of the DATA step, it can return a different value to a macro variable for each iteration of the DATA step, while SYMGET produces a static, single macro value. This is a complicated topic that is beyond the scope of this book. If you want to learn more about the differences between SYMGET and RESOLVE, see the SAS OnlineDoc and *SAS Macro Reference*.

Purpose: To assign one or more values of a DATA step variable to a macro variable.

Syntax: RESOLVE(*character-value*)

character-value is a character literal in single quotation marks, the name of a SAS character variable, or a character expression that the DATA step resolves to a macro text expression or a SAS statement.

Examples

For these examples, CHAR = '&MAC' and X=3. Note the use of single quotation marks here so that the macro processor does not resolve the argument. The value of &MAC is "Hello", and the value of &MAC3 is "Goodbye".

Function	Returns
RESOLVE(CHAR)	"Hello"
RESOLVE('&MAC' || LEFT(PUT(X,3.)))	"Goodbye"

Program 13.3: Using RESOLVE to pass DATA step values to macro variables during the execution of the DATA step

```
***Primary function: RESOLVE;

%LET X1 = 10;
%LET X2 = 100;
%LET X3 = 1000;
DATA TEST;
   INPUT N @@;
   VALUE = RESOLVE('&X' || LEFT(PUT(N,3.)));
   PUT _ALL_;
DATALINES;
1 3 2 1
;
```

Explanation

As the DATA step executes, the first value of N (1) is concatenated with the value '&X' and the result is the value '&X1', which in turn is resolved to the value of the macro variable X1, which is 10. The subsequent iterations of the DATA step assign different values for the argument of the RESOLVE function. The result is the various values for the variable VALUE as shown in the following four lines from the SAS log.

```
N=1 VALUE=10 _ERROR_=0 _N_=1
N=3 VALUE=1000 _ERROR_=0 _N_=2
N=2 VALUE=100 _ERROR_=0 _N_=3
N=1 VALUE=10 _ERROR_=0 _N_=4
```

Function: CALL EXECUTE

Purpose: This function allows you to execute a macro from within a DATA step. For example, based on data values of DATA step variables, you can conditionally execute macros. Since CALL EXECUTE executes during the execution phase of the DATA step and since macro values are needed prior to DATA step execution, see the SAS OnlineDoc or one of the books devoted specifically to macro programming for tips before you start.

Syntax: CALL EXECUTE (*character-value*)

character-value is a character literal in quotation marks, the name of a SAS character variable, or a character expression that the DATA step resolves to a macro text expression or a SAS statement.

Examples

For these examples, NAME = "%MYMACRO"

Function	Result
CALL EXECUTE ("%MYMACRO")	Executes a macro called MYMACRO
CALL EXECUTE(NAME)	Executes a macro called MYMACRO
CALL EXECUTE("%MAC(DSN)")	Executes a macro called MAC and passes the argument DSN to the macro

Program 13.4: Using CALL EXECUTE to conditionally execute a macro

```
***Primary function: CALL EXECUTE;

%MACRO SIMPLE(DSN);
   PROC PRINT DATA=&DSN NOOBS;
     TITLE "Simple Listing - Today is &SYSDAY";
   RUN;
%MEND SIMPLE;

%MACRO COMPLEX(DSN);
   PROC MEANS DATA=&DSN N MEAN STD CLM MAXDEC=2;
     TITLE "Complex Statistics - Friday";
   RUN;
%MEND COMPLEX;
```

```
DATA TEST;
   INPUT X Y @@;
DATALINES;
7 5 1 2 3 4 9 8
;
DATA _NULL_;
   IF "&SYSDAY" NE "Friday" THEN CALL EXECUTE('%SIMPLE(TEST)');
   ELSE CALL EXECUTE('%COMPLEX(TEST)');
RUN;
```

Explanation

The two macros SIMPLE and COMPLEX produce either a simple PROC PRINT listing or a
PROC MEANS summary of data, respectively. In this example, the data set TEST contains
two variables, X and Y, and the data set is used in the next DATA _NULL_ step. Finally,
the program tests the value of the automatic macro variable, &SYSDAY. If the value is not
"Friday," the SIMPLE macro executes; if the value of &SYSDAY is "Friday," the
COMPLEX macro executes. The listing below was produced when this program was run on
a Wednesday:

```
                  Simple Listing - Today is Wednesday

                             X    Y

                             7    5
                             1    2
                             3    4
                             9    8
```

Running this program on a Friday results in the listing below:

```
                    Complex Statistics - Friday

                    The MEANS Procedure

                                           Lower 95%      Upper 95%
     Variable   N       Mean     Std Dev   CL for Mean    CL for Mean
     ──────────────────────────────────────────────────────────────
     X          4       5.00      3.65       -0.81          10.81
     Y          4       4.75      2.50        0.77           8.73
     ──────────────────────────────────────────────────────────────
```

Program 13.5: A non-macro example of CALL EXECUTE

```
***Primary function: CALL EXECUTE;

DATA EXECUTE;
   STRING = "PROC PRINT DATA=EXECUTE NOOBS;
   TITLE 'Listing of Data Set EXECUTE'; RUN;";
   DROP STRING;
   INFILE 'C:\BOOKS\FUNCTIONS\DATA2.DAT' END=LAST;
   INPUT X;
   IF LAST THEN CALL EXECUTE(STRING);
RUN;
```

Explanation

This program demonstrates how CALL EXECUTE can work with any SAS code. In this example, CALL EXECUTE executes the code stored in STRING after the DATA step has read in the last data value.   The result of running this program is simply the output from the PROC PRINT as shown below:

```
                    Listing of Data Set EXECUTE

                              X

                              2
                              3
                              4
                              7
                              6
                              5
```

Function: SYMGET

Purpose: To obtain the value of a macro variable during DATA step execution.

Syntax: SYMGET(*character-value*)

character-value is a character literal in quotation marks, the name of a SAS character variable, or a character expression that the DATA step resolves to the name of a macro variable. Note: You do not include the ampersand (&) as part of this argument.

Examples

For these examples the statement %LET M = Monday was submitted in open code. Also, the statement: CHARVAR = "M"; was part of the DATA step.

Function	Returns
SYMGET('M')	"Monday"
SYMGET(CHARVAR)	"Monday"

Program 13.6: Using the SYMGET function to assign a macro value to a DATA step variable

```
***Primary function: SYMGET
***Other function: CATS;

%LET X1 = 5;
%LET X2 = 10;
%LET X3 = 15;
DATA TEST;
   INPUT TYPE $ VALUE @@;
   MULT = SYMGET(CATS('X',TYPE));
   NEW_VALUE = MULT * VALUE;
DATALINES;
1 5   2 5   3 5
;
PROC PRINT DATA=TEST;
   TITLE "Listing of Data Set TEST";
RUN;
```

Explanation

The value of TYPE is read from the input data. The CATS function concatenates the character "X" and TYPE, and also strips leading and trailing blanks. See Chapter 1, "Character Functions," for details. So, in the first iteration of the DATA step, the argument for the SYMGET function is "X1" and the value of the macro variable X1 is 5. Thus, the variable MULT is assigned a value of 5 in the first observation. The following listing of the data set TEST shows that MULT takes on the values of 5, 10, and 15 in the three observations, respectively.

```
                          Listing of Data Set TEST


                                                    NEW_
               Obs     TYPE     VALUE     MULT      VALUE

                1       1         5         5         25
                2       2         5        10         50
                3       3         5        15         75
```

Chapter 14

SAS File I/O Functions

Introduction

The functions in this chapter address SAS data sets. There are functions to determine the number of observations in a data set, the number of character and numeric variables, and the formats and labels associated with each variable. You can readily obtain much of the same information produced by PROC CONTENTS by using these functions.

If you need to obtain SAS variable information, the V functions are also available and may be more convenient to use. See Chapter 15, "Variable Information Functions."

Creating Test Data Sets

Two SAS data sets, TEST and MISS, are used to demonstrate many of the functions in this chapter. The two SAS programs below create these two data sets:

Program 14.1: Program to create two SAS data sets, TEST and MISS

```
DATA TEST(LABEL="This is the data set label");
   LENGTH X3 4;
   INPUT @1  SUBJ      $CHAR3.
         @4  DOB       MMDDYY10.
         @14 (X1-X3)      (1.)
         @17 F_NAME    $CHAR10.
         @27 L_NAME    $CHAR15.;
   LABEL SUBJ    = 'Subject'
         DOB     = 'Date of Birth'
         X1      = 'The first X'
         X2      = 'Second X'
         X3      = 'Third X'
         F_NAME = 'First Name'
         L_NAME = 'Last Name';
   FORMAT DOB MMDDYY10. X3 ROMAN.;
DATALINES;
00110/21/1946123George    Hincappie
00211/05/1956987Pincus    Zukerman
00701/01/19903..Jose      Juarez
;

DATA MISS;
   INPUT X Y A$ Z1-Z3;
DATALINES;
1 2 abc 4 5 6
999 5 xyz 999 4 5
999 999 xxx 9 8 999
2 8 ZZZ 999 999 999
;
PROC SORT DATA=TEST;
   BY SUBJ;
RUN;
PROC PRINT DATA=TEST NOOBS LABEL;
   TITLE "Listing of Data Set TEST";
RUN;

PROC PRINT DATA=MISS NOOBS;
   TITLE "Listing of Data Set MISS";
RUN;
```

The listing of these two data sets, output from PROC PRINT, is shown below:

```
                    Listing of Data Set TEST

     Third              Date of     The     Second   First
       X     Subject     Birth    first X     X       Name    Last Name

      III     001     10/21/1946     1         2     George   Hincappie
      VII     002     11/05/1956     9         8     Pincus   Zukerman
       .      007     01/01/1990     3         .     Jose     Juarez


                    Listing of Data Set MISS

              X      Y      A      Z1     Z2     Z3

              1      2     abc     4      5      6
             999     5     xyz    999     4      5
             999    999    xxx     9      8     999
              2      8     zzz    999    999    999
```

Functions That Determine if SAS Data Sets Exist, and That Open and Close Files

Function: **EXIST**

Purpose: To determine if a SAS data set exists. This is useful prior to opening the data set and attempting to determine data set attributes. The function returns a 1 if the data set exists and a 0 otherwise.

Syntax: EXIST(*member-name <,type>*)

member-name is a SAS data set name, a view, or a SAS catalog.

type is either data (default) or view. Note: See the SAS OnlineDoc for a list of other data types.

Examples

For these examples, TEST=`"MYLIB.MYDATA."`

Function	Returns
EXIST('MYLIB.MYDATA')	1 (if the data set exists), 0 otherwise
EXIST(TEST,VIEW)	1 (if the data view exists), 0 otherwise

See Program 14.2 for an example of the EXIST function.

Function: **OPEN**

Purpose: To open a SAS data set and return a data set ID. An ID is necessary for many of the functions in this chapter. If the data set cannot be opened, OPEN returns a 0.

Syntax: OPEN(*data-set-name* <,'*mode*'>)

data-set-name is a SAS data set name of the form: *libref.data-set-name*.

mode	is an optional argument that indicates the type of access.
I	is the default value and opens the file for input using random access if available.
IN	opens the file with sequential access, allowing you to revisit observations.
IS	opens the file with sequential access without allowing you to revisit observations.

Examples

For these examples, TEST=`"MYLIB.MYDATA."`

Function	Result
OPEN(TEST)	Opens MYLIB.DATA with random access
OPEN(TEST,"IN")	Opens MYLIB.DATA with sequential access
OPEN('MYLIB.FRED')	Opens permanent SAS data set MYLIB.FRED

See Programs 14.2 and 14.3 for examples of the OPEN function.

Function: CLOSE

Purpose: To close a SAS data set after it has been opened with the OPEN function. It is good practice to close data sets as soon as possible.

Syntax: CLOSE(*dsid*)

dsid is the data set ID returned by the OPEN function.

Examples

For this example, the statement: DSID = OPEN("TEST"); was previously submitted.

Function	Returns
CLOSE(DSID)	0 (if the operation was successful)

See Programs 14.2 and 14.3 for examples of the CLOSE function.

Functions That Return SAS Data Set Characteristics

The ATTRC and ATTRN functions return information about a SAS data set. Instead of using the SAS data set name as one of the arguments in the function, a SAS data set ID (DSID) is used instead. The value of this ID is returned by the OPEN function. This value can then be used as the DSID argument required by these functions.

Function: ATTRC

Purpose: To return various pieces of information concerning a SAS data set. The "C" in the function name refers to "character." The reason for that is that the various pieces of information obtainable by this function are character values. Some of the more useful attributes returned by this function are the data set label, the engine used to access the data set, and the LIBREF of the SAS library where the data set is stored.

Syntax: `ATTRC(dsid, 'attribute')`

dsid is the data set ID returned by the OPEN function.

attribute   is one of the following, placed in quotation marks.
Note: This is not a complete list. See the SAS OnlineDoc
for a complete list.

charset   returns a value for the character set of the machine that
created the data set. Possible values are: ASCII,
EBCDIC, ANSI (OS/2 ANSI standard ASCII), and
OEM (OS/2 OEM code format).

encyrpt   returns "YES" or "NO" depending on whether the data
set was encrypted.

engine   returns the name of the SAS engine needed to access
the data set.

label   returns the SAS data set label.

lib   returns the LIBREF of the SAS library where the data
set is located.

sorted by   returns the names of the BY variables. If the data set
is not sorted, the function returns an empty string.

Examples

For these examples, the statement: `DSID = OPEN(TEST);`   was issued.

Function	Returns
ATTRC(DSID,'LABEL')	This is the data set label
ATTRC(DSID,'ENGINE')	V9
ATTRC(DSID,'CHARSET')	ANSI
ATTRC(DSID,'ENCYRPT')	NO
ATTRC(DSID,'SORTEDBY')	SUBJ (if the data set was sorted)

See Program 14.3 for a sample program.

Function: **ATTRN**

Purpose: To return various pieces of information concerning a SAS data set. The "N" in the function name refers to the fact that this function returns numeric information concerning a SAS data set. Some of the more useful attributes returned by this function include whether there are any observations or variables in the data set, the number of observations and the number of variables, and whether the data set is password-protected.

Syntax: **ATTRN(*dsid*, '*attribute*')**

  dsid   is the data set ID returned by the OPEN function.

  attribute   is one of the following, placed in quotation marks. This is not a complete list. See the SAS OnlineDoc for a complete list.

  any   indicates if the data set has observations and/or variables.
  -1   indicates that there are no observations and no variables
  0   indicates that there are no observations.
  1   indicates that the data set has both observations and variables.

  crdte   is the creation date of the SAS data set as a date-time variable.

  modte   is the date the data set was last modified (also a date-time value).

  nlobs   is the number of logical observations (not including those marked to be deleted) and is unaffected by any WHERE clause that may be active. This is the attribute you will probably use, rather than either of the two that follow.

  nlobsf   is the number of logical observations (not including those marked to be deleted), including the effect of a FIRSTOBS=, OBS=, and any WHERE statement that may be in effect. Note: This option forces the system to read every observation and can consume large computer resources.

nobs   is the number of physical observations (including those marked for deletion).

Nvars   returns the number of variables in the data set.

pw   returns a 1 if the data set is password-protected, a 0 if it is not.

Examples

For these examples, the statement: DSID = OPEN(TEST); was issued.

Function	Returns
ATTRN(DSID,'ANY')	1
ATTRN(DSID,'NLOBS')	3
ATTRN(DSID,'NOBS')	3
ATTRN(DSID,'NVARS')	7

Program 14.2: Macro to determine the number of observations in a SAS data set

```
***Primary functions: OPEN, EXIST, ATTRN, CLOSE;

%MACRO NOBS(DSN);
   IF EXIST("&DSN") THEN DO;
      DSID = OPEN("&DSN","I");
      NOBS = ATTRN(DSID,"NLOBS");
   END;
   ELSE NOBS=.;
   RC = CLOSE(DSID);
%MEND NOBS;

Using the macro:

DATA USEIT;
   %NOBS(TEST);
   PUT NOBS=;
RUN;
```

Explanation

This short macro first checks to see that the data set exists, using the EXIST function. If it does, you open the data set and determine the number of observations, using the ATTRN function. If the data set does not exist, NOBS is set to a missing value. Finally, the CLOSE function closes the data set. You might want to create a macro variable (using CALL SYMPUT) with this value so you could conditionally execute SAS code, depending on the number of observations in a SAS data set. The single line written to the SAS log by this program is:

```
NOBS=3
```

See Program 14.3 for an additional sample program.

Function: **DSNAME**

Purpose: To return the SAS data set name associated with a SAS data set ID (returned by the OPEN function).

Syntax: DSNAME(*dsid*)

dsid is the SAS data set ID returned by the OPEN function.

Examples

For this example, the statement: OSCAR = OPEN("TEST"); was previously submitted.

Function	Returns
DSNAME(OSCAR)	TEST

Program 14.3: Determining the number of observations, variables, and other characteristics of a SAS data set using SAS I/O functions

---

```
***Primary functions: OPEN, ATTRC, ATTRN, CLOSE;

DATA _NULL_;
   DSID = OPEN ('TEST');
   ANY = ATTRN(DSID,'ANY');
   NLOBS = ATTRN(DSID,'NLOBS');
   NVARS = ATTRN(DSID,'NVARS');
   LABEL = ATTRC(DSID,'LABEL');
   ENGINE = ATTRC(DSID,'ENGINE');
   CHARSET =ATTRC(DSID,'CHARSET');
   DSN = DSNAME(DSID);
   RC = CLOSE(DSID);
   FILE PRINT;
   TITLE;
   PUT "Characteristics of Data Set Test" /
      40*'-'/
      "DSID ="     @11 DSID    /
      "ANY ="      @11 ANY     /
      "NLOBS ="    @11 NLOBS   /
      "NVARS ="    @11 NVARS   /
      "LABEL ="    @11 LABEL   /
      "ENGINE ="   @11 ENGINE  /
      "CHARSET ="  @11 CHARSET /
      "DSN ="      @11 DSN     /
      "RC ="       @11 RC;
RUN;
```

Explanation

The OPEN function returns a data set ID that is used with the ATTRC and ATTRN functions to identify the data set for which you want information. The three ATTRN functions return very useful information about a SAS data set: if there are any variables and/or observations, the number of observations, and the number of variables. The ATTRC function is used to determine other information about the SAS data set that may be important in a large system where the data sets are created on different platforms and may use different coding (such as ANSI, ASCII, or EBCDIC) for storing character variables. It is important to close the data set when you are done. Data sets opened in a DATA step are automatically closed, but it is a good habit to close any data set as soon as possible. The listing produced by this program is shown below:

```
                  Characteristics of Data Set Test
         ----------------------------------------
         DSID =    1
         ANY  =    1
         NLOBS =   3
         NVARS =   7
         LABEL =   This is the data set label
         ENGINE =  V9
         CHARSET = ANSI
         DSN  =    WORK.TEST.DATA
         RC   =    0
```

Functions That Return Variable Information

See Chapter 15, "Variable Information Functions," for an alternative way to obtain variable information using the V functions.

Function: VARFMT

Purpose: To determine the format assigned to a SAS data set variable. If the resulting variable is not previously given a length, the length will be set to 200.

Syntax: VARFMT(*dsid, var-number*)

dsid is the SAS data set ID returned by the OPEN function.

var-number is a number reflecting the variable's order in the SAS data set. This number is returned by the VARNUM function. You can also inspect the output from PROC CONTENTS.

Examples

For this example, the statement: DSID = OPEN("TEST"); was previously submitted.

Function	Returns
VARFMT(DSID,3)	The format for the 3rd variable in the data set with identifier DSID: MMDDYY10.
VARFMT(DSID,VARNUM(DSID,"DOB"))	The format for the variable DOB in the data set with identifier DSID: MMDDYY10.

See Program 14.4 for a sample program.

Function: **VARLABEL**

Purpose: To determine the label assigned to a SAS data set variable. If the resulting variable is not previously given a length, the length will be set to 200.

Syntax: VARLABEL(*dsid, var-number*)

dsid is the SAS data set ID returned by the OPEN function.

var-number is a number reflecting the variable's order in the SAS data set. This number is returned by the VARNUM function. You can also inspect the output from PROC CONTENTS.

Examples

For this example, the statement: DSID = OPEN("TEST"); was previously submitted.

Function	Returns
VARLABEL(DSID,3)	The label assigned to the 3rd variable in the data set with identifier DSID: Date of Birth
VARLABEL(DSID,VARNUM(DSID,"DOB"))	The label assigned to the variable GENDER in the data set with identifier DSID: Date of Birth

See Program 14.4 for a sample program.

Function: **VARLEN**

Purpose: To determine the storage length for a SAS data set variable.

Syntax: VARLEN(*dsid, var-number*)

dsid is the SAS data set ID returned by the OPEN function.

var-number is a number reflecting the variable's order in the SAS data set. This number is returned by the VARNUM function. You can also inspect the output from PROC CONTENTS.

Examples

For this example, the statement: DSID = OPEN("TEST"); was previously submitted.

Function	Returns
VARLEN(DSID,6)	The length format for the 6th variable in the data set with identifier DSID: 10
VARLEN(DSID,VARNUM(DSID,"F_NAME"))	The length for the variable F_NAME in the data set with identifier DSID: 10.

Program 14.4: Determining the format, label, and length attributes of a variable using the VARFMT, VARLEN, and VARNUM functions

```
***Primary functions: OPEN, VARFMT, VARNUM, VARLABEL, VARLEN, CLOSE;

DATA _NULL_;
   LENGTH FORMAT LABEL $ 32;
   DSID = OPEN("TEST");
   ORDER = VARNUM(DSID,"X3");
   FORMAT = VARFMT(DSID,ORDER);
   LABEL = VARLABEL(DSID,ORDER);
   LENGTH = VARLEN(DSID,ORDER);
   RC = CLOSE(DSID);
   PUT ORDER= FORMAT= LABEL= LENGTH=;
RUN;
```

Explanation

The OPEN function opens the data set TEST and assigns a data set identifier (DSID). The VARNUM function determines the order of variable X3 in the data set (1). Note: X3 is in position 1 because of the LENGTH statement. It is the first variable in the data set. The VARFMT function also returns the format (ROMAN) for variable X3. The VARLABEL function returns the label "Third X," and the VARLEN function returns a 4, the length assigned to the variable X3. The line printed to the SAS log by this program is:

```
ORDER=1 FORMAT=ROMAN. LABEL=Third X LENGTH=4
```

Function: VARNAME

Purpose: To return the name of a SAS variable, given the order in the SAS data set. This number is returned by the VARNUM function. You can also inspect the output from PROC CONTENTS.

Syntax: VARNAME(*dsid, var-number*)

dsid is the SAS data set ID returned by the OPEN function.

var-number is a number reflecting the variable's order in the SAS data set. This number is returned by the VARNUM function. You can also inspect the output from PROC CONTENTS.

Examples

For this example, the statement: `DSID = OPEN("TEST");` was previously submitted.

Function	Returns
`VARNAME(DSID,3)`	The variable name of the 3rd variable in the data set with identifier `DSID`: `DOB`

See Program 14.5 for a sample program.

Function: **VARNUM**

Purpose: To return the position of a SAS variable in a SAS data set, given the variable name. This function is basically the inverse of the VARNAME function.

Syntax: **VARNUM(*dsid, varname*)**

   dsid is the SAS data set ID returned by the OPEN function.

   varname is a name of a variable in the SAS data set with the identifier *dsid*.

Examples

For this example, the statement: `DSID = OPEN("TEST");` was previously submitted and `V = "DOB"`.

Function	Returns
`VARNUM(DSID,"DOB")`	The position of a variable called "DOB" in the SAS data set with identifier `DSID`: `3`
`VARNUM(DSID,V)`	The position of a variable called "DOB" in the SAS data set with identifier `DSID`: `3`

Program 14.5: Determining a variable name, given its position in a SAS data set and vice versa

```
***Primary functions: OPEN, VARNAME, VARNUM, CLOSE;

DATA _NULL_;
   ID = OPEN("TEST");
   VAR_NAME = VARNAME(ID,1);
   VAR_POS  = VARNUM(ID,"DOB");
   RC = CLOSE(ID);
   PUT "The name of the 1st variable in data set test is: " VAR_NAME /
       "The position of variable DOB is: " VAR_POS;
RUN;
```

Explanation

The data set TEST is opened with the OPEN function, and the data set identifier is assigned to the variable called ID. The VARNAME function returns the variable name assigned to the first variable in the data set TEST, and the VARNUM function returns the position of the variable DOB in the data set TEST. The two lines written to the SAS log are:

```
The name of the 1st variable in data set test is: X3
The position of variable DOB is: 3
```

Function: VARTYPE

Purpose: To determine if a SAS data set variable is character or numeric. For character variables, the function returns a 'C' and for numeric variables it returns an 'N'.

Syntax: VARTYPE(*dsid, var-number*)

dsid is the SAS data set ID returned by the OPEN function.

var-number is a number reflecting the variable's order in the SAS data set. This number is returned by the VARNUM function. You can also inspect the output from PROC CONTENTS.

Examples

For this example, the statement: DSID = OPEN("TEST"); was previously submitted.

Function		Returns
VARTYPE(DSID,1)	(variable X3)	"N"
VARTYPE(DSID,6)	(variable F_NAME)	"C"
VARTYPE(DSID,3)	(variable DOB)	"N"

Program 14.6: A general-purpose macro to display data set attributes such as number of observations, number of variables, variable list, variable type, formats, labels, etc.

```
***Primary functions: EXIST, OPEN, ATTRN, ATTRC, VARNAME, VARTYPE,
                       VARLEN, VARFMT, VARLABEL, and CLOSE;

%MACRO DSN_INFO(DSN);
   DATA _NULL_;
      FILE PRINT;
      IF NOT EXIST("&DSN") THEN DO;
         PUT "Data set &DSN does not exist";
         STOP;
      END;

      DSID    = OPEN("&DSN","I");
      NVARS   = ATTRN(DSID,"NVARS");
      NOBS    = ATTRN(DSID,"NLOBS");
      CHARSET = ATTRC(DSID,"CHARSET");
      ENGINE  = ATTRC(DSID,"ENGINE");
      ENCRYPT = ATTRC(DSID,"ENCRYPT");
      LABEL   = ATTRC(DSID,"LABEL");
      SORT    = ATTRC(DSID,"SORTEDBY");


      PUT "Information for Data Set &DSN" /
         72*'-' // ;
      IF LABEL NE " " then PUT "Data set Label is: " LABEL;
      PUT "Data set created with engine: " ENGINE /
         "Character set used: " CHARSET;
      IF ENCRYPT = "YES" then PUT "Data set is encrypted";
      ELSE PUT "Data set is not encrypted";
      IF SORT = " " then PUT "Data set is not sorted";
      ELSE PUT "Data set is sorted by: " SORT /;
      PUT
         "Number of Observations: " NOBS /
         "Number of Variables    : " NVARS /
```

```
               72*'-' /
               "***** Variable Information *****" //
               @1   "Variable Name"
               @20  "Type"
               @26  "Length"
               @34  "Format"
               @47  "Label"/
               72*'-';
           DO I = 1 TO NVARS;
               NAME = VARNAME(DSID,I);
               TYPE = VARTYPE(DSID,I);
               IF TYPE = "C" THEN TYPE = "Char";
               ELSE IF TYPE = "N" THEN TYPE = "Num";

               LENGTH = VARLEN(DSID,I);
               FMT = VARFMT(DSID,I);
               LABEL = VARLABEL(DSID,I);

               PUT @1      NAME
                   @20     TYPE
                   @26     LENGTH
                   @34     FMT
                   @47     LABEL;
           END;

           RC = CLOSE(DSID);
       RUN;
   %MEND DSN_INFO;
```

Explanation

This rather long macro uses most of the functions described in this chapter to produce a very compact equivalent of PROC CONTENTS. You may want to customize it to produce just the information you find useful. The VARTYPE function determines if a variable is character or numeric.

Calling the macro: %DSN_INFO(TEST); results in the following output:

```
Information for Data Set test
----------------------------------------------------------------------


Data set Label is: This is the data set label
Data set created with engine: V9
Character set used: ANSI
Data set is not encrypted
Data set is sorted by: SUBJ

Number of Observations: 3
Number of Variables   : 7
----------------------------------------------------------------------
***** Variable Information *****

Variable Name        Type  Length  Format       Label
----------------------------------------------------------------------
X3                   Num   4       ROMAN.       Third X
SUBJ                 Char  3                    Subject
DOB                  Num   8       MMDDYY10.    Date of Birth
X1                   Num   8                    The first X
X2                   Num   8                    Second X
F_NAME               Char  10                   First Name
L_NAME               Char  15                   Last Name
```

C h a p t e r 1 5

Variable Information Functions

Introduction

The functions in this chapter all return information about SAS variables. For example, VNAME returns the name of a variable, given an array reference. VTYPE is used to determine if a variable is character or numeric. The advantage of these functions over the VAR functions listed in the previous chapter is that the OPEN function is not needed to obtain variable information.

As a general class, there are Vname functions and VnameX functions. For example, there is a function called VTYPE and another function called VTYPEX. The difference is that the Vname functions need a variable name as the argument; the VnameX functions can evaluate an expression to determine the variable name.

I will not discuss the VnameX functions individually. A single example is shown for VTYPE and VTYPEX. Further, not all the V functions are discussed here. For information on some of the less frequently used functions, see the SAS OnlineDoc or *SAS Language Reference: Concepts*. Note: The wording of arguments in this book might differ from the wording of arguments in the *SAS OnlineDoc 9.1*.

Functions That Determine SAS Variable Information

Function: VTYPE

Purpose: To determine if a variable is character or numeric.

Syntax: VTYPE(*variable*)

variable is the name of a SAS variable.

Note: By default, the result of this function is a character variable of length 1. Values of C or N are returned for character and numeric variables, respectively.

Examples

Function	Returns
VTYPE(NUM) where NUM is a numeric variable	"N"
VTYPE(CHAR) where CHAR is a character variable	"C"

See Program 15.2 for an example.

Function: **VTYPEX**

Purpose: To determine if a variable is character or numeric.

Syntax: `VTYPE(expression)`

expression is an expression that evaluates to a SAS variable name.

Note: By default, the result of this function is a character variable of length 1. Values of C or N are returned for character and numeric variables, respectively.

Examples

Function	Returns
`VTYPEX('X' || '1')` where X1 is a numeric variable	"N"
`VTYPEX('CH' || 'AR')` where CHAR is a character variable	"C"

Program 15.1: Creating a test data set for use with most of the V functions

```
PROC FORMAT;
   VALUE YESNO 1='YES' 0='NO';
   INVALUE READ 0-5 = 777
                6-9 = 888
                OTHER = 999;
RUN;
DATA VAR;
   INFORMAT CHAR $CHAR1. Y READ2. Z 3.2 MONEY DOLLAR5.;
   INPUT @1  X       1.
         @2  CHAR    $CHAR1.
         @3  Y       READ2.
         @5  Z       3.2
         @8  MONEY   DOLLAR5.
         @13 (A1-A3) (1.)
         @16 DATE    MMDDYY10.;
   FORMAT X YESNO. MONEY DOLLAR8.2 Z 7.4;
   LABEL X = 'The X variable'
         Y = 'Pain Scale'
         MONEY = 'Housing Cost';
```

```
    ARRAY OSCAR[3] A1-A3;
DATALINES;
1B 31231,765987
ON 86549,123234
;
```

Program 15.2: Determining a variable's type (numeric or character) using VTYPE and VTYPEX

```
***Primary functions: VTYPE, VTYPEX;

DATA CHAR_NUM;
    SET VAR;
    TYPE_X = VTYPE(X);
    TYPE_CHAR = VTYPE(CHAR);
    TYPE_A1 = VTYPEX('A' || PUT(3-2,1.));
RUN;

PROC PRINT DATA=CHAR_NUM NOOBS;
    TITLE "Listing of Data Set CHAR_NUM";
RUN;
```

Explanation

Since variables X and A1 are both numeric, the VTYPE and VTYPEX functions return an "N". Note that the expression for TYPE_A1 evaluates to the value "A1" which is a numeric variable. This same expression could not have been used as the argument of VTYPE. TYPE_CHAR is a character variable and the VTYPE function returns a "C". Note that you do not have to predefine the length of the resulting character variables—they are set to 1 as the default length. A listing of output is shown below:

									TYPE_	
X	CHAR	Y	Z	MONEY	A1	A2	A3	TYPE_X	CHAR	TYPE_A1
YES	B	777	1.23	$1765.00	9	8	7	N	C	N
NO	N	888	6.54	$9123.00	2	3	4	N	C	N

Listing of Data Set CHAR_NUM

Function: **VLENGTH**

Purpose: To return the storage length (determined at compile time) for a variable. See the LENGTHM function in Chapter 1, "Character Functions", for a function with similar purpose.

Syntax: VLENGTH(*variable*)

variable is the name of a SAS variable.

Example

The variables in these examples are taken from Program 15.1.

Function	Returns
VLENGTH(CHAR)	1
VLENGTH(Y)	8
VLENGTH(MONEY)	8

Program 15.3: Determining the storage length of character and numeric variables

```
***Primary function: VLENGTH;

DATA _NULL_;
   LENGTH Y 4 NAME $ 20;
   X = 123;
   y = 123;
   CHAR = 'ABC';
   LONG = 'This is a long character variable';
   PAD = 'A    '; ***A followed by 4 blanks;
   NAME = 'Frank';

   L_X = VLENGTH(X);
   L_Y = VLENGTH(Y);
   L_CHAR = VLENGTH(CHAR);
   L_LONG = VLENGTH(LONG);
   L_PAD = VLENGTH(PAD);
   L_NAME = VLENGTH(NAME);
```

```
     PUT L_X = /
         L_Y = /
         L_CHAR = /
         L_LONG = /
         L_PAD = /
         L_NAME = ;
  RUN;
```

Explanation

The VLENGTH function is used to determine the storage length for the variables in the SAS data set. A portion of the output to the SAS log is shown next. Notice in particular that the length of PAD (5) is the storage length, not the value returned by the LENGTH function.

```
L_X=8
L_Y=4
L_CHAR=3
L_LONG=33
L_PAD=5
L_NAME=20
```

Function: VNAME

Purpose: To return the name of a SAS variable. It is most useful when you want to determine which variable a specific array element is referencing. Note there is also a call routine with the same name that accomplishes the same task.

Syntax: VNAME(*variable-reference*)

variable-reference is usually an array element. You should use a LENGTH statement to hold the result of this function. Otherwise, the result will be a character variable of length 200.

Examples

For these examples, the statement ARRAY NUMS [*] X2-X3 Y Z; was submitted previously.

Function	Returns
VNAME(NUM[4])	"Y"
VNAME(NUM[2])	"X2"

Program 15.4: Program to replace all numeric values of 999 with a SAS missing value and to provide a list of variable names where the changes were made

```
***Primary functions: VNAME, SYMPUTX
***Other functions: DIM;
***This data step determines the number of numeric
   variables in the data set and assigns it to a macro variable (N);

DATA _NULL_;
   SET MISS;
   ARRAY NUMS[*] _NUMERIC_;
   CALL SYMPUTX('N',DIM(NUMS));
   STOP;
RUN;

DATA _NULL_;
   SET MISS END=LAST;
   FILE PRINT;
   ARRAY NUMS[*] _NUMERIC_;
   LENGTH NAMES1-NAMES&N $ 32;
   ARRAY NAMES[&N];
   ARRAY HOWMANY[&N];
   RETAIN NAMES1-NAMES&N;
   DO I = 1 TO DIM(NUMS);
      IF NUMS[I] = 999 THEN DO;
         NUMS[I] = .;
         NAMES[I] = VNAME(NUMS[I]);
         HOWMANY[I] + 1;
      END;
   END;
   IF LAST THEN DO I = 1 TO &N;
      IF NAMES[I] NE ' ' THEN
      PUT HOWMANY[I] "Values of 999 converted to missing for variable "
         NAMES[I];
   END;
RUN;
```

Explanation

The first DATA _NULL_ DATA step uses the special name _NUMERIC_ to refer to all numeric variables in the MISS data set. The DIM function determines this number, and the value is converted to a character variable using the PUT function. Any leading blanks are removed with the LEFT function. Finally, the call to SYMPUT assigns this value to the macro variable N.

The next DATA step sets up one array, NUMS, to represent the 'N' numeric variables and another array, NAMES, to hold the variable names of these variables. Notice that the length of NAMES is set directly in the ARRAY statement (32) so that a LENGTH statement is not necessary. As the DO loop executes, each of the numeric variables tests if a value of 999 is found, and if so, converts it to a SAS missing value and increments a counter (HOWMANY[I]) to keep track of how many replacements were made. A listing produced by this program is shown below:

```
2 Values of 999 converted to missing for variable X
1 Values of 999 converted to missing for variable Y
2 Values of 999 converted to missing for variable Z1
1 Values of 999 converted to missing for variable Z2
2 Values of 999 converted to missing for variable Z3
```

Program 15.5: Writing a general purpose macro to replace all occurrences of a particular value (such as 999) in a SAS missing value in a SAS data set and produce a report showing the number of replacements for each variable

```
***Primary functions: VNAME, CALL SYMPUT
***Other functions: DIM, LEFT, PUT;

%MACRO REPLACE_MISSING (
                        DSN,        /* the SAS data set name */
                        MISS_VALUE /* the value of the missing value */
                        );
   DATA _NULL_;
      SET &DSN;
      ARRAY NUMS[*] _NUMERIC_;
      N_NUMBERS = LEFT(PUT(DIM(NUMS),5.));
      CALL SYMPUT('N',N_NUMBERS);
      STOP;
   RUN;
   DATA _NULL_;
      SET &DSN END=LAST;
      FILE PRINT;
      ARRAY NUMS[*] _NUMERIC_;
      ARRAY NAMES[&N] $ 32 _TEMPORARY_ ;
      ARRAY HOWMANY[&N] _TEMPORARY_;
      DO I = 1 TO DIM(NUMS);
         IF NUMS[I] = &MISS_VALUE THEN DO;
            NUMS[I] = .;
            NAMES[I] = VNAME(NUMS[I]);
```

```
            HOWMANY[I] + 1;
         END;
      END;
      IF LAST THEN DO I = 1 TO &N;
         IF NAMES[I] NE ' ' THEN
         PUT HOWMANY[I]
            "Values of &MISS_VALUE converted to missing for variable "
  NAMES[I];
      END;
   RUN;
%MEND REPlACE_MISSING;
```

Explanation

This macro is basically identical to the previous program. The only difference is that the data set name and the value to be replaced are calling arguments to the macro. Just to make sure it works, I called the macro like this:

```
%REPLACE_MISSING(MISS,999);
```

and produced output identical to the previous listing.

Function: **VLABEL**

Purpose: To return the label associated with a SAS variable. If no label is associated with the variable, the function returns the variable name. If no length is assigned to the variable holding the label, it is given a length of 200 by default.

Syntax: **VLABEL(*variable*)**

variable is the name of a SAS variable. VLABEL does not accept an expression for the variable name. Use VLABELX for that purpose.

Examples

For these examples `VAR1 = 'X'` and `VAR2 = 'Z'`

Function	Returns
VLABEL(VAR1)	"The X variable"
VLABEL(VAR2)	"Z"
VLABEL('X')	"The X variable"

See Program 15.7 for an example.

Function: **CALL VNEXT**

Purpose: To determine the name, type, and length of one or more variables in a SAS data set. Each successive call to the routine returns information on the next variable in the SAS data set.

Syntax: `CALL VNEXT (name <, type <,length>>)`

name   is the name of the variable that will hold the variable name. You should set the length of this variable with a LENGTH statement prior to calling the routine. If the value of NAME is blank or the routine is being called for the first time in the DATA step, NAME will be replaced by the name of the first variable in the SAS data set. On subsequent calls, NAME is given the name of each variable in the order they are in the SAS data set. After all the names have been returned, VNEXT will return a blank value to NAME.

type   is an optional argument. If included, it is the name of the variable that will hold the variable type ('C' = character, 'N' = numeric). Set the length of this variable to 1 before calling the routine.

length   is an optional argument. If you include it, you must also supply a variable name to hold the type value. This variable will be a numeric variable and will be the storage length for the variable.

Examples

The variables in these examples are taken from Program 15.1.

Function	Name	Type	Length
CALL VNEXT(NAME, TYPE, LENGTH) 1st call	X	N	8
CALL VNEXT(NAME, TYPE, LENGTH) 2nd call	CHAR	C	1

Program 15.6: Determining the name, type, and length of all variables in a SAS data set

```
***Primary function: CALL VNEXT;

DATA VAR_INFO;
   IF 0 THEN SET VAR;
   LENGTH VAR_NAME $ 32 VAR_TYPE $ 1;
   DO UNTIL (VAR_NAME = ' ');
      CALL VNEXT(VAR_NAME,VAR_TYPE,VAR_LENGTH);
      IF VAR_NAME NE ' ' THEN OUTPUT;
   END;
   KEEP VAR_:;
RUN;

PROC PRINT DATA=VAR_INFO NOOBS;
   TITLE "Listing of Data Set VAR_INFO";
RUN;
```

Explanation

The trick of using IF 0 (which is never true) allows you to determine variable information without having to actually read any data values from the data set. Notice that VAR_NAME and VAR_TYPE are both assigned lengths prior to calling VNEXT. Since VNEXT returns a blank value to the variable named in the first argument when there are no more variables to be read, it is used as a test to determine when to stop execution of the DO loop. The listing of VAR_INFO is shown below:

```
                    Listing of Data Set VAR_INFO

                                         VAR_
                 VAR_NAME      VAR_TYPE   LENGTH

                 X             N          8
                 CHAR          C          1
                 Y             N          8
                 Z             N          8
                 MONEY         N          8
                 A1            N          8
                 A2            N          8
                 A3            N          8
                 VAR_NAME      C          32
                 VAR_TYPE      C          1
                 VAR_LENGTH    N          8
                 _ERROR_       N          8
                 _N_           N          8
```

Functions That Determine Format Information

This set of related functions also has corresponding VnameX functions (VFORMATX, VFORMATNX, etc.) They all return information concerning formats.

Function: VFORMAT

Purpose: To return the format name associated with a variable. The name includes the $ if the format is associated with a character variable, and the width, if included. For numeric variables, the name also includes the value to the right of the decimal point. For example, possible returned values are $CHAR15 and DOLLAR8.2.

Syntax: VFORMAT(*variable*)

variable is a SAS variable name.

Examples

The variables in these examples are taken from Program 15.1.

Function	Returns
VFORMAT(CHAR)	$CHAR.
VFORMAT(MONEY)	DOLLAR8.2

See Program 15.7 for an example.

Function: VFORMATD

Purpose: To return the format decimal value associated with a variable.

Syntax: VFORMATD(*variable*)

variable is a SAS variable name.

Examples

The variables in these examples are taken from Program 15.1.

Function	Returns
VFORMATD(Z)	4
VFORMATD(MONEY)	2

See Program 15.7 for an example.

Function: VFORMATN

Purpose: To return the format name associated with a variable. The name includes the $ if the format is a character variable but not the width of decimal value.

Syntax: VFORMATN(*variable*)

variable is a SAS variable name.

Examples

The variables in these examples are taken from Program 15.1.

Function	Returns
VFORMATN(CHAR)	$CHAR
VFORMATN(MONEY)	DOLLAR

See Program 15.7 for an example.

Function: VFORMATW

Purpose: To return the format width associated with a variable.

Syntax: VFORMATW(*variable*)

variable is a SAS variable name.

Examples

The variables in these examples are taken from Program 15.1.

Function	Returns
VFORMATW(CHAR)	1
VFORMATW(MONEY)	8

See Program 15.7 for an example.

Functions That Determine Informat Information

This set of functions is similar to the VFORMAT functions described in the previous section except that they return informat information.

Function: **VINFORMAT**

Purpose: To return the informat name associated with a variable. The name includes the $ if the informat is associated with a character variable, and the width, if included. For numeric variables, the name also includes the value to the right of the decimal point. For example, possible returned values are $CHAR15 and DOLLAR8.2.

Syntax: VINFORMAT(*variable*)

variable is a SAS variable name.

Examples

The variables in these examples are taken from Program 15.1.

Function	Returns
VINFORMAT(Y)	READ2.
VINFORMAT(MONEY)	DOLLAR5.
VINFORMAT(CHAR)	$CHAR1.

See Program 15.7 for an example.

Function: VINFORMATD

Purpose: To return the informat decimal value associated with a variable.

Syntax: VINFORMATD(*variable*)

variable is a SAS variable name.

Examples

The variables in these examples are taken from Program 15.1.

Function	Returns
VINFORMATD(Z)	2
VINFORMATD(MONEY)	0

See Program 15.7 for an example.

Function: VINFORMATN

Purpose: To return the informat name associated with a variable. The name includes the $ if the informat is associated with a character variable but not the width of the decimal value.

Syntax: VINFORMATN(*variable*)

variable is a SAS variable name.

Examples

The variables in these examples are taken from Program 15.1.

Function	Returns
VINFORMATN(Y)	READ
VINFORMATN(MONEY)	DOLLAR

See Program 15.7 for an example.

Function: **VINFORMATW**

Purpose: To return the informat width associated with a variable.

Syntax: `VINFORMATW(variable)`

variable is a SAS variable name.

Examples

The variables in these examples are taken from Program 15.1.

Function	Returns
VINFORMATW(Z)	3
VINFORMATW(MONEY)	5

See Program 15.7 for an example.

Program 15.7: Demonstrating a variety of SAS V functions

```
***Primary functions: VFORMAT, VFORMATD, VFORMATN, VFORMATW, VINFORMAT,
***VINFORMATD, VINFORMATN, VINFORMATW, VLABEL;

DATA VFUNC;
   SET VAR(OBS=1);
   LENGTH VFORMAT_X VFORMAT_Y VFORMAT_CHAR VFORMAT_MONEY
          VFORMATN_X VFORMATN_Y VFORMATN_CHAR VFORMATN_MONEY $8.
          VINFORMAT_X VINFORMAT_Y VINFORMAT_CHAR VINFORMAT_MONEY
          VINFORMATN_X VINFORMATN_Y VINFORMATN_CHAR VINFORMATN_MONEY $8.
          VLABEL_X VLABEL_Y VLABEL_CHAR VLABEL_MONEY $ 40;

   ***Format functions;
   VFORMAT_X = VFORMAT(X);
   VFORMAT_Y = VFORMAT(Y);
   VFORMAT_CHAR = VFORMAT(CHAR);
   VFORMAT_MONEY = VFORMAT(MONEY);
   VFORMATN_X = VFORMATN(X);
   VFORMATN_Y = VFORMATN(Y);
   VFORMATN_CHAR = VFORMATN(CHAR);
   VFORMATN_MONEY = VFORMATN(MONEY);
   VFORMATW_X = VFORMATW(X);
   VFORMATW_Y = VFORMATW(Y);
   VFORMATW_CHAR = VFORMATW(CHAR);
```

```
   VFORMATW_MONEY = VFORMATW(MONEY);
   VFORMATD_X = VFORMATD(X);
   VFORMATD_Y = VFORMATD(Y);
   VFORMATD_CHAR = VFORMATD(CHAR);
   VFORMATD_MONEY = VFORMATD(MONEY);

   ***Informat functions;
   VINFORMAT_X = VINFORMAT(X);
   VINFORMAT_Y = VINFORMAT(Y);
   VINFORMAT_CHAR = VINFORMAT(CHAR);
   VINFORMAT_MONEY = VINFORMAT(MONEY);
   VINFORMATN_X = VINFORMATN(X);
   VINFORMATN_Y = VINFORMATN(Y);
   VINFORMATN_CHAR = VINFORMATN(CHAR);
   VINFORMATN_MONEY = VINFORMATN(MONEY);
   VINFORMATW_X = VINFORMATW(X);
   VINFORMATW_Y = VINFORMATW(Y);
   VINFORMATW_CHAR = VINFORMATW(CHAR);
   VINFORMATW_MONEY = VINFORMATW(MONEY);
   VINFORMATD_X = VINFORMATD(X);
   VINFORMATD_Y = VINFORMATD(Y);
   VINFORMATD_CHAR = VINFORMATD(CHAR);
   VINFORMATD_MONEY = VINFORMATD(MONEY);

   ***Label information;
   VLABEL_X = VLABEL(X);
   VLABEL_Y = VLABEL(Y);
   VLABEL_CHAR = VLABEL(CHAR);
   VLABEL_MONEY = VLABEL(MONEY);
RUN;

PROC PRINT DATA=VFUNC NOOBS HEADING=H;
   TITLE "Listing of Data Set VFUNC";
   VAR V:;
RUN;
```

Explanation

This program is straightforward. Each of the V functions is used on four of the variables from the data set VAR. The informat name for the numeric variables is F. except where an explicit INFORMAT statement is used. The decimal value for the character variable is 0. Inspection of the listing below will help you to clarify this group of V functions.

```
                      Listing of Data Set VFUNC

VFORMAT_    VFORMAT_    VFORMAT_    VFORMAT_    VFORMATN_   VFORMATN_   VFORMATN_
   X           Y          CHAR       MONEY         X           Y          CHAR

YESNO3.     BEST12.      $1.        DOLLAR8.     YESNO       BEST          $

VFORMATN_   VINFORMAT_  VINFORMAT_  VINFORMAT_   VINFORMAT_  VINFORMATN_
  MONEY        X           Y          CHAR         MONEY        X

DOLLAR        F.         READ2.      $CHAR1.      DOLLAR5.      F

VINFORMATN_ VINFORMATN_ VINFORMATN_                                       VLABEL_
   Y           CHAR        MONEY     VLABEL_X     VLABEL_Y                  CHAR

 READ         $CHAR       DOLLAR     The X variable Pain Scale             CHAR

            VFORMATW_   VFORMATW_   VFORMATW_    VFORMATW_   VFORMATD_   VFORMATD_
VLABEL_MONEY   X           Y          CHAR        MONEY        X           Y

Housing Cost   3          12          1            8           0           0

VFORMATD_   VFORMATD_   VINFORMATW_  VINFORMATW_  VINFORMATW_  VINFORMATW_
  CHAR        MONEY         X            Y           CHAR        MONEY

   0           2            0            2            1           5

VINFORMATD_   VINFORMATD_   VINFORMATD_    VINFORMATD_
    X             Y            CHAR          MONEY

    0             0             0             0
```

C h a p t e r   1 6

Bitwise Logical Functions

Introduction

I doubt you will find any routine uses for these bit manipulation functions in your everyday programming. However, they are fun, and I thought a short program demonstrating the four logical functions (AND, NOT, OR, Exclusive OR) would be interesting. I left out the remaining two functions which shift bits right or left. One reason I decided to include these four bitwise functions is that the exclusive OR function (BXOR) has applications in ciphers and I have long been interested in codes and ciphers.

This collection of functions performs logical operations on bit strings. As a quick review, recall that A AND B is true if both A and B are true; NOT A reverses the value (0 to 1 or 1 to 0); A OR B is true if either A or B is true or if both A and B are true; A XOR (exclusive OR) B is true if A or B, but not both are true. The table below summarizes these rules:

Operation	A	B	Result
NOT A	1		0
	0		1
A AND B	0	0	0
	0	1	0
	1	0	0
	1	1	1
A OR B	0	0	0
	0	1	1
	1	0	1
	1	1	1
A XOR B	0	0	0
	0	1	1
	1	0	1
	1	1	0

A program demonstrating these functions follows the descriptions.

Function: BNOT

Purpose: To negate an argument, i.e., 1's are turned into 0's and vice versa.

Syntax: BNOT(*numeric-value*)

numeric-value is a numeric value that is 0 or positive and not missing.

Examples

For these examples let X = 5 (0101 in binary) and Y = 12 (1100 in binary).

Function	Returns
BNOT(X)	1010 right-most 4 bits in binary, remaining bits are 1's. (Equal to 4294967290)
BNOT(Y)	0011 right-most 4 bits in binary, remaining bits are 1's (Equal to 4294967283)

Function: **BAND**

Purpose: To perform a logical AND function between two bit strings. As a review, recall that the AND function between two logical variables is true (1) only when both arguments are true. It is false (0) otherwise.

Syntax: BAND(*numeric-value-one, numeric-value-two*)

numeric-value-one is a numeric value that is zero or positive and is not missing.

numeric-value-two has the same properties as the above.

Examples

For these examples let X = 5 (0101 in binary) and Y = 12 (1100 in binary).

```
       X = 0 1 0 1 =  5
       Y = 1 1 0 0 = 12
BAND(X,Y)  = 0 1 0 0 =  4
```

Function	Returns
BAND(X,Y)	4 (0100 in binary)

Function: **BOR**

Purpose: To perform a logical OR function between two-bit strings. As a review, recall that the OR function between two logical variables is true (1) if either one or both arguments are true. It is false (0) otherwise.

Syntax: BOR(*numeric-value-one, numeric-value-two*)

numeric-value-one is a numeric value that is 0 or positive and is not missing.

numeric-value-two has the same properties as the above.

Examples

For these examples let X = 5 (0101 in binary) and Y = 12 (1100 in binary).

```
X = 0 1 0 1 =  5
Y = 1 1 0 0 = 12
BOR(X,Y)  = 1 1 0 1 = 13
```

Function	Returns
BOR(X,Y)	13 (1101 in binary)

Function: **BXOR**

Purpose: To perform a logical exclusive OR function between two bit strings. As a review, recall that the exclusive OR function between two logical variables is true (1) if one (**but not both**) of the arguments is true. It is false (0) otherwise. (Actually, an exclusive OR is just an OR that resides in an upscale neighborhood.)

Note: There are some interesting applications to encoding and decoding text messages using the exclusive OR function. These will be discussed following the encryption and decryption program.

Syntax: BXOR(*numeric-value-one*, *numeric-value-two*)

numeric-value-one is a numeric value that is 0 or positive and is not missing.

numeric-value-two has the same properties as the above.

Examples

For these examples let X = 5 (0101 in binary) and Y = 12 (1100 in binary).

```
        X = 0 1 0 1 =  5
        Y = 1 1 0 0 = 12
BXOR(X,Y)   = 0 0 0 1 =  1
```

Function	Returns
BXOR(X,Y)	9 (1001 in binary)

Program 16.1: Demonstrating the bitwise logical functions

```
***Primary functions: BAND, BNOT, BOR, BXOR;

DATA _NULL_;
   TITLE "Demonstrating the Bitwise Logical Functions";
   FILE PRINT;
   INPUT @1  X BINARY4. /
         @1  Y BINARY4. /
         @1 AFRAID BINARY8.;

   AND = BAND(X,Y);
   NOT = BNOT(AFRAID); ***Get it, Be not afraid?;
   OR  = BOR(X,Y);
   XOR = BXOR(X,Y);
   FORMAT X Y AND OR XOR BINARY4.
         AFRAID NOT BINARY8.;
   PUT X= Y= AFRAID= / 60*'-' //
       AND= OR= XOR= NOT=;
DATALINES;
0101
1100
11110000
;
```

Explanation

Although the bitwise logical functions work on any numerical arguments, it makes more sense when you either read or output the numbers as binary strings. In this program, the values of X and Y are read in using the BINARY4. informat while the variable AFRAID is read using a BINARY8. informat. Likewise, the values produced by the functions are also output using BINARY formats. A listing of the output is shown below:

```
Demonstrating the Bitwise Logical Functions
X=0101 Y=1100 AFRAID=11110000

-----------------------------------------------------------

AND=0100 OR=1101 XOR=1001 NOT=00001111
```

Program 16.2: Enciphering and deciphering text using a key

```
***Primary functions: BXOR, RANK, BYTE
***Other functions: SUBSTR (used on both sides of the equal sign), DIM;

DATA ENCODE;
   ARRAY L[5] $ 1;
   ARRAY NUM[5];
   ARRAY XOR[5];
   RETAIN KEY 173;
   INPUT STRING $CHAR5.;
   DO I = 1 TO DIM(L);
      L[I] = SUBSTR(STRING,I,1);
      NUM[I] = RANK(L[I]);
      XOR[I] = BXOR(NUM[I],KEY);
   END;
   KEEP XOR1-XOR5;
DATALINES;
ABCDE
Help
;
PROC PRINT DATA=ENCODE NOOBS;
   TITLE "Encoded Message";
   VAR XOR1-XOR5;
RUN;

DATA DECODE;
   ARRAY L[5] $ 1;
   ARRAY NUM[5];
   ARRAY XOR[5];
   RETAIN KEY 173;
```

```
      LENGTH STRING $ 5;
      SET ENCODE;
      DO I = 1 TO DIM(L);
          NUM[I] = BXOR(XOR[I],KEY);
          L[I] = BYTE(NUM[I]);
          SUBSTR(STRING,I,1) = L[I];
      END;
      DROP I;
   RUN;

   PROC PRINT DATA=DECODE NOOBS;
      TITLE "Decoding Output";
      VAR STRING;
   RUN;
```

Explanation

This program is an interesting application of the exclusive OR function to the science of cryptography. First, let me explain why the exclusive OR is so useful here. Suppose you have a binary string 11010000 and a key 10101010. If you use an exclusive OR between these two strings, you get: 01111010. What is interesting about this is that you can **reverse** the process by using the exclusive OR again with the encoded string and the key. Thus, the exclusive OR of the result 01111010 and the key 10101010 is the original binary string, 11010000.

Since this is only a demonstration program, the length of the text string was set to five. Obviously, you can expand this to anything you like. You can also use a longer key if you choose. By the way, the RETAIN statement is used both to keep the KEY value in the PDV (program data vector) for the duration of the program and also to set its initial (and only) value to 173.

Before you start to turn your text into code, you use the SUBSTR function to place each of the letters in the original string into the elements of an array, one character to each variable. Since you want to turn text into code and the bitwise logical functions work only on numerical arguments, you use the RANK function to associate a number (the ASCII or EBCDIC collating sequence) with each of the letters. For example, an uppercase A is equal to 65, and uppercase B to 66, and so forth. The BXOR function is used to perform an exclusive OR with each of the numerical values and the KEY. So, if you want to be a spy, you can send the ENCODE data set to someone and make sure the recipient has the key.

The encoded text looks like this:

```
Encoded Message

XOR1     XOR2     XOR3     XOR4     XOR5

236      239      238      233      232
229      200      193      221      141
```

The decoding section of the program is similar to the encoding section. The exclusive OR is performed on every coded value and the key. The resulting letters are the original text, and they are placed in the proper position in the new string using the SUBSTR function on the left-hand side of the equal sign. This use (see Chapter 1) allows you to place individual characters in any position of a character variable. The decoded text is turned back to the original message and is shown below:

```
Decoding Output

STRING

ABCDE
Help
```

Encrypting and Decrypting Macros

The two macros that follow are general purpose encrypting and decrypting macros that make use of the exclusive OR function (XOR) and the uniform random number function. Rather than use a single key to perform the encryption, the key is actually a random number seed which, in turn, generates a whole series of keys, one for each character in the document to be encrypted. It turns out that if you have a truly random key the same length as the document you want to encrypt, it is theoretically unbreakable! In the spy business, high-security messages can be transmitted using a "one-time pad" (or so I'm told). The problem with this system is that the recipient of the coded message needs to keep a copy of the keys somewhere, probably in a safe, and it could be stolen or somehow compromised.

The macros presented here rely on the SAS random number function (RANUNI) to generate a random, but repeatable, sequence of keys. All that you need to reproduce the series of random numbers is the seed value. So, this makes for a fairly secure code if you choose a key with a large number of digits (say 9 or 10). Following the two macros, there will be a fairly detailed explanation.

Program 16.3: Writing general purpose encrypting and decrypting macros

---

```
***Primary functions: BXOR, RANK, BYTE
***Other functions: SUBSTR (used on the left-hand side of the equal
sign), DIM, RANUNI;

%MACRO ENCODE(DSN,           /* Name of the SAS data set to hold the
                                encrypted message */
             FILE_NAME,    /* The name of the raw data file that holds
                               the plain text */
             KEY           /* A number of your choice which will be the
                              seed for the random number generator. A
                              large number is preferable */
             );
   %LET LEN = 80;
   DATA &DSN;
      ARRAY L[&LEN] $ 1 _TEMPORARY_; /* Each element holds a character
                                        of plain text */
      ARRAY NUM[&LEN] _TEMPORARY_;   /* A numerical equivalent for each
                                        letter */
      ARRAY XOR[&LEN];               /* The coded value of each letter */
      RETAIN KEY &KEY;
      INFILE "&FILE_NAME" PAD;
      INPUT STRING $CHAR&LEN..;
      DO I = 1 TO DIM(L);
         L[I] = SUBSTR(STRING,I,1);
         NUM[I] = RANK(L[I]);
         XOR[I] = BXOR(NUM[I],RANUNI(KEY));
      END;
      KEEP XOR1-XOR&LEN;
   RUN;
%MEND ENCODE;

%MACRO DECODE(DSN,           /* Name of the SAS data set to hold the
                                encrypted message */
             KEY           /* A number that must match the key of
                              the enciphered message */
             );
   %LET LEN = 80;
   DATA DECODE;
```

```
     ARRAY L[&LEN] $ 1 _TEMPORARY_;
     ARRAY NUM[&LEN] _TEMPORARY_;
     ARRAY XOR[&LEN];
     RETAIN KEY &KEY;
     LENGTH STRING $ &LEN;
     SET &DSN;
     DO I = 1 TO DIM(L);
         NUM[I] = BXOR(XOR[I],RANUNI(KEY));
         L[I] = BYTE(NUM[I]);
         SUBSTR(STRING,I,1) = L[I];
     END;
     DROP I;
   RUN;
   PROC PRINT DATA=DECODE NOOBS;
     TITLE "Decoding Output";
     VAR STRING;
   RUN;
%MEND DECODE;
```

Here is a sample calling sequence:

```
%ENCODE (CODE,C:\I_SPY\PLAINTEXT.TXT,17614353);
%DECODE (CODE,17614353);
```

Explanation

The calling arguments are the name of the output SAS data set that will hold the coded message; the full path and file name of the raw, plain text message; and a key value (which is really the seed for the random number function).

To make the program easier to adapt, I assigned the maximum length of each line of text to a macro variable (LEN). If you wish, you could just replace the &LEN values in the macro with a fixed value, such as 80.

The L array stores each of the individual characters in the plain text message. The NUM array assigns a numerical equivalent to each of the character values, using the RANK function. The BXOR function performs an exclusive OR between each of the numerical equivalents and a random number generated using the RANUNI function (and seeded with the KEY value). Since you don't need any of the L or NUM variables in the data set, these arrays are defined as _TEMPORARY_ to make the program more efficient.

The resulting data set is what you can transmit to your spy friends. Hopefully, you have arranged for him or her to know the value of the key. Perhaps the key value can be computed from the date in some manner.

The deciphering macro just reverses the process. Here, you use the same seed for the random number function, so you generate the same series of random numbers. I suspect that the random series may be system dependent, so you may want to be sure that you and your spy friends are both on PCs or mainframes, etc. Also, you need to be sure that both systems use the same coding system (ASCII or EBCDIC).

Once the DECODE macro has recomputed the numerical values for each letter, the BYTE function (the inverse of the RANK function) turns these numbers back into the plain text letters. Finally, the SUBSTR function places each of these characters in the proper position in the STRING variable. I have no idea whether the NSA and their super-computers could break this code easily or not. But, if they didn't run SAS on their machines, they would have lots of problems!

Anyway, I hope you enjoyed this novel use of the BXOR function. I had a lot of fun writing it!

List of Functions

Index

Y

Z

Special Characters

Call your local SAS office to order these books
from Books by Users Press

A Step-by-Step Approach to Using the SAS® System for Factor Analysis and Structural Equation Modeling
by **Larry Hatcher** . . . . .Order No. A55129

A Step-by-Step Approach to Using the SAS® System for Univariate and Multivariate Statistics
by **Larry Hatcher**
and **Edward Stepanski** . . . . .Order No. A55072

Step-by-Step Basic Statistics Using SAS®: Student Guide and *Exercises*
(books in this set also sold separately)
by **Larry Hatcher** . . . . .Order No. A57541

Strategic Data Warehousing Principles Using SAS® Software
by **Peter R. Welbrock** . . . . .Order No. A56278

Survival Analysis Using the SAS® System: A Practical Guide
by **Paul D. Allison** . . . . .Order No. A55233

Table-Driven Strategies for Rapid SAS® Applications Development
by **Tanya Kolosova**
and **Samuel Berestizhevsky** . . . . . . .Order No. A55198

Tuning SAS® Applications in the OS/390 and z/OS Environments, Second Edition
by **Michael A. Raithel** . . . . .Order No. A58172

Univariate and Multivariate General Linear Models: Theory and Applications Using SAS® Software
by **Neil H. Timm**
and **Tammy A. Mieczkowski** . . . . . . .Order No. A55809

Using SAS® in Financial Research
by **Ekkehart Boehmer, John Paul Broussard,**
and **Juha-Pekka Kallunki** . . . . .Order No. A57601

Using the SAS® Windowing Environment: A Quick Tutorial
by **Larry Hatcher** . . . . .Order No. A57201

Visualizing Categorical Data
by **Michael Friendly** . . . . .Order No. A56571

Web Development with SAS® by Example
by **Frederick Pratter** . . . . .Order No. A58694

Working with the SAS® System
by **Erik W. Tilanus** . . . . .Order No. A55190

Your Guide to Survey Research Using the SAS® System
by **Archer Gravely** . . . . .Order No. A55688

JMP® Books

Basic Business Statistics: A Casebook
by **Dean P. Foster, Robert A. Stine,**
and **Richard P. Waterman** . . . . .Order No. A56813

Business Analysis Using Regression: A Casebook
by **Dean P. Foster, Robert A. Stine,**
and **Richard P. Waterman** . . . . .Order No. A56818

JMP® Start Statistics, Second Edition
by **John Sall, Ann Lehman,**
and **Lee Creighton** . . . . .Order No. A58166

Regression Using JMP®
by **Rudolf J. Freund, Ramon C. Littell,**
and **Lee Creighton** . . . . .Order No. A58789

support.sas.com/pubs